THE FIRST CHRISTIAN

by A. POWELL DAVIES

American Destiny
The Faith of an Unrepentant Liberal
America's Real Religion
Man's Vast Future
The Temptation to be Good
The Urge to Persecute
The Language of the Heart
The Meaning of the Dead Sea Scrolls
The Ten Commandments
The First Christian

THE FIRST CHRISTIAN

A Study of St. Paul and Christian Origins

by
A. POWELL DAVIES

FARRAR, STRAUS AND CUDAHY
NEW YORK

Published simultaneously in Canada by
Ambassador Books, Ltd., Toronto
Manufactured in the United States of America
American Book–Stratford Press, Inc., New York

ACKNOWLEDGMENTS

For the privilege of including quotations long enough to require special permission, thanks are expressed to the following publishers:

Harper Bros. for permission to quote from CHRISTIAN BEGINNINGS, by Morton Enslin, 1938 & 1956; the Macmillan Co. for permission to quote from PAUL AND HIS INTERPRETERS, by Albert Schweitzer, 1912, 1951; John Murray (Publishers) Ltd., and Scribners for permission to quote from THE MYSTERY RELIGIONS AND CHRISTIANITY, by Samuel Angus, 1925; and the Viking Press for permission to quote from a translation of the Thanksgiving Psalms in THE DEAD SEA SCROLLS by Millar Burrows, 1956.

For assistance in research and untiring labors in the preparation of the manuscript I am particularly indebted to Miss Jane Grey Wheeler; and to her and Mrs. O. H. Wheeler for reading proof and preparing the index. To Captain William N. Price, U.S.N., and Mrs. Price I am grateful for a critical reading of the manuscript from the standpoint of the lay reader. To my congregation at All Souls Church in Washington which for many years now has encouraged me in combining a confident religious faith with a conscientious search for truth, my thanks are inexpressible.

A.P.D.

CONTENTS

INTRODUCTION: CHRISTIANITY
AND ITS HISTORY

The traditional story of Christian origins is well known and there are many who do not wish to subject it to closer examination. To these good people the work of scholars seems meddlesome and even destructive; they are sure they know all they need to know merely by reading the Bible. This book is not intended for those who hold this belief; it is written for the general reader who, no matter what his religious faith, has confidence in scientific methods and whose desire in all things is to arrive at truth.

This kind of reader probably already knows that the New Testament presents problems—textual, literary and historical—that scholars conscientiously attempt to solve. Their criterion is not and cannot be the defense of a tradition; they must be guided by the evidence. In analyzing Scripture, they do not permit themselves to determine in advance what their conclusions will be; they accept the facts precisely as they find them and draw the inferences that honesty requires.

They are not, as some would have it, attacking Christianity. Most Biblical scholars are members of a church (or synagogue) and many of them are professors in institutions devoted to the education of the ministry. What they believe (and their critics apparently do not) is that fidelity to truth is a sacred obligation and that nothing that suppresses truth is genuinely religious.

But then, it is objected, even though this be so, should not the findings of scholars be restricted to those who make a special study of such matters—other scholars and perhaps the educated clergy? Is it wise to share this knowledge

1

with the uninitiated layman? What this really means is that the layman's faith must be based upon ignorance or it may fall apart—an assumption which, when plainly stated, is rather shocking. Actually, there is no more reason why the layman's faith should be damaged by knowledge of the truth than the faith of scholars or the clergy.

As to the effect of scholarship upon faith, let us take an illustrious example. Albert Schweitzer is a scholar. He rejects the traditional view of Christian origins, and for that matter, even the traditional view of Jesus. But Schweitzer, as is widely known, instead of being a man whose faith has been destroyed by his scholarship is a modern saint who has devoted his life to the welfare of African tribesmen in remote Lambarene. What stronger proof could there be that no conflict exists between a consecrated life and a scientific view of Christian history?

Let us say at once: there is indeed a great deal in the New Testament that scholars do not and cannot accept as fact. Certain incidents, for example, in the gospels are described by the justly esteemed French scholar, Maurice Goguel, as "simply figments of the imagination."[1] But Goguel does not regard the New Testament as anything less than a great literature: he gives his life to the devoted study of it. Again, Johannes Weiss, one of the most renowned of German scholars, tells us that the story of early Christianity in the New Testament is "a pure idealization of the church's evolution which cannot stand in the light of historical facts."[2] Yet no one can read Weiss without recognizing the importance he attaches to the facts behind the New Testament narrative—or without feeling that his diligent scholarship is inspired by a high-minded religious faith.

Bultmann, another German scholar who is held in high regard, describes Christianity as "a complex phenomenon" which "at a very early stage in its development came into contact with Hellenistic paganism, a contact which was to exercise a profound influence on Christianity itself," which he finds to be a "syncretistic phenomenon."[3] But however syncretistic Christianity may be, in Bultmann's view it deserves the close attention that he gives it and has much to reveal to us of the principles that should guide a truly religious life.

To come to an American scholar, Morton Enslin, who also is in the front rank of his profession, we read as follows: "The claim for Christianity is often made that it is the 'faith once and for all delivered to the saints.' To the student of history such a claim is not only false; it is positively absurd. . . . Christianity was the child of Judaism . . . [which] within a score of years became a Gentile cult . . . adopted new conceptions, took on a totally different character, borrowed from all with which it came into contact."[4] What this means is not that Christianity is discredited because it evolved in a natural way and grew with history but that it is a marvelous synthesis, containing precisely the same values, spiritually and ethically, as when it was supposed to be "once and for all delivered to the saints." These are a few out of many scholars who might be cited, who, though differing at numerous points in their opinions, are united in rejecting the traditional view of Christian origins.

One of the contentions frequently encountered when it is proposed to convey the findings of modern scholarship to the layman is that the layman is not equipped to understand them and may thus be exposed to "the little knowledge" that is "a dangerous thing." What is meant, of course, is that the layman knows no ancient languages and is unfamiliar with the critical apparatus and will therefore not appreciate the points at issue. This is not a valid contention. For while it is true that there are considerations that cannot be presented fully to those who have no technical background, just as there are points that cannot be demonstrated without some knowledge of Greek, Hebrew or the

Aramaics, these are not vital to the main inquiry. The fact is that, to an extent that is quite sufficient for the purpose, it is possible to present evidence and develop arguments in language that is easily understood by the general reader.

Our purpose then, in the present study, is to introduce the general reader to the problems of Christian origins as modern scholarship investigates them. Since it was his influence upon the new movement that determined the direction it took, we shall be much concerned with the Apostle Paul. His place in any study of Christian beginnings must always be prominent; in the case of our own study it will be central. How Christianity would have developed if Paul had had no part in it is a moot question: history does not reveal its alternatives. As events actually happened, his was the decisive role.

Our inquiry divides itself into three parts. In the first, we discover the difficulties with the traditional story and then describe the resources with which scholars meet them. In the second, we set the story of Christian origins in its historical and cultural context, showing how, especially through the work of Paul, the new movement was affected by pagan as well as Jewish influences. In the third, with the help of the knowledge we have now accumulated we inquire into the beginnings of the movement at Jerusalem, finding it far different from the "primitive church" traditionally portrayed, and then return to Paul's missions in Asia Minor and Europe, completing the study with an evaluation of the reasons for Paul's arrest in Jerusalem and imprisonment in Rome. In a brief conclusion, we summarize our findings and take leave of Paul.

If, after following the present inquiry, the reader feels stimulated to pursue the study further, suggestions for his guidance are provided at the end of the book.

NOTE: Biblical quotations in this book are from the Revised Version (RV), except where otherwise noted.

CHRONOLOGICAL TABLE

NOTE: Events recorded in the New Testament can be dated only approximately and with considerable difference of informed opinion. While the arrangement adopted in the text is based upon the table given below, the main conclusions reached do not depend upon precise dating.

B.C.

63 Pompey enters Jerusalem. Palestine under Roman rule.

43 Octavian victorious survivor of Roman triumvirate.

37-4 A.D. Herod the Great client-king in Palestine.

27 Octavian becomes Caesar Augustus.

6 BIRTH OF JESUS

4 Dead Sea sect returns to Qumran monastery from "Damascus." Its scriptures, including *Manual of Discipline, Habakkuk Commentary,* together with other Jewish scriptures not included in the Bible, known and used by New Covenanters at Jerusalem.

4 B.C.-6 A.D. Archelaus ethnarch of Judea; 4 B.C.-39 A.D. Herod Antipas tetrarch of Galilee; 4 B.C.-34 A.D. Philip tetrarch of northern Palestine.

A.D.

6 Judea becomes Roman province ruled by procurators. Census of Quirinius. Revolt of Judas ("the Zealot").

14 Tiberius becomes emperor.

18-36 Caiaphas Jewish high priest.

26-36 Pontius Pilate procurator of Judea.

28 Execution of John the Baptist by Herod Antipas.

29 CRUCIFIXION OF JESUS by Pontius Pilate.

34 Paul in Jerusalem. His journey to Damascus. Traditional date of his conversion.

36 Marcellus procurator of Judea. Paul's fifteen days with Peter and James at Jerusalem.

5

37   Accession of Emperor Gaius Caligula. Marullus procurator of Judea.

38   Severe persecution of Jews at Alexandria where they formed large colony.

40-41   Caligula orders his statue set up in Jerusalem Temple. His instruction is frustrated; this, plus other "signs" attracts Gentiles to Judaism and to New Covenanters. Paul brought by Barnabas to Antioch to assist in making conversions.

41   Accession of Claudius. Herod Agrippa, client-king of Judea. Revolt of Theudas.

42 or 43   Paul leaves Antioch for preaching mission in Cyprus and Asia Minor.

45-50   Paul's campaign in cities of Asia and Europe around Aegean Sea.

50   Jews banished from Rome. Paul accused of being agitator against Roman rule.

     Publication of *Epistle of James* (or earlier).

51   Paul in Corinth. He returns to Antioch. Conference with James "the Lord's brother" at Jerusalem concerning the application of the Mosaic Law and circumcision to Gentile believers. No firm agreement, but Paul undertakes to collect fund from his Gentile congregations for the patriarchal community at Jerusalem.

52   Felix procurator of Judea.

     Between 50 and 54 Paul's letters to the *Thessalonians* (from Corinth), to the *Corinthians* (from Ephesus), to the *Galatians* (from Ephesus?), to the *Romans* (from Corinth?) were written.

54   Nero becomes emperor. Paul arrested by the Roman guard during a riot in the Temple at Jerusalem.

58   Festus procurator of Judea. Paul appeals to Caesar and is ordered to Rome. Arrival of Paul in Rome in 58 or 59.

     Paul's letters to *Philippians, Colossians, Philemon* written during imprisonment in Rome (unless one or more were written during a hypothetical imprisonment in Ephesus several years earlier.)

62 Assassination of James the Just ("brother of the Lord") on orders of Ananas, the Jewish high priest.

64 Fire of Rome. Persecution of Messianic believers by Nero. EXECUTION OF PETER AND PAUL (according to tradition).

65 Epistle to the *Hebrews* (erroneously ascribed to Paul).

66 Jewish revolt in Palestine. War with the Romans, 66-73 A.D.

68-69 Roman civil war. Galba, Otho, Vitellius.

69 Vespasian becomes emperor.

70 FALL OF JERUSALEM

75 Publication of early form of *Mark's Gospel*.

79 Accession of Titus.
    About this time or a few years later, publication of *Matthew's Gospel*.

81 Domitian becomes emperor. Persecution of believers in Rome and Asia Minor.
    Letters of *I Peter* and *Jude* (?)

90 General persecution of Jews and Christians. Synod of Jamnia establishes Jewish Bible (Old Testament), according to tradition.

95 Publication of book of *Revelation* during time of persecution (or earlier).

96 Nerva becomes emperor.

98 Accession of Trajan.

100 Pliny (the younger) corresponds with Trajan on disputed civil rights of Christians.

105 Publication of *Luke-Acts* as two volumes of one work.

110 Collection of Paul's letters, stimulated by Luke-Acts, perhaps initially by the Church at Ephesus. Prefatory letter provided by compiler, writing in Paul's name, later called letter to the *Ephesians*.

113 Jewish revolts in Cyprus and elsewhere.

115 Martyrdom of St. Ignatius.
    Publication of *Pastoral Epistles* (*I & II Timothy & Titus*) in Paul's name and of *I John* (?).

117 Hadrian becomes emperor. Jewish revolt in Palestine. Publication of *II* and *III John* (?).

135 Rome suppresses revolt of Jews in Palestine under the "Messiah" Bar Kochba. Jerusalem becomes Roman colony Aelia Capitolina. Jews excluded from Aelia upon penalty of death.

Publication of *John's Gospel* (or perhaps much earlier).

The *Epistle of Barnabas* (not in New Testament).

138 Atoninus Pius becomes emperor.

145-155 Marcion's heresy causes disturbance in churches.

Marcion's Gospel (Luke) and *Apostolicon* (ten letters of Paul—edited by Marcion). Publication of *II Peter,* based in part on Pauline sources or traditions.

Gospels of *Peter, Thomas,* etc., *Acts of Paul and Thecla,* and many other scriptures not included in New Testament published in this period.

161 Marcus Aurelius. Early form of Apostles' Creed by this time.

325 Council of Nicaea. Christian orthodoxy established.

PART ONE

PROBLEMS OF THE
TRADITIONAL STORY

THE STRANGER FROM TARSUS

At Tarsus, the capital of Cilicia in the southeastern corner of Asia Minor, East met West as perhaps in no other city of the Roman Empire. Nowhere could an environment have been found more suited to the needs of one whose chosen mission would require the blending of Judaic and Hellenistic thought. Although its schools could scarcely rank with the famous universities of Athens and Alexandria, Tarsus, according to Strabo, the Greek geographer, had more enthusiasm for education than did either of these greater cities. Whether he attended the university or not, no Greek-speaking Tarsian could escape this hunger for Hellenistic learning.

Nor could he be unaffected by the Greek gymnasium and theater. To a strict Jew, participation in the games would be forbidden, but it was hardly possible not to observe them. In the case of the Tarsian Jew with whom we are concerned, we know from the allusions in his letters that he was at least a keen spectator. Strict Jews might not attend the theater (though in some cities special sections of the seating space were reserved for Jews and this may have been the case in Tarsus), but whether they did or not they would surely come to know something of Greek tragedy with its moral dilemmas, its wistful despairs and its unsparing portrayal of reality. Whoever lived in Tarsus and spoke Greek breathed the Hellenistic spirit no matter what his faith or nationality.

The port of Tarsus was an inland harbor formed by a

spring-fed lake through which ran the River Cydnus.[1] Here might be seen the ships of every coastal city in the empire. It was up the Cydnus that the royal barge of Cleopatra had been rowed when she went to meet Anthony, displayed (one hesitates to say attired) as a reclining Venus, attended by make-believe Cupids and Graces beneath a canopy of gold. Less glamorous perhaps, but of more substantial interest, were the vessels plying regularly between Egypt and Asia Minor, bringing sometimes, besides their cargoes and more ordinary passengers, famous theologians and philosophers from Alexandria.

Yet Tarsus was Oriental as well as Greek. The Aramaic of Syria was the language of a large part—possibly the greater part—of its populace. Many women wore veils in the Eastern manner as they walked through the streets. The religions of Asia had lost little of their hold; they were still the religions of the majority. For many centuries after the Greek and Roman conquests, the images of Asian deities were stamped on Tarsian coins.

To a Jew, of course, these religions were idolatry. But it was an insidious idolatry that affected even the mind that repulsed it. The salvation cults with their cryptic rituals, their *mater dolorosas*, their dying redeemers, spoke darkly but powerfully of things that went deep. There were pageants, passion plays, public liturgical dramas, and an inquiring mind would want to know what they were saying. There was something in all this that had entered into the common currency of ordinary thought and was inescapable. A Jew could be strict but he could not live in Tarsus as though it were Jerusalem.

The Tarsian Jew with whom we are concerned was known by three names: in Hebrew, Shaul; in Greek, Paulos; in Latin, Paulus. Much has been written about his change of name from Shaul (Saul) to Paul (Acts xiii, 13). The simplest explanation, but not necessarily a sufficient one, is that where Aramaic was spoken,* it was natural to call him Shaul, and this is what he is called in the book of Acts when he is in an Aramaic-speaking environment. But when, on the Isle of Cyprus, he changes to a Greek-speaking environment in which, as he moves forward on his journeys, most of the rest of his life will be spent, he is called by his Greek name, Paulos. His Latin name would be seldom used since the common language of the Roman Empire was Greek.

The curious fact that the Greek form of his name is taken from what seems to be a Roman cognomen, *Paulus*, instead of from his Hebrew name may perhaps be explained by noting that *saulos* is an offensive word in Greek, meaning an effeminized man, and therefore would have been objectionable. It is true that the composer of the book of Acts uses *Saulos* until the sudden change occurs, but in rendering *Shaul* into Greek, *Saulos* is the inevitable equivalent. Possibly it was used in translating an Aramaic source, and not without embarrassment. Certainly, no time is lost in making the change to *Paulos* as soon as Paul's journeyings provide the logical opportunity.

It is often mentioned that Paul's Latin name is also not flattering since *paulus* means small. This in turn recalls the tradition that Paul was short of stature, which has led some to conjecture that Paulus was a nickname. More likely, the suitability of name to stature was a coincidence. If Paul had been given a nickname, it would not have been in the little-used Latin but in Greek. Moreover, we know that Paulus was the cognomen of Roman families of high standing (for example, the Aemilian *gens*) where it could have had no derogatory meaning, and it may well have been from such a family that, in accordance with a well-

* Aramaic belongs to the same language group as Hebrew and for most purposes had gradually replaced it in the last centuries B.C. Such traditional Hebrew names as Shaul remained the same. The reason for the form *Saul* instead of *Shaul* is that there is no "sh" sound in Greek.

established custom, Paul received his Roman name.* In full, the latter must have been in triple form as was always the case with Romans, but we do not know what it was. Without committing ourselves to these opinions, since we intend to take up the question again later, for the present we shall leave the matter and be content to speak of Paul.

The only description we have of his appearance comes from the apocryphal *Acts of Paul and Thecla,* where we are told, as just noted, that he was "a man little of stature." The rest of the description is that he was "thin-haired upon his head, crooked in the legs, well preserved in body, with joined eyebrows and somewhat hooked nose, full of grace: for sometimes he seemed like a man and sometimes had the countenance of an angel."[2]

The authenticity of this portrait has been much debated. Those who favor it emphasize that it is unflattering. If it were false, Paul would have more hair, straight legs and separated eyebrows! Then there is the paradoxical assertion, unlikely to be invented, that so ugly a man could seem at times to have "the countenance of an angel"! To the defenders of the portrait this means that although ill-favored in his ordinary appearance, Paul could become so radiant in inspired moments that the effect was moving and beautiful. Those who deny that the description is authentic point to differences in esthetic standards as between the early Christian centuries and our own and remind us that the *Acts of Paul and Thecla* is mostly fiction. For ourselves, we doubt that esthetic standards have ever favored baldness or bandy-leggedness, even among ascetics; nor is there any reason why historical persons should not be correctly described in fiction. On the whole, therefore, this portrait, the only one we have, might well be cautiously adopted.

* It is reasonably well established that Paul, at least by the time he made his last visit to Jerusalem, was a Roman citizen. How and at what point he became one is a baffling problem to be taken up later.

About Paul's years in Tarsus we have no direct information and must depend upon our knowledge of time and place and upon inferences to be drawn from his letters. He may or may not have attended the university. His Greek is not excellent. He freely admits that he is unpolished in speech* but insists that he is not lacking in knowledge (II Cor. xi, 6). He then goes on to say that he was always easily understood—which may have been true of his discourse but is certainly not of his letters! As the author of II Peter puts it, in the writings of "our beloved brother Paul" there are "some things hard to be understood" (iii, 15, 16), a sentiment that has endeared this unknown author (he was not Peter) to many a New Testament scholar!

One of the most puzzling questions concerning Paul's education is raised by a speech attributed to him in Acts** in which he says that he was born in Tarsus but brought up in Jerusalem where he sat at the feet of the great Rabbi Gamaliel (xxii, 3). Scholars view this speech with considerable suspicion (for reasons which will be taken up later on) but if Paul was taught by Gamaliel it must have been during some interval when he was living in Jerusalem, for he cannot have been brought up there. If there is anything that is certain it is that Paul was not Palestinian; he was Saul of Tarsus, a Grecian Jew.

It is as such that he thinks and writes. If Paul had been brought up in Judea "according to the strict manner of the Law," his knowledge of Greek would have been at most superficial and meager. Even the accomplished Josephus never fully mastered Greek and complains that his Jewish education discouraged it. In Judea, he says, learning con-

* AV and RV translate ἰδιώτης τῷ λόγῳ (idiōtēs tō logō) "rude in speech." This is too literal and heedless of the context. Paul is deliberately exaggerating. (AV = Authorized Version—or King James Version of the Bible; RV = Revised Version.)

** Scholars do not use the misleading term "Acts of the Apostles." Acts gives only a fragmentary account even of those apostles who are included in the story (many are not mentioned). The greater part of the narrative has to do with Paul.

sists of being fully acquainted with the Mosaic Law and proficiency in its interpretation.[3]

As to his station in life, if Paul was a tentmaker (in Tarsus this would have included sail-making) he certainly was not a hired hand, tied to his trade. He was free to travel. Perhaps he was at one time an *apostolos* of the Temple hierarchy, one who collected and carried to Jerusalem the contributions of Jews who lived abroad, which was a regular annual practice.[4] That he had learned a trade means only that he had followed an established Jewish custom. Even the rabbis learned a trade while they were being schooled in the Mosaic Law, and afterward frequently worked at it. Among the well-to-do it was a precautionary measure, so that, if it became necessary they could maintain themselves by their own exertions—which was definitely the case with Paul during his journeys as a preacher. He tells the Philippian community (probably near the end of his life) that he has learned "both to be filled and to be hungry, both to abound and to be in want" (Phil. iv, 12). Which means that he had sometimes been well off and at other times was hard put to it to find the money even to buy food. It is reasonable to suppose that at Tarsus he was prosperous, as he possibly was for some time after he joined the believers in the Risen Jesus, but that some time during his work abroad his funds ran out —or he may have donated them to the treasury of the Antioch believers in accordance with what may have been the rule of the community (cf. I Cor. xiii, 3).

We have emphasized his Hellenistic environment—and correctly. He was indeed a Grecian Jew. Nevertheless, he was not, as some writers would have him, Greek first and Jew last. No matter how much he came from Tarsus, he was of the Jewish faith, steeped in the tradition of his fathers, a Pharisee, "brought up according to the strict manner of the Law." It is as such that we shall meet him in Jerusalem, "making havoc," as he later put it, "of God's Community."

THE EARLY YEARS:
A CONFUSED CHRONICLE

1. *The Community of First Believers*

Soon after the crucifixion of Jesus, the belief arose among some of his followers that he had risen from the dead. His execution had not meant the failure of his mission; it was a supreme sacrifice, divinely foreordained, the necessary prelude to his triumph. Shortly he would reappear to rule the world. They would await his coming at Jerusalem.

Pared down to what is most surely historical, this was the beginning of the movement from which would grow the Christian Church. Of such an outcome, however, the first believers had no inkling. They were wholly engrossed with the anticipated return of Jesus. This was their "gospel" or "good news" which they were eager to make known. The great "Day of the Lord" which Messianic Jews had been awaiting was now imminent, the present world order would at last be ended and in its place would come the rule of God's "Anointed," who was none other than the Risen Jesus.

Within a remarkably short time there were communities which had joyfully received this "good news," not only in Jerusalem but in Damascus and Antioch and perhaps in other cities. Whether these communities were founded upon this "good news" or had existed before it reached them is a question to be considered at a later time when

17

more of the evidence is before us. But in any case, upon the basis of what we learn in the book of Acts, the "good news" was swiftly spread.

By the fifth year after the crucifixion, Greek-speaking Jews from abroad had become active in the movement. They were Jews of the Dispersion, some of them no doubt on temporary visits to their homeland, others permanent settlers in Jerusalem. They were unfamiliar with Aramaic, the language of the Jews of Palestine, so they had their own synagogues where the Scriptures were read in Greek.* They are called "Hellenists" in the New Testament, and it is evident that they included Gentile converts as well as Grecian Jews by birth.

It was in connection with the Hellenists that the first disturbance occurred within the new movement, an episode of some importance of which unfortunately we have only a meager and confused account. What we are told is that "when the number of the disciples was multiplying, there arose a murmuring of the Hellenists against the Hebrews because their widows were neglected in the daily ministration" (Acts vi, 1). This mention of a "daily ministration" reminds us that in the new movement, as in the Essenic sects to which it bore such close resemblance, there was a common fund to which members were invited to contribute their "possessions" and from which there was daily disbursement to pay the community's expenses and minister to individual needs. In the case of the Essenic sects, or at least of their more ascetic settlements, cash payments would rarely be necessary because the community lived together and shared common meals. We are told of the early believers in the Risen Jesus that they too "had all things in common," but we have no detailed knowledge of what this means (Acts iv, 32).

---

* Aramaic- and Greek-speaking Jews would know a smattering of each other's language: enough for the market place but not nearly enough for religious discourse.

In any case, according to the book of Acts a solution to the problem of discrimination against the Hellenist widows is suggested by a committee called "the Twelve." These are not the twelve disciples of Jesus, as we shall later see, but a *Twelve* that has been given authority over the Jerusalem believers, including (according to the book of Acts) the Hellenists. It is not fitting, says the *Twelve*, that they should "forsake the word of God and serve tables," so they propose the selection of "seven men of good report" to be appointed by the *Twelve* to relieve them of "this business" (vi, 2-6). The seven appointed are all Hellenists as is evident from their Greek names. It is they and not the Judaic believers who are best fitted to "serve tables."*

But on any rendering, this story will not do. The *Twelve* are the leaders of the Judaic believers, the selected *Seven* are obviously the leaders of the Hellenists. One of them in particular, Stephanos or Stephen, is the boldest protagonist in the entire movement. His skill in debate is so formidable that he reduces his opponents to enraged silence, so that they are driven to turn to the authorities and lay information against him.

What the dispute was actually about, it is impossible to tell. The composer of the book of Acts has reason, perhaps, for not allowing us to know. As one scholar puts it, "in the form in which we have it the story has been so conventionalized and revamped that reconstruction is hopeless."[6] What we do see, half hidden behind the narrative as it comes to us, is that there were already differences between the Judaic and Hellenist believers which the composer of Acts tries to smooth out by making the Hellenist leaders subordinate to the Judaic *Twelve*. But he is not able to go on with his story without allowing Stephen to

---

* Serving tables has usually been taken to mean the supervision of the common meals, but it has recently been suggested that since, in Aramaic, money-changers are called "table-men," it is more probable that the function intended was the disbursement of funds from the common treasury.[5]

take the prominent part which the development of his theme demands and thus he discloses that the leadership of Stephen was independent and that his views differed enough from those of the Judaic believers to provoke his arrest while even the leaders of the latter were left undisturbed (Acts viii, 1).

To this we shall return. Meanwhile, another foreign Jew appears in Jerusalem, a zealous heresy hunter who first persecutes the new movement—or at least the part of it of which Stephen was a leader—and then, by joining it, so changes it eventually that it is a question whether he did not do it less violence as a persecutor than he did as an adherent.

2. *The Stoning of Stephen*

According to the New Testament narrative, when Stephen, the first of the martyrs, was stoned after trial by the Jewish Council or *Sanhedrin*, Paul "was consenting unto his death." Stephen's accusers, who were obliged by Jewish law to cast the first stones, "laid down their garments" at Paul's feet (Acts vii, 58-60). "And there arose on that day," the story continues, "a great persecution against the community* that was in Jerusalem; and they were all scattered abroad throughout the regions of Judea and Samaria, except the apostles . . . And Saul (Paul) laid waste the community, entering house after house, hauling away both men and women and throwing them into prison" (viii, 1-3).

Why was Stephen stoned? To the uncritical reader, it looks as though it was for blasphemy. Stephen has been brought before the Sanhedrin, charged with disparaging

---

* To translate ἐκκλησία (ekklēsia) as "church" is anachronistic. There was as yet no church as we understand that term. *Ekklēsia* means *an assembly,* originally one summoned by the city crier for municipal purposes, but eventually a regularly meeting assembly bound together by a common and continuing aim, and thus in the present context, a *community.* Even the word κοινωνία (koinōnia) although it means a communion or fellowship does not mean "church" as we understand that term.

the Temple and the Mosaic Law and declaring that Jesus of Nazareth will destroy "this place" and change the customs of Moses. He makes an exceedingly long speech (according to the narrative), rehearsing Jewish history from the standpoint of those of the Hebrew prophets who had condemned Temple sacrifice; then he attacks the members of the Council itself, accusing them of being the custodians of a Law which they do not keep. Hearing this they "gnash their teeth" at him, to which he responds by saying that he sees "the heavens opened and the Son of Man standing on the right hand of God" (vii, 56). It is for this, apparently, that the members of the Council, without waiting to pass sentence as prescribed by law, rush him out of the city and stone him to death.*

But why is it that a general persecution immediately follows? Other members of the believing community, far from disparaging the Temple are said to visit it day by day, notably Peter and John. It is true that the latter are said to have been haled before the Council and told to stop preaching, but they are certainly not charged with blasphemy. Then, when the persecution disperses the believers —or some of them—we are given the remarkable information that although others fled, *the apostles remained!* (viii, 1). The apostles were the leaders. Why were they not the first to be apprehended?

This is a problem that has preoccupied scholars for several generations. Not surprisingly, the proffered solutions are far from harmonious. It has been suggested that only the Hellenists were persecuted, Stephen being their leader, and that they were not Grecian Jews but Gentiles.[7] The former is probable, the latter exceedingly unlikely. Upon

* As many Jewish scholars have pointed out, the only blasphemy that is a crime in Jewish law is pronouncing the sacred name of God (Yahweh), which Stephen did not do (Mishna: San. VII, 5). It is possible of course that the crowd standing by took matters into its own hands and stoned Stephen illegally. But if so, why the formality of the accusers "casting the first stones"? The narrative is indeed far from clear.

what basis would the Roman procurator permit a persecution of Gentiles by order of the Jewish Council? Moreover, this explanation fails to deal satisfactorily with the assertion in Acts that the trouble broke out in the synagogues of the Libertines (*sic* Libyans?),[8] Cyrenians, Alexandrians, and "of them of Cilicia and Asia." If it was in synagogues that the opposition to Stephen arose, it was also from synagogues that he most likely drew his support. Yet we cannot be certain.

Other scholars, notably the Abbé Loisy, suggest that Stephen and his following were the first to declare in public that Jesus had risen from the dead and would shortly appear as the Messiah. The Galilean followers had been more cautious, and the stories about the boldness of Peter and John, as related in Acts, are not to be credited.[9] Thus the quiet propaganda of the Judaic believers went unnoticed by the authorities or was not counted dangerous, whereas the open proclamations of Stephen and the Hellenists were immediately recognized as unbearably heretical. Loisy also supposes that Stephen's attack on the Temple and his assertion that the Messiah would make drastic changes in Mosaic regulations had aggravated his offense in the eyes of the Council.

The composer of Acts, so it seems, is masking the true story because he does not want to reveal that there was any real difference between the Hellenist believers and the Judaic ones. He wishes to show the new movement as proceeding with only minor discords from its founding at Jerusalem to its mission to the Gentiles. Actually, the cleavage was deep even near the beginning but we cannot be certain of the cause of it.

Here the reader who knows the New Testament well may be thinking of Stephen's long speech and perhaps fears that we have not sufficiently considered it. If there is one thing we may be sure of, it is that Stephen never made this speech. In ancient times, no means existed for recording speeches, no shorthand, no method whatever for making a verbatim report. Short utterances might be remembered. But scarcely a speech of over a thousand words! Moreover, Stephen, being a Hellenist, presumably spoke Greek. The trial must have been conducted in Aramaic. The Sanhedrin would not have conducted a trial in Greek even if it had been capable of it, which it was not. Was it through an interpreter then that Stephen cried out that he saw the heavens opened and the Son of Man at the right hand of God? Perhaps so; yet it seems to have been overlooked in the dramatic portrayal of Stephen's impact on the Council!

But to come to realities, no serious modern scholar believes that the speeches appearing in the New Testament are verbatim records of what the speaker said. Even as conservative a scholar as Headlam has to admit that the speeches are "in a sense"—he does not say what sense—the author's "own compositions." He also admits that they are in the author's style, no matter who is supposed to be speaking.[10] Schmiedel, in his article on Acts in the *Encyclopedia Biblica*, says unreservedly that "it is without doubt that the author constructed [the speeches] in each case according to his own conception of the situation." Schweitzer thinks the speeches in Acts may be "based upon traditions of speeches . . . actually delivered, but in the form in which we have them they doubtless belong to the author of Acts and are adapted to his representation of the facts."[11]

The simplest statement of the matter is made by Enslin, who says that "no classical student will need to be warned that the speeches in the book of Acts are the free composition of the author, precisely as are those of Josephus, Philo, Thucydides or Livy." And he goes on to quote Thucydides who admits that he himself composed the speeches in his *History* to represent what he thinks the several speakers might most appropriately have said, having re-

gard to the "subjects under consideration [and] the senti-
ments most befitting the occasion." This was the universal
ancient custom.[12]

It was the composer of Acts, then, who wrote Stephen's
speech in a book published about sixty or seventy years
after any speech by Stephen could have been spoken.
What it reflects is the attitude of Gentile Christians to the
Jewish rejection of Jesus, as it had developed two generations after the death of Stephen. At the time of the stoning,
there was no way of knowing how many Jews would reject
Jesus. Most of them as yet had not even heard of him.

The best assumption seems to be that Stephen was
stoned for an intolerable Jewish heresy and at a time when
feelings were running so high that mob rule broke into the
judicial procedure. Whatever heresy it was it must have
been the same that Paul was eager to stamp out and it
applied only to the Hellenist believers. That is, unless we
are willing to conclude, with a minority of the more radical scholars, that Paul was not there and that Acts brings
him in for dramatic effect to make his conversion more
striking.[13] But Paul himself admits that he persecuted "the
community of God" (Gal. i, 13) and where else did he do
it if not at Jerusalem?

We can also argue that we shall not be far wrong if we
suppose that the heresy Paul was persecuting was the one
that he would presently accept at the time of his conversion. If this is correct, then Stephen's crime in the eyes of
the Sanhedrin may not have been solely his proclamation
of the Risen Jesus as the coming Messiah but also an assertion that in some way contrary to the Mosaic Law, Jesus
would find converts among the Gentiles. For it is certain
that Paul quickly came to this belief.

In this event it is apparent that the Judaic believers did
not need to take flight since they did not share Stephen's
views. Here, if we are right—and there is no way of being
sure of it—we get a glimpse of what the trouble was be-

tween the Jewish community ruled by the *Twelve* and the Hellenist community ruled by the *Seven*. It was a question of relationship to Gentiles. Perhaps "the Hellenist widows" were "neglected in the daily ministrations" because they were not "of Moses' Law" even though they were believers in the Risen Jesus. If so, this was a symptom of a wider cleavage. A further possibility, which will be better understood later in our inquiry, is that only a minority of the Judaic believers had accepted as yet the Messiahship of the Risen Jesus, and that as compared with the Hellenists, they were much quieter in communicating their gospel.

The reader will now begin to see the sort of problem we encounter when we try to get at the realities hidden in the narrative. Any interpretation of the early chapters of Acts must explain what Acts itself does not disclose, i.e., why the Hellenist believers* were persecuted and the Judaic believers left in peace, not even the apostles being arrested. If Peter and his associates were the leaders of the entire movement they would have been seized by the authorities at the same time as Stephen. But Paul (whom we are assuming to have been a leading persecutor) did not even know of them. Three years after this persecution he goes to Jerusalem to *become acquainted* with Peter (Gal. i, 18).**

The believers, then, whom Paul was persecuting were Hellenists, Greek-speaking Jews like himself for whose errant faith he might feel a special animosity. Some of them even came from Cilicia, his own territory. If their heresy

---

* It will have been noted before this that we are careful not to call the early believers *Christians*. To refer to them as such is quite inaccurate. It has been argued in defense of the practice that although the term "is not strictly appropriate at this period nor for many years," its use is justified to avoid "roundabout phrases."[14] Perhaps so; but the reader will be better reminded of the actual situation if the term is avoided, even at the expense of some inconvenience. In this book, instead of such terms as "primitive Christians" and the like we shall use the word "believers."

** The word ἱστορῆσαι (historēsai) should not be translated *see* but *become acquainted with*, as in RV margin.

were to spread, it could undermine the Jewry of Tarsus—indeed of the entire Dispersion. This the Judaic believers were not threatening. They had quarreled with the Hellenists. They were not dangerous to Judaism. And thus, the Judaic believers at Jerusalem enjoy peace, while Paul, having taken his part in driving the Hellenists out of the Holy City, is now preparing to pursue them to Damascus.

3. Was There a Journey to Damascus?

In the ninth chapter of the book of Acts, we are told that Paul, who was "breathing threatenings and slaughter against the disciples of the Lord," went to the Judean high priest to request "letters to Damascus, unto the synagogues" authorizing him to arrest "any that were of the Way," that he might bring them as prisoners to Jerusalem.

The term "any that were of the Way" is not explicit and raises many questions, but upon the basis of the assumptions which for the present we have adopted must be taken to mean Hellenist believers and particularly the followers of Stephen.

It must then have been followers of Stephen that Paul was hoping to bring back from Damascus. Armed with his letters from the high priest and accompanied by a police escort he sets forth to arrest them. But just before he reaches the city "a light out of heaven" blinds him and he falls to the ground. While prostrate he hears a voice saying to him in Aramaic, "Saul, Saul, why persecutest thou me?" "Who art thou, Lord?" he asks. "I am Jesus whom thou persecutest," the voice replies, "rise and enter into the city and it shall be told thee what thou shalt do."

Blinded by the heavenly light, Paul has to be led by the hand into Damascus where he fasts for three days. Then a believer named Ananias comes to him, prompted by a vision, and lays his hands upon him. Paul immediately receives back his sight and, as the story puts it, "straightway in the synagogue he proclaimed Jesus."

To most Bible readers, this familiar story raises only one question: what really happened when Paul was struck by the blinding light and heard a voice speaking to him? Was it a supernatural visitation or an hallucination? Or was it an experience, internal to Paul's own mind, that was neither the one nor the other? The answer most often given (except answers based upon faith alone and therefore not open to the methods of historians) is that Paul was brooding over the death of Stephen, which had deeply affected him, when suddenly he had some kind of seizure, perhaps epileptic, perhaps prostration due to the heat of the sun. While thus afflicted he thought he heard the voice of Stephen's Master, Jesus, reproaching him, which led to his conversion to the faith he had been persecuting.

What is not generally known, however, is that there are other difficulties with this story, much harder to handle than the conjectural question of the nature of Paul's "vision." They are not difficulties raised by skeptics who are bent upon subjecting the narrative to unsympathetic investigation; they are problems within the narrative itself which, if they are not resolved, leave us with a bewildering and inconsistent chronicle, too confused to be understood.

There is the initial problem, for instance, of how Paul expected to make arrests in a city under foreign jurisdiction. He had obtained warrants, the story tells us, from the Jerusalem high priest and had been given a patrol of armed guards to bring his prisoners safely to Judea. Are we to suppose that he would be allowed to march these guards through the gates of a Syrian city, make his arrests and carry off his prisoners, all without interference from the municipal authorities? It is possible, of course, that he had secured the cooperation of the Nabatean king, Aretas, who at this time (it is said) appointed the governors of

Damascus. It may have been such a Nabatean governor who later attempted to capture Paul when, after his conversion, he had caused a disturbance by his preaching, but Paul eluded him by being "let down in a basket" over the city wall (II Cor. xi, 32). A more plausible explanation of this latter incident, however, is that the Nabateans were waiting for Paul outside the city gates and that he was let down over the wall to elude them. In this event it would appear that they had no authority within the city (and that King Aretas did *not* appoint the governors) or they would have made a search, as Paul himself was apparently proposing to do (according to Acts) so that he could arrest the believers.

But how could Paul make a search if the Nabateans were unable to do so? Upon what basis did he get permission from the Damascus authorities? Or did he somehow proceed without permission? Upon the basis of the record as it comes to us, the problem is insoluble.

Let us assume, nevertheless, that because of facts unknown to us the stated purpose of Paul's journey was feasible. What of the journey itself? It is described three times in the book of Acts, once in the third person and twice as coming from the mouth of Paul himself. When we compare these versions attentively we are at once struck by variations in detail. In the first version, for example (chap. ix), when the light from heaven blinds Paul and he hears Jesus speaking to him, we are told that "the men who journeyed with him stood speechless, *hearing the voice* but beholding no man." In the second version, we are told that those who were with Paul "beheld the light but they *heard not the voice*" (xxii, 9), while in the third version, instead of these companions *standing* speechless, as the first version says they did, they all *fall* to the ground when Paul does (xxvi, 14).

These contradictions, it must be remembered, occur

within the brief space of a rather short book, where even in detail it is natural to expect harmony.

There are other differences, some of them subtle but not for that reason inferior in significance. In the first version, Ananias is a "disciple" and the impression given is that he belongs to the Hellenist believers. This impression is much reinforced by the statement that after his interview with Ananias, Paul "straightway" preaches Jesus in the synagogues. It is this preaching that gets him into trouble with the Jews so that he is forced to escape from Damascus. In the second version, Ananias becomes "a devout man according to the Law," which means that he is an orthodox and pious Jew, and we hear nothing of Paul causing disturbances in the synagogues. Instead, he comes to Jerusalem and, quite unlike a Hellenist believer, betakes himself to the Temple where he has a trance in which "the Righteous One" (presumably but not certainly Jesus) commissions him to be an apostle to the Gentiles (xxii, 11-21). In this version, it may be noted, Paul is defending himself before a hostile Jewish audience, so what we have, no doubt, is a speech constructed by the composer of Acts to suit a difficult occasion.

The most striking inconsistency, however, is in the words attributed to Jesus during his appearance to Paul on the road to Damascus. In the first version, Jesus, after identifying himself, tells Paul to "rise, and enter into the city, and it shall be told thee what thou must do" (ix, 6). In the second version, we have substantially the same instructions: here, too, it is not until he arrives in Damascus that Paul learns of the mission to which he has been appointed. But in the third version, we read as follows (xxvi, 15 ff.): "I am Jesus whom thou persecutest. But arise and stand upon thy feet: for to this end have I appeared unto thee, to appoint thee a minister and a witness both of the things which thou hast seen and of the things wherein I will appear unto thee; delivering thee from the people, and from the Gentiles, unto whom I send thee, to open their eyes to turn them from darkness to light and from the power of Satan unto God, that they may receive remission of sins and an inheritance among them that are sanctified by faith in me."

Here there is no command to go to the city for instructions but a full commission to apostleship, together with a brief outline of the eventual Pauline theology. This version occurs in a speech placed in the mouth of Paul during his appearance before King Agrippa and the Roman procurator, Festus, and once more we see how the composer of Acts has created an utterance suited to an occasion—indeed, the appropriateness of a speech to its circumstances is more important to him than avoiding contradictions in the narrative!

4. *Paul on Oath Denies the Sequel*

We turn now to the most serious difficulty of all. In the first version of the "Journey" story, we are told that Paul, after his escape from Damascus, came to Jerusalem where, after some not unnatural hesitation on the part of the believers, he was admitted to the community through the good offices of Barnabas. "And he was with them," this version says, "going in and out at Jerusalem, preaching boldly in the name of the Lord: and he spake and disputed against the Grecian Jews; but they went about to kill him" (ix, 28-29). In the second version, there is a riot before he can reach this point in his recital, so we pass on to the third. Here the first version is elaborated: "I was not disobedient to the heavenly vision," he says, "but declared both to them at Damascus first, and at Jerusalem, and throughout all the country of Judea . . . that they should repent and turn to God" (xxvi, 19-20).

These assertions are not inconsistent with each other but are damaging for another reason: they are contra-

dicted by Paul himself in his letter to the Galatians (chaps.
i & ii). "When it was the good pleasure of God," he says,
"who separated me [even] from my mother's womb, and
called me through his grace to reveal his Son in me, that
I might preach him among the Gentiles, immediately I
conferred not with flesh and blood, neither went I up to
Jerusalem to them that were apostles before me: but I
went away into Arabia; and again I returned to Damascus.
Then, after three years I went up to Jerusalem to become
acquainted with Cephas, and remained there fifteen days.
But other of the apostles saw I none, except James the
Lord's brother."

Here he interposes an oath, turning his recital into an
affidavit. "Now touching the things which I write you, behold, before God I lie not." And continuing, he says,
"Then I came into the regions of Syria and Cilicia; I was
*still unknown by face unto the communities of Judea
which were in Christ.*"

To the story in Acts, this contradiction is disastrous.
There never was a preaching campaign "at Jerusalem and
through all the country of Judea!" (Acts xxvi, 20). If Paul
was unknown to the Judean communities, then he had undertaken no mission among them. In fact, he had never
joined the Judean movement or even attempted to join it.
He saw only Cephas (Peter) and James the Lord's brother.
Even of the other apostles, not to mention more ordinary
believers, "saw I none," he says. Instead of his having gone
"in and out at Jerusalem, preaching boldly in the name of
the Lord," the Jerusalem community had not even known
that he was there. "They only heard say," he tells us, "that
he who once persecuted us now preacheth the faith of
which he made havoc"; but they never heard him preach
it in Judea!

Now, if there is any portion of the New Testament that
is authentic, it is Paul's letter to the Galatians. If we cannot rely upon this letter, we can rely upon nothing and

may as well close our inquiry. But the fact is that we *can* rely upon it. The letter to the Galatians is from Paul himself and by every test is genuine. But could Paul perchance have been mistaken? Had he overlooked something? Were there imperfections in his memory?

In this letter, Paul is replying to accusations made against him by enemies who would like nothing better than to tear his testimony to pieces. Never has he had more reason to be accurate than in these chapters. This he knows and puts himself on oath. If there had been any inaccuracy, any substantial omission in what he says of himself in these two chapters, it would have been ruinously exploited. Our assumption must therefore be that we have in Galatians the firm truth by which everything in Acts must always be tested. This would be so even if Galatians and Acts had been written at the same time, but the fact is that Galatians (besides being Paul's own testimony) was written at least forty years earlier and is thus much closer to the events described.

What then becomes of Paul's journey to Damascus? The reader, perhaps, like some of the scholars, may be ready to abandon it.[15] But this is too drastic. The narrative of Acts is difficult but not hopeless; if it poses hard questions, it also reveals important information. Concerning Paul's journey, let us note that in Galatians he does say that he "returned to Damascus." He had therefore been there more than once, just as Acts indicates. In another place he tells us how he escaped from Damascus (II Cor. xi, 32). This evidence has weight. Damascus was important in the life of Paul. There *could* have been a first eventful journey. Let us try to reconstruct it.

5. *Can the Journey Be Reconstructed?*

What seems most likely is that Paul, a strictly brought up Jew of Tarsus, a Pharisee who looked for the coming of the Messiah, was resident for a time in Jerusalem. During the latter part of the reign of the Emperor Tiberius and while Pontius Pilate was still procurator in Judea—say about 34 A.D.—he first heard of the belief that a Galilean who had been crucified was the Messiah. This belief was causing a disturbance among the Greek-speaking Jews and their proselytes. The authorities began to suppress it, and this led to the stoning of Stephen and a general persecution of the Hellenist believers in which Paul joined.

Of the Judaic first believers he probably knew nothing, or if he had heard of them, regarded them as soundly Jewish. It was Stephen's Hellenists upon whom his wrath was vented. These he hounded out through all Jerusalem. He fastened chains upon them. He watched them die. Then something began to happen to him.

Brooding and troubled, Paul was taking second thought. Could it be possible that these fanatics were right? Could it be that the Jewish Messiah, like the redeemers of the pagan religions familiar in Tarsus, must die and rise again? Was this the Father's purpose? Must it be by suffering that the Anointed One was perfected? To die—like Attis and Osiris—then to rise again? But as *Israel's* Messiah! Or would he be more than this? Was God doing something new and wonderful? Was the old Jewish Law that condemned sin but could not prevent it being somehow superseded? Was it faith, not law, that saved men? Then faith in what—and whom?

Reviewing much that had come to him from his Hellenistic environment, and perhaps searching afresh the Hebrew Scriptures, new concepts began to form in his mind. He was no longer persecuting but spent most of his time alone. One day, while praying in the Temple (Acts xxii, 18) it seemed to him that Jesus spoke to him. He was to preach the faith of the Hellenist believers, develop it fully, make it transmissible to the Gentiles.

But he could not begin in Jerusalem. There he would

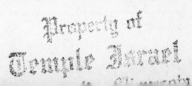

share the fate of Stephen. He would go to those whom he had scattered, beginning at Damascus.

The Jerusalem believers knew nothing of Paul's inward change. When they heard where he had gone, they supposed that it could only be to persecute. When they learned that he had had a vision, some thought that it was in the Temple (Acts xxii), others that it must have been just before he arrived at Damascus (Acts ix). For in that city he had done no persecuting. The vision must have intercepted him. The Risen Jesus who had appeared first to Peter had appeared also to Paul and had rebuked him. The inference was inescapable. As the believers saw it, Paul had left Jerusalem a persecutor, had arrived in Damascus a believer. A miracle had happened on the way. And thus a legend grew. Like other legends, it had several forms. They did not need to be consistent. Legend is not concerned with facts: it portrays the inner workings of men's minds.

This, at least, is one possible reconstruction. Others have been suggested, placing the vision and conversion *after* the arrival of Paul in Damascus. But if this is where it took place there is nothing in the New Testament that prompts even a guess about the circumstances. As one scholar who holds this view confesses, he can do nothing to support it, for "we have no knowledge of what brought him to that city, nor do we know whether he had previously been a zealous opponent" of the community of believers elsewhere. "The inner process which issued in his conversion is not to be discerned either in the Epistles or in Acts."[16]

Strictly speaking, this is true. The reconstruction we have outlined is admittedly precarious but has perhaps the merit of conserving the main substance of the Acts story so far as this is possible. In any case, since the three versions in Acts do not agree within themselves, and since some of the main assertions are sharply contradicted by Paul himself in Galatians, the conventional view collapses. We must therefore either give up the question or suggest, for whatever it may be worth, what seems to us a plausible hypothesis.

To complete this portion of the narrative: from Damascus Paul went to Arabia, for what purpose we do not know —though later we shall venture a conjecture. Returning to Damascus he became interested in what was told him of the Judaic first believers, the community at Jerusalem. He decided upon a visit—an extremely quiet one. For Paul, Jerusalem was now a place of jeopardy: he did not wish to be seen there. During fifteen days, he conferred with Peter. He also saw James "the Lord's brother," the superintendent of the community. But he saw no others. Then, passing through Syria into Cilicia he went home to Tarsus. What he did there we are not told. The next event, as recorded in the narrative, is his prompt response to an invitation brought to him by Barnabas to come to Antioch.

CHAPTER II

FROM ANTIOCH TO ROME:
A STUDY IN CONFLICTING TESTIMONY

1. *Some Questions of When and Where*

To readers who have received conventional instruction in Christian origins, nothing is more familiar than Paul's three "missionary journeys." Most Bibles contain a map upon which these so-called journeys are charted and no hint is given that *upon the basis of the New Testament itself* the three itineraries are, to say the least, the subject of no small amount of controversy. Yet they have been retained, even by writers who are fully aware of the dilemmas involved, partly because of unwillingness to acknowledge the defectiveness of the Acts narrative, and partly no doubt because the "journeys" make a neat pattern into which the better-known events of Paul's life can be fitted with optimum convenience.

Nevertheless, no attempt to preserve this pattern has ever succeeded except at the price of unbalancing the evidence and allowing the "wish-to-believe" to distort the shape of history. In the first place, and quite incontrovertibly, Paul describes in his letters events of which Acts makes no mention. As the Dominican scholar, Father Grollenberg, puts it, "Comparison with the Letters of St. Paul shows that the account contained in the Acts of the Apostles is far from complete."[17] This is about as frugal a statement of the matter as a conscientious scholar could make.

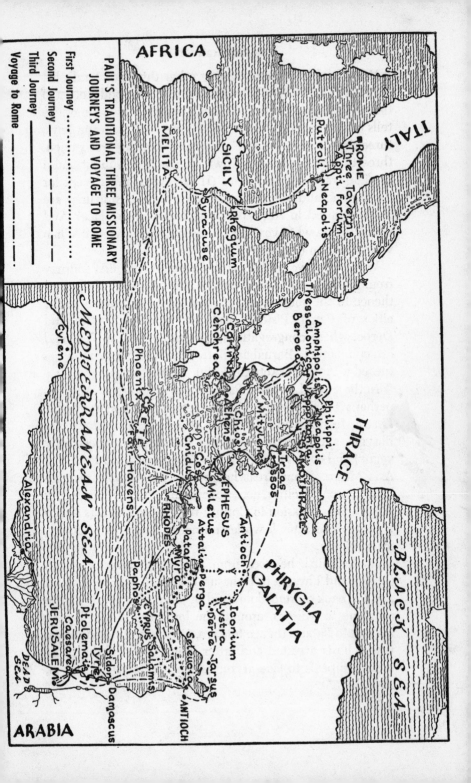

PAUL'S TRADITIONAL THREE MISSIONARY
JOURNEYS AND VOYAGE TO ROME

First Journey ·············
Second Journey — — —
Third Journey ————
Voyage to Rome — · — · —

What he has in mind, among other things, is Paul's list of his adversities in what we know as his Second Letter to the Corinthians (actually it is his Fourth). Five times, he tells us, he received "forty stripes save one" from the Jews, three times he was beaten "with rods," once he was stoned, three times he suffered shipwreck, and for "a night and a day" he was adrift in the sea (II Cor. xi, 24 ff.). Except for the stoning and one of the beatings these misfortunes are not recounted in Acts. Where did they take place? And when? Upon what voyages did he suffer shipwreck? When was he beaten by Jews?

What we have in Acts is the account of a first journey from Antioch, the Syrian capital, to the island of Cyprus, thence to the south coast of Asia Minor and north to the cities of Perga, Pisidian Antioch, Iconium, Lystra and Derbe, where congregations were organized by Paul and his companion, Barnabas, both of whom thereupon returned to Antioch (Acts xiii & xiv).

In the second journey, Paul goes overland from Antioch, perhaps to Tarsus, revisits the congregations in Derbe, Lystra, Iconium and Pisidian Antioch, then ventures into Phrygia and Galatia (here the itinerary is exceedingly vague) and comes eventually to Troas on the west coast of Asia Minor. From Troas he goes to Macedonia, evangelizes the coastal cities, goes down into Achaia and is deeply engaged in a mission in Corinth from which he sets sail to Ephesus and after a while returns to Caesarea (Acts xv, 36—xviii, 22).

In the third, he goes from Antioch overland through Galatia and Phrygia to Ephesus, thence to Macedonia and Achaia, back to Macedonia and by ship to Troas, down the coastline to Miletus, around the lee shore of the Isle of Rhodes to Patara, thence to Tyre, Caesarea and Jerusalem, where he is arrested and, after being tried by the procurator, appeals to Caesar and is sent to Rome (Acts xviii, 23—xxiii, 35).

We need not doubt that the composer of Acts is describing in his own way some—perhaps most—of the campaigns that Paul actually undertook.[18] He has before him what on the whole must have been reliable sources. It is his treatment of them that raises difficulties. That he would arrange his material to suit his purposes we might already suspect from the way in which on necessary occasions he provided Paul with suitable speeches. In this, as we have seen, he was no innovator. He followed the pattern usual at the time. He was a Greek historian and as such, in the words of Dean Inge, "invented speeches for his principal characters."[19]

What then of the "missionary journeys?" Were they not "invented" on much the same basis? As Bishop Barnes puts it, rather cautiously, the story told by Acts "was written more than sixty years after the crucifixion of Jesus. Its early information as to Paul is not always easy to reconcile with that given in Galatians and elsewhere. . . . We must sharply distinguish such information from facts to be regarded as certain."[20] Most modern scholars go further than this. At the turn of the century, it could still happen that an eminent scholar, as for example Headlam, could write an introduction to Acts without warning the reader that the subject was full of uncertainties.[21] Such an attitude, unworthy of a true historian, has happily become more rare. We now know with Goguel that the composer of Acts supplemented his source material with "various traditions of a somewhat legendary character,"[22] and with Weiss that his arrangement "is quite artificial."[23] This, in general, is the viewpoint of modern scholarship and competent critics increasingly accept it.

Bereft then of the pattern followed in Acts, we have to find a new one. This, let us admit at once, is by no means easy. The chronology of Paul's life is a baffling puzzle which scholar after scholar has attempted to solve, with the not unnatural result that there is wide disparity of opinion. Some scholars feel that there is one date at least in which they can have confidence: that of Paul's appearance before the proconsul, Gallio, in Corinth, sometime between the spring of 51 and the autumn of 52 A.D. This is because an inscription recovered at Delphi fixes the term during which Gallio served at Corinth.[24]

But unfortunately, as we have seen in examining the story of the Damascus journey, we cannot rely upon the composer of Acts for precise history: Paul may not have appeared before Gallio any more than he conducted a preaching mission in Judea. The reasons for doubting the authenticity of the Gallio incident will be developed later; for the moment, we note only that even in the case of the "firmest" date that can be postulated, there is no certainty; such is the difficulty of constructing a Pauline chronology.

The truth is that the problem is insoluble. Even if we could arrive at a satisfactory arrangement of the events recorded in Acts, there are the other events mentioned by Paul but not in Acts which we could only fit in by recourse to sheer guessing without a shred of reliable information upon which to base our guesses. This is not to say that there are no writers who have "solved" the problem to their own satisfaction, but such solutions immediately become targets for other writers to riddle with objections. Fortunately, in the case of the present study precise dating is not necessary. All that is required is a rather general view of main events, suitably grouped and—so far as this is possible—in their correct sequence.

This means that for the most part we can accept the report in Acts as to the cities visited but not necessarily in the order given or without assuming that there were visits to other cities of which there is no mention. We have to allow, for instance, for the shipwrecks mentioned by Paul but not in Acts. Where did they take place? In visits to Cyprus, to cities on the Aegean Sea, or to places of which

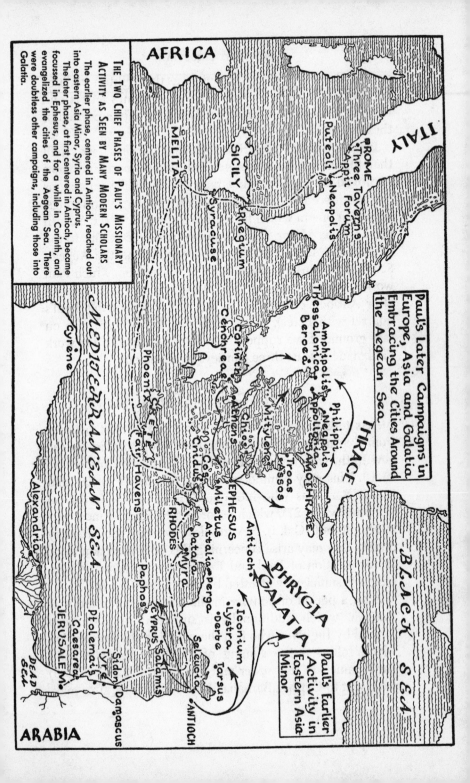

THE TWO CHIEF PHASES OF PAUL'S MISSIONARY ACTIVITY AS SEEN BY MANY MODERN SCHOLARS

The earlier phase, centered in Antioch, reached out into eastern Asia Minor, Syria and Cyprus.

The later phase, at first centered in Antioch, became focussed in Ephesus, and for a while in Corinth, and evangelized the cities of the Aegean Sea. There were doubtless other campaigns, including those into Galatia.

Paul's Later Campaigns in Europe, Asia and Galatia Embracing the Cities Around the Aegean Sea.

Paul's Earlier Activity in Eastern Asia Minor

AFRICA

ITALY

ROME
Three Taverns
Appii Forum

Puteoli Neapolis

MELITA

SICILY
Syracuse
Rhegium

Cyrene

MEDITERRANEAN SEA

Phoenix
CRETE
Fair Havens

Corinth
Cenchreae

Amphipolis
Thessalonica
Beroea

Philippi
Neapolis
Apollonia

THRACE

SAMOTHRACE

Athens
Chios
Mitylene
Troas
ASSOS

Cnidus
Cos
Miletus

EPHESUS
Attalia Perga
Patara
Myra

RHODES

Paphos

CYPRUS Salamis

Sidon Damascus
Tyre
Ptolemais
Caesarea
JERUSALEM

Alexandria

DEAD SEA

ARABIA

BLACK SEA

Antioch

PHRYGIA
GALATIA

Iconium
Lystra
Derbe Tarsus

Seleucia
ANTIOCH

neither Paul's letters nor Acts gives us the slightest inkling? We cannot suppose that we have *all* of Paul's letters and nothing is more plain than that Acts tells only a portion of the story.

Instead of the traditional three "journeys" we shall therefore adopt the rather general pattern more and more approved by modern scholars in which Paul's campaigns are considered as belonging within two large groupings, an earlier one in which he worked in Syria and the eastern parts of Asia Minor, and a later one which took him to the cities, both Asian and European, which line the Aegean Sea. For the earlier campaigns, the center from which Paul worked was Antioch, the Syrian capital; for the later ones, after Antioch ceased to be the center (following Paul's quarrel with Peter), it was Ephesus. And we are also on safe ground if we suppose that in the course of his work Paul made at least three journeys to Jerusalem.

2. *The Gathering Storm*

Acts tells us that it was Barnabas, a Hellenist believer from Cyprus and himself a prominent propagandist for the new faith, who brought Paul from Tarsus to Antioch (xi, 25 ff.). This may remind us that Acts tells us earlier that it was Barnabas who introduced Paul to the Jerusalem community (ix, 27), which according to Paul he most certainly did not (Gal. i). Nevertheless, we may set aside any doubts that may arise concerning this later assertion since the association of Paul and Barnabas in missionary campaigns is sufficiently attested by the letters (Gal. ii, 1).

After a period of activity in the thriving community at Antioch, which traditionally is supposed to have been formed by fugitives who fled there during the persecution which followed the stoning of Stephen, Barnabas and Paul (named in that order and the latter still called Saul) were sent to Cyprus, Barnabas' homeland. Here, after making conversions and organizing the believers, most of whom were Gentile, Saul, who is now called Paul, takes the initiative away from Barnabas and proposes more adventurous missions. He "and his company" (including the subordinated Barnabas) set sail for Pamphylia in the south of Asia Minor and in this area succeed in founding new societies. There are scholars, however, who believe that this itinerary should be revised. It was only Barnabas, they think, who went to Cyprus; Paul went directly to Pamphylia.[25] The association of the two is supplied by the composer of Acts to show that Paul was on excellent terms with the respected Barnabas, thereby disproving assertions that were being made during the latter part of the first century (when Acts was written) that Paul had broken with Antiochian orthodoxy. If the good Barnabas was his comrade, the charges against Paul could not possibly be true.

However this may be, there is no doubt that Paul organized communities in Asia Minor and that he did so on a basis more "liberal" (as we would put it) than was being done by anyone else. At least, if there were others who went as far as Paul did, we have no knowledge of them. Paul's deviation from the original requirements, briefly stated, consisted in his remission of the obligation of circumcision on the part of Gentile new believers and his subordination of the Mosaic Law. Salvation was by faith in the Messiah. Jews should be circumcised because they were Jews, not as a condition of salvation. Jews should follow their dietary regulations; but for Gentiles these things were not necessary. So Paul removed them and it was this that brought upon him so much trouble.

From the beginning there had been uneasiness—perhaps this is too mild a word—between the Judaic and the Hellenist believers, as we saw when we considered the martyrdom of Stephen. We said at that time that Stephen's death and the persecution that followed might be explained by supposing that Stephen was preaching boldly that the Risen Jesus was the coming Messiah whereas the Judean community was much more quiet about it. It also seemed possible, even probable, that Stephen had spoken disparagingly of the Temple sacrifices and that he had abrogated some of the authority of Mosaic Law. But it is not likely that he had released his followers from the obligation of circumcision, especially since, presumably, most of them were Jewish. Yet, the feeling persists that what Paul completed may well have been begun by Stephen.*

In any case, what we see in Acts, partly disguised by the composer, and in the letters entirely undisguised, is that Paul was going further than *the Hellenist communities* (not merely further than the community at Jerusalem) in admitting Gentiles to the movement simply upon confession of faith and by baptism and without requiring circumcision or observance of the Mosaic Law.

3. *Negotiations at Jerusalem*

That thorny questions were taken up with the leaders at Jerusalem, both Paul and Acts agree, though they diverge sharply as to how and when. According to Acts, Paul (once more with the ever-useful Barnabas) went to Jerusalem to hand over to the community's treasury a relief fund collected in Antioch in a time of famine. We know from external evidence that there was such a famine at about this time and there is thus good reason to credit the story (xi, 29) so far as the relief fund is concerned, setting aside the question as to whether one of the emissaries was Paul. But there is nothing said about the Judaic-Gentile question

---

* It may be thought that if Stephen had departed from Judaic obligations to any considerable extent it is he and not Paul who is entitled to be called "the first Christian," but this does not allow for Paul's fusion of the idea of the Messiah with that of the Redeemer and Lord. To Stephen, Jesus was the coming Messiah. To Paul, he was this and also—eventually —the Savior who had replaced the pagan redeemers of the salvation cults. Historically, it is the Redeemership of Jesus, not his Messianic office, that is distinctive of the Christian cultus.

having been taken up at this meeting. On the contrary, a later visit is devoted to it (xv), the so-called Council of Jerusalem. On this occasion, the issue is formally debated, Peter *defending* the Pauline position, and the result is a decree issued by James, the superintendent, to the effect that all that is required from Gentile believers is that they abstain from food "sacrificed to idols, and from blood, and from things strangled, and from fornication." This means that Jewish dietary rules must be followed and (probably) that there must be no consorting with the temple prostitutes of pagan deities.

Of this "Council" Paul knows nothing. If we take it (as seems certain to the present writer) that Galatians was a late writing, no meeting of this sort could have taken place at least until most of Paul's work was done. Nor could Paul have been present, as Acts says he was. This is tacitly admitted in Acts itself when on Paul's final visit to Jerusalem and just before his arrest, James is described as informing him that he (James) had circulated a letter containing this very decree, just as though this was news to Paul—who was supposed to have been a principal negotiator at the "Council" when the decree was issued! (xxi, 25).

According to some scholars, as for example Weiss, this Jerusalem convocation never took place and the decree of James "simply did not exist."[26] Another view is that the story of the earlier visit of Paul and Barnabas to Jerusalem was contained in a source coming from Antioch which did not admit that Antiochian believers went to Jerusalem to have their orthodoxy adjudicated and which therefore based the visit on the relief fund. There was also, however, a Jerusalem source which in speaking of the same visit mentioned the decision of James but omitted reference to the relief fund and the famine. These two accounts of one visit, each of which omitted what its writer found embarrassing, the composer of Acts treated as relating to two visits the last of which he considerably elaborated.

It may furthermore be held that since Peter in the "Council" story does most of the talking and almost as though Paul and Barnabas were not present, the fact is that they were indeed not present and the "Council" was settling an issue raised not by them but by Peter. Peter's "liberal" tendencies are clear both in Acts and in Galatians and it may very well be that a time arrived when he too wanted concessions (though fewer than Paul's) made to the Gentile believers.

As for Paul, he did not even accept the prohibition of "meats offered to idols." It was by no means easy outside of sizable Jewish communities to obtain meat that had *not* been "offered to idols." This practice was merely the donation of a certain portion of the animals butchered for market to the temple of one of the sacrificial cults, there to be burned on an altar or eaten by the priests. It was quite similar to the practice at Jerusalem except that at the Jewish Temple the sacrifice was offered to the "one true God" and not to "idols." The remaining meat which was then put on sale was considered to have been "blessed" by whatever god had "received" his appropriate portion. (Relatively few animals were entirely consumed on the altars either in the pagan cults or in the Hebrew ritual; an instance of it in the latter is the "whole burnt offering.")

To a pious Jew, the question of which god had "blessed" the meat was vital; he could only eat it if it had been "blessed" by the one and only God, Jehovah. Hence the requirement set forth by James. But Paul regarded the matter as almost trivial. In his First Letter to the Corinthians he tells his Gentile converts that idols are nothing anyway and that to intelligent people the question of whether food has been offered to nonexistent deities is unimportant; the only thing to beware of, he says, is the possibility that an enlightened person's example may cause a weaker brother "to stumble" (chap. viii).

To know what really happened at the Jerusalem interview (it was not a council), we must go to Paul himself (Gal. ii). There had been trouble in the congregations he had founded, stirred up by Judaic believers who insisted that the new faith could not dispense either with the Mosaic Law or with circumcision. To join the new movement it was necessary in effect to become a member of the Jewish nation, just as it was in the Pharisaic synagogues which received proselytes. There was evidently something of the same trouble in Antioch. So Paul "by revelation"—that is, moved inwardly by his own resolve and not by command from anyone else—takes Barnabas and Titus (the latter an important colleague in his campaigns abroad) to Jerusalem to see James and Peter.

At this conference there was evidently no real decision. According to the Galatians story as it appears in certain manuscripts, Paul was compelled to have Titus circumcised even though he was a Gentile, presumably because he was taking a prominent part in the movement and was in fact one of its missionaries. According to other manuscripts (from which our Galatians is translated), Paul utterly refused to have Titus circumcised. It is difficult to choose between these two opposing versions. But even if the circumcision took place it was a special case: perhaps a kind of appeasement.[27] What happened in the end was that James and Peter gave Paul and Barnabas "the right hand of fellowship" on the broad basis that as Peter was an apostle to the Jews ("the circumcision"), so Paul was an apostle to the Gentiles ("the uncircumcision").

There was, however, one other requirement and to Paul it was of the utmost importance. He was to "remember the Poor": which meant that he was to take up a collection among his Gentile congregations for the benefit of the Jerusalem community—which evidently sometimes called itself by the Essenic title, "the Poor." What the attitude of James was, it is hard to conjecture. Most probably, his viewpoint was entirely Jewish and he did not regard the Messiah as coming to the Gentiles except as he came through the chosen people, Israel. In this event, it may not have mattered to him very much what Jewish rites the Gentile believers observed since their position in the coming Kingdom would be secondary and derivative. But he could not give his endorsement to Paul's attitude. He could merely understand and tolerate it. The Messiah in any case would soon arrive. Then it would be seen what should be done about the Gentiles. Meanwhile, the financial situation was acute. Just as foreign Jews sent their annual contributions to the Temple, why should not the Gentile congregations take up at least one generous offering for the relief of the Jerusalem community? To this Paul gave his prompt assent; he saw at once how useful it would be in proving that between himself and the Jerusalem apostles there was a basis of agreement.

4. *The Quarrel with Peter*

At an unspecified time after the Jerusalem conference, Paul had a harsh encounter with Peter at Antioch. The latter, while a guest of the community in the Syrian capital, had been eating regularly with the mixed company of Jewish and Gentile believers. (This may mean that he participated in a sacramental meal or in the ordinary community supper which was in any case to some extent sacred, or both.) But when "certain came from James," Paul goes on, meaning members of the Jerusalem community over which James presided, Peter became intimidated and withdrew from the combined fellowship. Moved by his example, Barnabas did the same "and the rest of the Jews with him" (Gal. i & ii). Paul saw at once that this meant a division of the Jewish and Gentile believers which might never be healed. Nor do we know that it ever was.

A time came when Paul returned no more to the Antioch community and was no longer supported as one of its missionaries. The break might have come—and indeed we can confidently say that it did—at this very moment.

But reckless of this aspect of the outcome, Paul bitterly reproached Peter. "You are not standing upon the basis of the 'good news,'" he said. "First, you, a Jew, live in Gentile fashion, then you withdraw and demand that Gentiles live in Jewish fashion! We who are *born* Jews and have the Law nevertheless acknowledge that reliance upon the Law will not save us but only faith in Jesus the Messiah. If we return to Mosaic regulations," he argues, "where is our faith in the Messiah? And if it is this faith that saves even ourselves who are Jews, why should Gentiles follow the Law of Moses when it can save neither them nor us? Why then are you withdrawing from the Gentiles who are saved even as we are saved? Surely, you are betraying your faith in Jesus who put his trust in you—and in salvation through him as the Messiah!" (Gal. ii, paraphrased.)

Such was the line of Paul's argument, and such his reproach. But we may be certain that Peter and Barnabas—and perhaps most of the other Jewish believers—had never really given up the Law. They were just no longer sure how they ought to regard it. Their condition was one of irresolution: they could come to no satisfactory decision. If it was faith in the Messiah which alone brought salvation, Jewish regulations *could* logically be dispensed with. But *should* they? They were certainly a great hindrance in converting the Gentiles. The dietary laws were bad enough, but circumcision was thoroughly abominated. To a Gentile convert it meant the mockery of men and the repugnance of women among the Greek-speaking unconverted. Yet to a Jew it was the sign of his nation as well as of his faith, given to him by the God of his fathers. Could Gentiles share the Jewish heritage and not adopt the Jewish sign? Could they enter into the Covenant and disregard its sacred Law? After all, it was a Jewish Messiah who was coming—to the Jews first, then to the world.

Peter, according to strong but nonetheless uncertain tradition, eventually went a long way toward Paul's position. Before the incident at Antioch, Paul may well have thought that he had already very largely adopted it, although for his own part confining his missionary work to Jews (Gal. ii, 8). But it was impossible to go as far as Paul had gone without absorbing the Hellenistic elements in his theology. This Peter had not done. And so there was the continuing struggle, subdued in Acts, conspicuous in Paul's letters, as manifested by the quarrel with Peter at Antioch.[28]

5. *Collection for the Saints: A Suppressed Episode*

We are not for the moment describing Paul's campaigns; they will be better understood when we know more of the background. Our purpose for the present is only to introduce the story and to show how it is treated in Acts. We come therefore without further delay to the final phase in which Paul takes up his collection for the community at Jerusalem. In his letters the accumulation of this fund is of the utmost importance. In Acts there is no mention of it.

Various attempts have been made to explain this by saying that the collection was a continuing affair like that sent by the Jews of the Dispersion to the Temple treasury at Jerusalem. But the only basis for this supposition is a rather fine point of grammar,* assisted by the thesis that Galatians was written before Paul's final period of activity in the cities of the Aegean.

The argument here is a rather technical one and we

---

* μνημονεύωμεν (mnēmoneuōmen) means *remember* in the present tense of continuous action. Grammatically, however, there is no indication one way or the other whether the continuous action has already begun. The reference is to the request of James that Paul's Gentile communities "*remember* the Poor" (Gal. ii, 10).

postpone its discussion to a more suitable context in the next chapter. For the moment let it merely be mentioned that the point it seeks to make is that if there had been a number of offerings on a continuing basis, this last collection would not have been thought remarkable. But this is not in the least the impression conveyed by the letters of Paul.

Irrespective of when Galatians was written and of whether there were previous collections, the emphasis Paul places upon the fund he brought to Jerusalem on this final occasion requires that it was nothing less than the acknowledged purpose of his journey and that the composer of Acts, who must have known of it, had a reason for not mentioning it. In I Corinthians (xvi, 1 ff.), Paul speaks of carrying it himself to Jerusalem rather than merely sending it (and also says, "As I gave orders to the communities of Galatia, so also do ye," bringing Galatians on any natural basis close in date to this letter); in II Corinthians he devotes more than a chapter to it (parts of viii and all of ix); in Romans xv, he explains that it is important that he himself take this offering to Jerusalem (25-32) although he is anxious to make his first visit to Rome and then go on to Spain.

Evidently, no matter what else Paul was eager to do, conveying this offering to the Jerusalem community and handing it over in his own person had a higher priority. That the Jerusalem visit was perilous to Paul is made perfectly plain both in the letters and in Acts. Why was he willing to take such risks? Acts makes it appear that his whole purpose was to renew his relationship with the parent society with which he was in communion, thus demonstrating that the Pauline churches (as they eventually became) were legitimate in their descent from the first believers. So Paul goes to Jerusalem (and the composer of Acts may have believed this in spite of his sources) an esteemed envoy returning to the patriarchal community with no slightest hint that the nobility of the occasion had been somewhat clouded by the presence of a large financial contribution.

As to the real situation, as one scholar puts it, "The only bond between [Paul] and Jerusalem now is his collection of money for the benefit of the community there: he had promised that, and he would keep his part of the bargain."[29] It was a benefaction that he could bestow upon the Jerusalem leaders which would oblige them to recognize his work. If they accepted the contributions of his followers they were acknowledging the legitimacy of his apostleship. Whatever they thought of the basis upon which he had built his Gentile following, here was proof tangible that he had been successful and that the communities he had founded were worthily commending themselves to the movement's patriarchate.

Nor would it diminish Paul's treasured independence. He did not hold his apostolate from the Jerusalem community. It had been given him in a vision by Jesus himself. This was vital to Paul. Under no circumstances could he bow to Jerusalem authority. But a large gift of money was not "bowing." It had exactly the right significance for a dignified, equalitarian relationship. James could receive it gracefully as a generous tribute, Paul could transmit it proudly as a testimony to his work.

Yet Paul after all was somewhat ambivalent. In Galatians he could speak of "those who are reputed to be somewhat" and say that "whatsoever they were, it maketh no matter to me"; but it did matter. James at least was important to Paul and he wanted his approval. If this was more than he could get for his preaching, he would have it for his eager recognition that Jerusalem had a claim upon the rest of the movement's philanthropy. It was a kind of recognition which was palatable to Paul and at the same time acceptable to James. Besides the value of the money, which was doubtless much needed, it signified a salute to the Judaic community which raised no questions of theology.

But the composer of Acts was not satisfied with this. Paul and the patriarchate at Jerusalem had to be in full communion even though, admittedly, there were differences of emphasis between them. So Paul goes to Jerusalem resembling a Judaic believer: as Judaic indeed as the composer of Acts can make him while still allowing him to remain the apostle to the Gentiles. There was no real difficulty, according to this narrative, between him and the believers under James the Just's superintendency. The trouble was all between the believers in the Risen Jesus and the unbelieving Jews.

Here, however, we must not go so far as to suppose that Paul, after his arrest, did not make out the best case he could for his Judaism, even though the speeches attributed to him cannot have been his. That he stressed the Judaic side of his outlook is entirely likely. He was on trial for his life, accused of apostasy to his religion upon a basis that made him also a provocateur, endangering the peace of the empire. If he could show that, although believing some things that other Jews did not, he was nevertheless a faithful son of Israel and a man of peace, it would go a long way toward satisfying Roman law. But he certainly never said, "I came to bring alms to my nation, and offerings, in presenting which they found me purified in the Temple" (xxiv, 18). The alms and offerings went to James and the community of Judaic believers and not to the Jewish nation. Here the composer of Acts may even have turned the neat trick of converting the collection solicited by James into a contribution from Paul to the Temple treasury, thus at one blow explaining the tradition of a collection and giving further evidence that Paul in spite of everything was both a believer in Jesus the Messiah and at the same time a pious Jew.

Anyone who after reading this section of the Acts narrative (xxii-xxvi) will turn to Paul's letters (say Galatians iii and v) will find it difficult to believe that he is dealing with the same man. In a sense, of course, he is not. In the letters he has Paul's own words, his arguments, his impassioned pleas. In Acts he has a story put together almost half a century later, compiled to fit a pattern and edited to a tendentious purpose. "If ye receive circumcision," says the Paul of Galatians, "Christ will profit you nothing." And again, "There can be neither Jew nor Greek . . . for ye are all one in Christ Jesus." And in this case, he continues, those who belong to Christ are the real inheritors of the Jewish covenant, "Abraham's seed, heirs according to promise" (iii and v). Which means that believers in his doctrine who are baptized into the faith have *replaced* the Jews, irrespective of whether by birth they were Jews or Greeks, and are thus God's chosen people! But in Acts he says he serves "the God of our fathers, believing all things which are according to the Law," and even that the only real issue between himself and other Jews is his belief in the resurrection of the dead! (xxiv).

And thus we see once more that if we are to recover the story of what really happened in those early days—or as much of it as is recoverable—we shall never do it by remaining close to the surface.

6. *The Unfinished Story*

The story of Paul's voyage as a prisoner to Rome is considered by many scholars to have been edited only slightly by the composer of Acts, most of it coming directly from one of his sources. Other scholars dispute this warmly, urging that the composer is here displaying his greatest skill. Either way we can be grateful for it since it is one of the finest brief descriptive narratives ever written. In form at least, and probably in fact (at any rate until Italy is reached), it is an eyewitness account, vivid in its details, precise as to time and place. It ends with the words, "When we had entered Rome, Paul was allowed a private lodging, with the soldier who guarded him" (xxviii, 16).

With the voyage complete, we return to the composer and must be on our guard again. The book ends on the polemical note that God's salvation, which the Jews have refused, will surely be received by the Gentiles. Thus the thesis is complete, however full of inconsistencies. Pauline Christianity has been traced from the original Judaic believers, with whom Paul was in full communion, to the Gentile churches which adopt it as their legitimate inheritance. What began in Jerusalem has safely arrived in Rome.*

Here Paul resided "two whole years," the concluding verse informs us, "and received all that went in unto him, preaching the kingdom of God and teaching the things concerning the Lord Jesus Christ with all boldness, none forbidding him" (xxviii, 30).

But what we are not given is the end of Paul's story. If he was released from imprisonment and went on to Spain, as one tradition (not much believed by modern scholars) supposes, Acts tells us nothing about it. Paul has arrived in Rome and is preaching with all boldness. It is on this note that the story must end. Of the other tradition, by far the more likely, that Paul perished in the Neronian persecution (64 A.D.), not a word is said. The climax has been reached; there must be no anticlimax. Particularly must nothing be said that would confirm the Roman suspicion that Christians from the beginning were rebels, praying for "the end of the world," "haters of the human race." It was hard enough to explain the crucifixion of Jesus by Pilate, though this could be laid to the instigation of the Jews. Must it also be revealed that Paul was condemned by Nero? Having come all this way to show that Christianity

---

* Jerusalem was destroyed in 70 A.D., about a generation before Acts was composed but not before some of its sources were written.

is continuous with Judaism, a legally recognized religion, must it be disclosed that the leading founder of the Gentile churches was executed as a criminal?

And thus the story is brought to a close where its composer's purpose is fulfilled, which is polemical rather than historical. Yet we must not judge him by any standard other than his own. He was writing of events as they *should* have happened and therefore *must* have happened in accordance with his faith. If we had his sources, they would be a treasure beyond price. But since these are lost to us, let us at least be grateful that we have a narrative that used them. For although the remaining New Testament Scriptures would still reveal to us something of early Christian thought and of the struggles that had shaped it, without the book of Acts very little could be known about the first communities of believers.

CHAPTER III

THE SOLUTION OF THE PROBLEMS:
THE METHODS OF MODERN CRITICISM

1. *Understanding the New Testament*

The problems of the Acts narrative as noted in the preceding two chapters have made it plain that the New Testament cannot be understood merely by reading it. Unless we are willing to brush aside contradictions and inconsistencies, suppressions and distortions, thus confessing that we are not concerned with what is true and what is false, we must have recourse to the methods of modern scholarship.

Actually, of course, in a certain measure all who read the Bible have been dependent upon these methods all along, though frequently they have not known it. The English translation of the New Testament was not made for us by angels. It is the result of immense labors begun by ancient scholars such as St. Jerome, labors that modern experts are still continuing. For there is no *one* settled text of the Greek New Testament. Any given translation, such as the King James or the Revised or the Revised Standard Version has been made upon the basis of *agreements among scholars*—upon such matters, e.g., as which documents shall be preferred in each of many thousands of doubtful instances.

To this extent, therefore—and it is far greater than the average layman has any idea of—the reader of an English translation of the New Testament is already relying upon the judgment of scholars. Besides the chief manuscripts and more important versions* which specialists must study, there are large "families" of other documents *within* and *between* which painstaking comparisons must be made. There is often difference of opinion. The New Testament in English (as also the Old Testament) is thus the product of a consensus among the scholars who made the translation, in arriving at which a majority necessarily (but not inerrantly) overrode a minority on disputed points.** Many defects in the King James Version (1611 A.D.) were corrected by the Revised Version (1884), and the latter in turn was further corrected by the recent Revised Standard Version. But no one who knows anything about the matter would contend that the process is complete. For as far ahead as we can look there will be *textual criticism*.

This kind of scholarship, however, is concerned only with bringing us as close as possible to what was written in the original documents. To understand the writings after we have arrived at an approximately authentic text, we need *literary* and *historical* criticism. Here we shall pause to note that to some people the word *criticism* as applied to the Bible is objectionable, largely, no doubt,

* By *manuscript* is meant a hand-written copy of the New Testament or a portion of it in Greek, the language of its composition. There are no originals (autographs) in our possession; nor is it likely that there ever will be. What we have are copies of copies several times removed (we do not know how many) from the originals, all of which contain errors and defects which pose questions for scholars. The chief *manuscripts* are four in number, dated in the fourth century A.D., to which, since 1931, has been added the third-century Chester Beatty papyri. The *versions* are translations from the Greek (into Latin, Syriac, etc.) and are often important because they may translate an older *manuscript* than those available to us or may in other ways provide significant indications. The total number of documents and fragments that scholars must consult runs into thousands.

** A curious example of an Old Testament case in which the majority has almost certainly been wrong, even in the recent Revised Standard Version, is the rendering of the word *tappūach* as *apple* (Song of Songs, ii, 5). There were no apple orchards in Palestine in Old Testament times. Some of the minority thought it should be *apricot* but they were overruled.

because they misconstrue its meaning. *Criticism* in this context does not imply a hostile attitude. Its meaning is derived from the Greek *kritikos*, which means *skilled in judgment*. Biblical criticism is thus the painstaking effort to acquire and use the scientific skills which in the case of *textual criticism* assure us that we have a text as close as possible to the original, and in the case of *literary criticism* enable us to identify and evaluate the various elements that enter into the Bible books, while *historical criticism* improves our comprehension of the Scriptures through setting them in the correct context of time and circumstance.

Because the New Testament comes to us as an entity, usually bound together (in morocco) with the Old Testament to make a single volume, we tend to think of it as though it had always been such. Nothing could be further from the truth. What a changed view we would have if we could see the piles of papyrus (ancient paper made from the pith of reeds) on a scribe's table, blown sometimes (as Schweitzer surmises) to the floor by a gust of wind and then put back in the wrong order—which may in part explain the confused condition of II Corinthians![30] There was nothing morocco-bound about the early manuscripts of the New Testament! Moreover, and of greater importance, the New Testament is a selection from a much wider literature, gradually agreed upon by Church authorities; and for the most part it was not produced for the purposes for which we use it.

There are many other gospels than our four—the gospels of Peter, Thomas, Philip, Hebrews, etc.; there are other books of Acts besides our "Acts of the Apostles," so-called —Acts of John, Peter, Andrew, Thomas, etc.; and there is an immense amount of further literature only a portion of which (but enough to fill 550 pages, closely printed) has been preserved.[31] Besides these scriptures, known as the Apocryphal New Testament, there are others that were much used in the early Church: the *Didache*, the letter of

Barnabas, the *Shepherd of Hermas* are prominent examples. The "Shepherd" in fact was for a time included in the New Testament.

But this was when there came *to be* a New Testament! For a long time it was the *Old* Testament that was the Christian Bible. It was to this Jewish Bible, which Christians had taken as their own, that believers went in search of "proof texts" of the mission and significance of Jesus as Messiah and Lord. This was the evidence that was then regarded as conclusive: Jesus was found (in ways that would astonish modern readers unfamiliar with this ancient practice) to have fulfilled the inspired prophecies. The literature which eventually became what we know as the New Testament was at first regarded as quite secondary.

Nor is it in the least true, as is often thoughtlessly assumed, that the Church was somehow founded upon the New Testament. (The early communities were not of course a Church, but the Church properly so called had undergone considerable development before there was a New Testament.) We might put it that instead of the New Testament producing the Church, the Church produced the New Testament. It did so in providing for its changing needs: the needs, that is, of a movement which was *becoming* a Church.

For the first half of the first century or more, the interest of believers was largely focused upon the imminent second coming of Jesus as Messiah. No permanent institution was envisaged. Nor was there need of a record of the life of Jesus: he would shortly return! As for a history of the movement, those who expect the end of history do not trouble to write it! There were indeed such writings as Paul's letters, not intended for preservation but written to meet an immediate situation, and it seems probable that they were largely neglected for nearly half a century. There were sacramental formulas, rituals of initiation, Jewish Messianic literature, sermons, memoirs—and above all catechetical material for the instruction of believers. The latter grew in volume as conditions called it forth. It was based on what there was of written tradition and on what had long been orally transmitted. As Nock puts it, "Under changed conditions it was necessary not only to supply the answers to some of the questions which piety asked, but also to reinforce that piety in daily life when it was no longer lived in the first intensity."[32]

It was to meet this need that a considerable part of the New Testament was produced, although by no means all of it. The book of Revelation, for instance, is a fiery summons to get ready for the cataclysm which will usher in the Messianic reign; it does not in the least contemplate an institutional church. In the "New Jerusalem" which will come down from heaven there will be no house of worship. "For the Lord God, the Almighty, and the Lamb are the temple thereof" (Rev. xxi, 22). The letter to the Hebrews which, in contrast, does not mention the Messianic reign, also belongs in a distinctive category. But the gospels and the book of Acts quite definitely were produced to meet the needs of a movement which, though still Messianic, was fast becoming an institutional church, and it is this literature that we must now subject to critical examination.

2. *Why the Gospels and Acts Were Written*

When it became evident that the Messianic reign was delayed and that it was questionable whether the Risen Jesus would soon return, interest in his life and work began to grow much stronger. To the second and third generations of those who were now called Christians it was not enough to be told of the blessedness in store for true believers or to hear repeated the exposition of the various elements of the primitive theology. They needed to know more about the beginnings of the movement. This was not merely to provide a firmer foundation for their own faith through establishing its reference points in history but also so that critics might be answered, for by the end of the first century there was no small amount of controversy.

The Jews in particular were attacking the belief in the Risen Jesus with increasing vigor. Jerusalem had been destroyed (70 A.D.) in the hapless revolt against the Romans, and Judaism was rallying itself to face a bleak future. There was thus a new concern for Jewish solidarity and it was particularly exasperating to hear the Gentile believers claiming to be the true Judaism and accusing Jews who were such by "race" of rejecting their Messiah. These same Gentile believers had also appropriated to themselves the Jewish Bible in its Greek translation, the Septuagint,* which they were using to prove their case against the Jews.

As to the original Jerusalem community from which the movement had taken its rise, James, its presiding officer, had been stoned to death on the orders of the high priest, Ananas, during an interval between procurators while Roman authority was weak (62 A.D.); and a few years later when the siege of the city was imminent, the entire society seems to have fled across the Jordan to Pella, where it was known as the sect of the Nazoreans, a name changed by Gentile Christians to Nazarenes. Faithful to the Law of Moses, the Nazoreans remained Judaic and survived obscurely in the eventual sect of the Ebionites. Ephesus and Rome—and perhaps Alexandria—were now the leading centers of the movement that had begun in Jerusalem.

Besides the Jews, there was rivalry with other Messianic sects, particularly the followers of John the Baptist, who did not in the least concede that their master had been only a "forerunner" of Jesus. There was also an increasing need for a clearer historical framework for the sacramental

---

* So called because according to tradition it was translated by seventy (or seventy-two) Jewish elders in Egypt, perhaps in the second century B.C.

ritual, so close to those of the mystery cults. In all respects, authoritative guidance had become necessary and the believers hoped to find it in the life and work of Jesus and in the history of their movement.

What directions, they asked, had Jesus given to his followers? What was his attitude to his Jewish fellow countrymen? Had he understood that they would reject him? What during his lifetime was his attitude to the Gentiles? Did he preach to them also? Had he known that it would be they who would receive him? What line did he take toward the Roman authorities? How did he appoint those who would organize his Church? Under what circumstances was he crucified? What was the accusation against him? What part did the Jews take in his crucifixion? Upon what day did he rise from the dead? What proof was there that he had risen? What was his relationship to John the Baptist? When did he ordain the sacraments? These and a hundred other questions cried out for answers.

The result was the emergence of a kind of literature that had not previously existed and which is represented in our four gospels. When similar questions were asked about the early believers and the heroes of the apostolic period, the result was such writings as the book of Acts. Neither the gospels nor Acts were written as what we would call history. They were answers to questions contrived in the form of a narrative. In the language of modern scholarship, they are *evangelical catechesis*.[33]

Now it is here most probably that the reader may need to make a determined effort to set aside his preconceptions. The gospels are *not* biographies but—so to speak—*explanations*. And since their composers saw many things differently, each from the other, the explanations are often at variance. The intention, however, is in all cases the same: to provide instruction according to a definite pattern; and the same is true of Acts. That is why we use the word *catechesis* which, like the commoner word "catechism" comes from the Greek.* The purpose of the gospels and Acts is to indoctrinate the reader (or more often the "hearer" in a class or congregation) through a vehicle of instruction which gives approved answers to the questions that arise in maintaining one's faith: thus a *catechesis*.

Earlier, there had been an *eschatological*** catechesis, or a pattern of instruction looking toward the coming of Jesus to reign as Messiah. Paul's letters to the Thessalonians are *catechesis* of this type in the emergent (and indeed almost impromptu!) stage of its development. Much of the *eschatological catechesis* was drawn from the Old Testament, which it must not be forgotten was at that time the Bible of the believers just as it was—and remains—the Bible of the Jews. By finding special meanings hidden in the Hebrew Scriptures it was possible to see not only that Jesus was predicted as God's Vicegerent and Messiah but that the time and place of his birth, the manner of his death, the miracle of his resurrection were all foretold. So were events still to come, especially the reappearance of Jesus in glory and the judgment of the world. This, then, was the *eschatological catechesis* and it did not immediately disappear when, to meet new conditions, the *evangelical catechesis* was developed.

The term *evangelical* is from the Greek word which in Anglo-Saxon is translated "gospel" ("good" + "spiel" or "spoken word") and in modern English "good news." It has become specific, however, for our New Testament gospels (and their continuation in Acts), thus indicating the derivation of doctrine or tradition from these sources. In the case of *evangelical catechesis* we go back to the time when these Scriptures were composed; it is the *gospels and Acts*

---

* From κατ-ηχεώ (*kat-ēcheō*) meaning *to sound into one's ears;* to teach orally in a repeated pattern so that what is taught is retained in memory to be reproduced by rote.

** From ἔσχατος (*eschatos*) meaning *uttermost;* doctrines of final things, death, the judgment, future life. Here, these things plus the end of the existing world order and the beginning of the Messianic reign.

themselves, considered as a response to the new need that had arisen, that become the *catechesis.*

Of our four gospels (*evangels*) that comprise this *catechesis* (of which Acts is the extension), the first to be written was Mark, though not quite in the form in which we have it. According to tradition, Peter, who could not speak Greek, used John Mark as his interpreter when addressing the Gentile communities. That Peter ever went to the Gentiles cannot be proved but is widely assumed. According to the church father, Eusebius (260-340 A.D.?), the second century Bishop Papias (whose writings are lost) reported that Mark, who had been Peter's interpreter, "wrote down accurately all that he remembered, though admittedly not in order, of what was said and done by the Lord."[34] Here then, though many scholars doubt it, we may have the nucleus of the gospel "according to Mark."

As it comes to us in the New Testament, however, Mark is not a series of memoirs translated from Peter's sermons but *catechesis* in the form of a tensely dramatic story the chief purpose of which is to show that the opposition to Jesus, though vicious, in the end completely failed. The crucifixion of Jesus merely fulfilled his mission of giving his life "a ransom for many" and was succeeded by his triumphant resurrection. Mark, whose gospel ends as abruptly as it begins, describes no *appearances* of the Risen Jesus. He is content to have the resurrection *announced* by a young man "arrayed in a white robe," who requests that Peter and the disciples be informed that Jesus "goeth before" them into Galilee (xvi, 5-7). The section following this announcement (Mark xvi, 9-19) is a later addition, universally admitted to have been absent in the original text, and may be disregarded.

The chief question that Mark's *catechesis* answers is the one brought forward from the earliest days: how can one crucified be God's Messiah? Mark's answer is that the suffering and death of Jesus were undertaken voluntarily,

God having appointed him the "Son of Man" or "Child of the Human Race," which race he thus redeems; and that the outcome of his crucifixion was his resurrection, the prelude to his Messianic triumph which was soon to be. He also answers some other important questions. If Jesus was the Messiah, why did his disciples not know it until his resurrection? Because, says Mark, Jesus kept it a secret. But in the telling of his story this inflicts on Mark some awkward moments. He cannot develop his theme without revealing the Messiahship of Jesus *to the reader*. Yet the disciples must not recognize it. And thus he must depict them as extremely unperceiving.

The moving back of the assumption of the Messiahship from the resurrection (where it occurs, for example, in the *Apocalypse of Peter*[35]) to the baptism involved such difficulties as these. As long as the emphasis was on the Risen Jesus who had been appointed God's Messiah at his resurrection, and whose *parousia** was imminent, the question of what he had been during his earthly life scarcely arose. Everything began (as it did for Paul) with the crucifixion and the resurrection. But when it became necessary to portray Jesus as the Messiah during his lifetime, and to do so in face of the fact that the second generation of believers were well aware that even the disciples themselves had not recognized Jesus as the Messiah until after his crucifixion, there was nothing for it but to describe the disciples as not bright enough to make this recognition.

Yet, not only had the Messiahship to be clear enough for Mark's readers to find it unmistakable; it had to be sufficiently apparent so that blame rested upon the Jews who rejected Jesus. If it was not plain that he was the Messiah, how could the Jews be held culpable for regarding him as a pretender? With these problems the writer of Mark in

---

* παρουσία (*parousia*) *a becoming present, an arrival.* Used especially of the hour when the anticipated Messiah would arrive and would be recognized as such.

its eventual version (whose identity we do not know but conventionally call him Mark) had to struggle as best he could. Hence we have Jesus reproaching his disciples for their dullness—and sometimes their unbelief! Which is a rather embarrassing element in a story which must also in the end exalt them as the original apostles. Here we may note how Mark takes care in his opening chapter to have the secret promptly divulged by demons that Jesus casts out of a man "with an unclean spirit" (i, 24). Since his readers believed deeply in demons and their percipiency, this evidence was impressive. Demons would know what was hidden from the disciples.

It is noteworthy, too, that in Mark's *catechesis* Jesus is announced, after his resurrection, as preceding his disciples into Galilee. The writer knows, no doubt, of the strong tradition that it was in Galilee that the Risen Jesus was seen by the apostles and he stays with this, saying nothing of the appearances in and about Jerusalem. So far as he can, he keeps his story unencumbered.

Mark's *catechesis* also sees to it (as do the others, following his lead) that the question is answered as to the relationship of Jesus to John the Baptist. That Jesus had been baptized by John was well known and it seemed to make him John's disciple. John's followers at the time that *Mark* was written were certainly exploiting this fact for everything that was in it. But Mark's *catechesis* has the answer. John is quoted as saying (and the quotation may apply to the Messiah "in general" and not to Jesus and thus be genuine): "There cometh after me he that is mightier than I, the latchet of whose shoes I am not worthy to stoop down and unloose," (i, 7) and this is so placed in the narrative that although there is no actual statement that it applies to Jesus, the inference is almost inescapable.

This, however, is as far as we can go with Mark's *catechesis* in a brief treatment. Indeed, the reader may be wondering why we begin with Mark, instead of going directly to Luke-Acts, our primary field of interest. One reason is that, in addition to Mark's priority and usefulness as a standard of comparison, he is extensively used by Matthew and Luke, the two other "synoptics,"* as the narrative source of their own evangels. A second reason will become plain in the next section.

Of Matthew's gospel, it may be noted in passing that the questions of the *catechesis* are largely answered by showing how Jesus fulfilled Bible (Old Testament) prophecy. To bring about these fulfilments, episodes such as the journey into Egypt ("Out of Egypt have I called my son") are invented. There is also the "massacre of the innocents" of which Herod was certainly capable but which, had it taken place, would never have escaped the watchful eye of Josephus who liked nothing better than to report the crimes of Herod. The story is undoubtedly produced for no other purpose than to provide a motive for the flight of the holy family to Egypt (which occurred only as a fulfilment of prophecy) and to fulfil the further prophecy of Rachel weeping for her children. As Enslin states the matter, "While Mark's narrative is not to be accepted uncritically as a plain chronicle of actual facts, but must be closely examined, Matthew's additions are palpably legendary."[36]

Matthew—to give the unknown writer the conventional name—is also much concerned with the controversies of Jesus with the Pharisees since the catechumens who will read his book will need this reinforcement in their current conflicts with the Jews. Whether Jesus was actually as harsh on the Pharisees as the *catechesis* indicates is quite uncertain; perhaps he was. But in any case, there is no doubt whatever that at the time the *synoptics* were written,

* From the Greek, συνοπτικός (*sunoptikos*), *taking a common view*. It is universally recognized by scholars that Matthew and Luke base their gospels upon Mark and upon another source or sources which they both use, often called Q (from *Quelle*: German for source). John's gospel also probably uses Mark to some slight extent but is different in so many ways from the others that it constitutes a quite separate problem. Nevertheless, it also is a *catechesis*, and in fact the most highly developed one.

there was extreme bitterness between the Jews of the Dispersion (who were nearly all of the Pharisaic party) and the Gentile believers. Hence, the controversy had to be represented in the *catechesis* as going back to Jesus.

There are further advances made by Matthew beyond Mark, and studies are available which pursue this important interest.[37] For our own part, having, we hope, sufficiently introduced the *evangelical catechesis,* we turn to Luke-Acts and the central interest of our study.

3. *The Catechesis in Luke-Acts: Clues to a Solution*

That Luke's gospel and the book of Acts are two parts of one work has long been recognized. As Goodspeed expresses it, "No finding of modern New Testament study is more assured than that Luke and Acts are not two books, written at different times, but two volumes of a single work, conceived and executed as a unit."[38] This is a matter of no small importance since it allows us to study the composer of Acts in his role as a gospel writer and therefore in the light of the other gospels. We thus become familiar with his methods in ways that would not be available to us if we knew him only through Acts. To employ an analogy from the physical sciences, in the case of Luke's gospel we can use the other gospels as "controls," but in the case of Acts, although there are other books which purport to deal with the apostolic period, their kinship is not close enough to permit their use as "controls."

What we mean by kinship is sufficiently illustrated if we remind the reader that Mark is one of Luke's sources. Indeed, the entire narrative portion of Luke, as also of Matthew, is taken from Mark. If, then, we can observe how Luke treats Mark as a source, we shall have a good idea of how he treats his sources in Acts.

First, let us note how he modifies Mark's language. This, as might be expected, is much more apparent in Greek

than in the English translation, although anyone who will
take up a "Harmony" of the gospels will see that even in
English the modifications are unmistakable. Mark tells us,
for instance, that after his baptism "immediately the spirit
driveth [Jesus] into the wilderness" (i, 12). In Matthew,
Jesus is *"led up* of the spirit into the wilderness" (iv, 1). In
Luke we are told, "And Jesus being full of the Holy Ghost
returned from Jordan and was *led* by the Spirit into the
wilderness" (iv, 1). (All the above from the King James
Version.)

So much in English. But let us turn to the Greek. The
word used by Mark for "driveth" is extremely strenuous
and means in this context a "seizure" in which Jesus is
violently propelled into the wilderness by the spirit which
has possessed him.* Both Matthew and Luke find this
language impossible. The former substitutes a verb which
means "to lead" or "carry up,"** the latter, a still gentler
verb which is often used for being led in the sense of
"guidance."*** In Mark's version, we may also note the
stark simplicity of the statement that Jesus is "spirit-
driven" whereas in Luke he is "full of the Holy Ghost."

Here, in a single striking example, we see how Luke alters the language of his sources to produce the impression
he desires. Everywhere in his gospel he is at pains to re-
move all evidence that Jesus could be moved by emotion
—or that he acted in any way that was not appropriate to
Luke's conception of the Messiah. As Dean Robinson puts
it, in his enumeration of passages altered or omitted on
this basis, "acts expressive of emotion" are not permitted to
Jesus in Luke.[39]

We note also the protection that is given to the dignity
of the apostles. In Mark, Jesus turns to Peter and says,

---

* The word ἐκβάλλει (*ekballei*) from ἐκβάλλω (*ekballō*), to *cast out,
strike out,* or *banish.*

** ἀνήχθη (*anēchthē*) from ἀνάγω (*anagō*), to *lead, take up to a higher
place.*

*** ἤγετο (*ēgeto*) from ἡγέομαι (*hēgeomai*), to *go before* or *lead the way.*

"Get thee behind me, Satan: for thou mindest not the things of God, but the things of men!" (viii, 33) Luke, in reproducing Mark's story, omits this episode entirely! It does not suit his *catechesis* to have the first of the apostles called "Satan" by his Master; nor can he allow Jesus to express his vexation: it is too discordant with the portrait he wishes to present of a Messiah serenely in command of all that happens around about him, moving confidently to the grand fulfilment of his destiny.

Another revision made by Luke is in the story of the cleansing of the Temple. In Mark, this is a very vigorous affair, involving the overturning of tables and benches, but in Luke no force is used. Nor can Luke afford to have Jesus say, as he does in Mark, that he will destroy the Temple. To report this would be to admit that the Jews were right in saying that Jesus had been provocative: how could it be claimed that he had given his fellow countrymen every opportunity to receive him if it must be confessed that he had threatened the Temple itself? Here we get a clue to Luke's purpose in Acts. Just as Jesus had to be represented as the Messiah who had come to the Jews —who had rejected him—as well as to the Gentiles—who had accepted him—and that he had "fulfilled" the Law, so Paul, the apostle to the Gentiles, had to be shown to be both loyally Jewish and faithful to his Master's universal mission. This was no easy undertaking, and as history it could not have succeeded, but it was satisfactory as *catechesis*.

Let us now, however, consider the *catechesis* in the several stages of its development. When we were speaking of Mark, we mentioned that at his, the first stage, it was sufficient to end his story with an empty tomb and a promise that Jesus would meet his disciples in Galilee. The believers to whom this was read were able to supply the sequel from the instruction that had been given them: Jesus did meet his disciples in Galilee and from thence went to heaven. Soon he would return as the Messiah. But after a while, this was not enough. Questions were asked that at first had not been thought of. "How much is proved by an empty tomb?" "Nothing," said the Jewish controversialists, "except that the disciples of Jesus stole his body and carried it away." So it was necessary to elaborate the story. Hence, Matthew adds an earthquake and has an angel descend from heaven to roll away the stone from the door of the sepulchre. Matthew is also careful to provide witnesses, a Roman patrol, which, when it sees the angel, falls to the earth in terror. The message that in Mark was given by the young man in white robes, whose appearance suggested no further comment, is in Matthew transferred to the angel, whose "appearance was as lightning." The message is nevertheless substantially the same. "Lo, he goeth before you into Galilee; there shall ye see him."

At this point, interrupting the narrative (and representing no doubt a later insertion) Jesus himself appears and confirms the message. He will meet his disciples in Galilee. Then comes an episode in which the patrol returns to the city and informs the "chief priests" of what has happened. The latter, quite unsubdued apparently by the awesome news of a resurrection, and the visit of an angel, promptly give the guardsmen money, telling them to say, "His disciples came by night, and stole him away while we slept." And this saying, Matthew tells us, continued to be spread abroad by the Jews "until this day" (xxviii, 1-15). Thus the *catechesis* provides the answer, as of Matthew's time, to Jewish challenges. An earthquake, an angel, the appearance of Jesus himself—and a fantastic story of bribery! (Could anyone be bribed to say he had not seen an angel if he was sure that he had?)

But this is not good enough for Luke. He dispenses with the earthquake, which after all is not specific, considered as evidence, and produces *two* "men in dazzling apparel" who tell the disciples who have come to the tomb that everything is happening exactly as predicted by Jesus during his ministry in Galilee. He then, in anticipation of the story he will tell in Acts, moves the scene to Judea. He wants the movement which will eventually result in the Gentile churches to begin at Jerusalem, the capital, not in Galilee which means nothing to the Gentile converts. Instead of the disciples dispersing, they remain at Jerusalem, almost as though they were awaiting the resurrection. Soon they will become the Jerusalem patriarchate from which, through Paul, Luke will trace the Gentile churches' legitimacy. For all this, Luke prepares the way with his adaptation of the resurrection story.

In addition, he meets an objection that Matthew had not had to contend with. Evidently, the adversaries of the Gentile believers were now claiming that "visions" were not conclusive. They could be hallucinations. Jesus had risen from the dead only in the imagination of his followers. Luke's expedient is rather desperate. When Jesus appears to a group of disciples they are unconvinced; they wonder if he may not be a ghost. So, besides inviting them to touch him to confirm that he is flesh and blood, he asks for food and proves his corporeality by eating "a piece of broiled fish" (xxiv, 42, 43).

This, however (besides being grotesque), involves Luke in what must have been an unanticipated difficulty. So long as Jesus went straight to heaven at the time of his resurrection, leaving nothing but an empty tomb behind him, the disposal of his body need not be explained. His appearance was in visions, and spiritual. But now he was still on earth in flesh and blood. The exigencies of controversy had required it. But now there was a new exigency. "What," asked the controversialists, "did he do with his body before he began to appear in visions, as he did to Paul?" And in answer to this objection, the *catechesis*, as developed by the resourceful Luke, created the ascension.

Having done this in his gospel, in Acts he improves upon it, keeping Jesus at or near Jerusalem for "forty days," instructing his disciples in their future mission; and finally, after Jesus has "ascended," produces "two men in white apparel" who inform them that "this Jesus, which was received up from you into heaven, shall so come in like manner as ye behold him going into heaven" (i, 11).

The *catechesis* of the resurrection does not stop here but continues through John's gospel to Peter's (which was not admitted to the New Testament), in which Jesus is followed from the sepulchre by his cross, and the latter, which seems to be alive, answers a question about his having preached "unto them that sleep."[40] But our purpose does not require us to go further than Luke. In this example, we see down to the point in which we are most interested, how the *catechesis* developed step by step from the simple report of an empty tomb and promised visions in Galilee to the corporeal presence of Jesus in Judea for forty days culminating in an ascension. It was a development, not at or near the time of the alleged events, but during a period from seventy to a hundred years afterward. As to the steps taken by Luke, it proceeded as it did because, as Professor Knox puts it, "Jesus was actually known, within the experience of the early church, in the Spirit, not in the flesh; there must then have been a time when this radical passage from flesh to Spirit took place; if it did not occur at the moment of the Resurrection, a later moment must be found for it. That moment was the Ascension."[41]

Now it would be possible, of course, to illustrate the development of the *evangelical catechesis* indefinitely, taking passage by passage and seeing how Luke treats it. This, however, is a study in itself and we can pursue it only far enough to show the freedom with which Luke used his sources when the purpose that he had in view required it. We can be sure that just as he does this in his gospel, so also he does it in Acts. Yet we must not suppose for a moment that he does it irresponsibly. He *adapts* Mark's narrative, changes its language, omits what does not suit his standpoint, elaborates where he thinks necessary, invents where he believes a more adequate story requires it. But he still remains with his sources. What this means is that he can be a difficult problem when it comes to reconstructing history, yet there is history to be reconstructed.

Another respect, long recognized, in which Luke uses his material in accordance with his own judgment is the distribution of the "direct teaching" of Jesus throughout his gospel instead of consolidating it into a single passage as Matthew does in the Sermon on the Mount. Here, although his arrangement is no more historical than Matthew's, Luke, unless he uses an older version than Matthew does, is more faithful to the wording of the common source. We may surmise then, that while he would be equally likely to make his own distribution of the material in Acts, he may often, in reproducing the details of his sources, be surprisingly reliable.

Here we must introduce another factor, and one, unfortunately, that does not simplify the problem. Down to now, we have been proceeding as though what we have in Luke-Acts is the composition as Luke wrote it. But this is not so. Later hands have been at work, possibly suppressing, certainly supplementing. Suppressions we can seldom identify, and even when we can, we do not know what it is that has been removed from the text. Supplements, however—or *surcharges,* to use the more technical term—can often be recognized. At the beginning of Acts, for instance, in one important ancient manuscript we have the following (i, 1-3):

"I composed the first book, O Theophilus, on all that Jesus, from the beginning, did and taught, until the day when, *having given command to the apostles, whom he*

*had chosen by the Holy Spirit, he was taken away. They
also it was to whom he presented himself alive after his
passion by many proofs . . ."* (Codex Alexandrinus).

In another important ancient manuscript, the passage
reads as follows:

"I composed the first book, O Theophilus, on all that
Jesus, from the beginning did and taught, until the day
when he was taken away, *having given command to the
apostles whom he had chosen by the Holy Spirit, and to
whom he gave orders to preach the Gospel. They also it
was to whom he presented himself . . ."* (Codex Bezae).

Now it is obvious that the italicized clauses are not
identical, the reason being that they have been inserted by
later hands into the original text, in one way in one family
of manuscripts, in another way in another. We know how
this kind of editing was practiced from experience with
other documents, as for example the letters of Ignatius,
which were enlarged by an unknown ecclesiastic of the
fourth century, who doubtless thought he was improving
them! A comparison with his version and the authentic
letters reveals exactly how he did his work. We are not so
fortunate in the case of Acts: we lack an "unretouched"
version with which to compare the manuscript as it comes
to us. Still, experience makes it plain that we shall not be
in error if we say that originally the verses in question
went as follows:

"I composed the first book, O Theophilus, on all that
Jesus, from the beginning, did and taught, until the day
when he was taken away."

Looking at this far simpler introduction and comparing
it with the two others which are loaded with what the
Abbé Loisy calls a "violent surcharge,"[42] it immediately

occurs to us that the entire book may have been dealt with in the same way. It undoubtedly has, and especially those parts of it that refer to the gift of the Holy Spirit. This is because a time came when it was necessary to make the earthly life of Jesus, which formerly had been pointed toward his imminent return as the Messiah, move toward fulfillment at Pentecost when the Holy Spirit was given. Jesus, it was said, had already come. His *parousia*, it was true, was still in the future. But he had come to his church in the Holy Spirit, in accordance with what had always been his intention and promise. So a later hand edited Acts accordingly!

We are now, perhaps, sufficiently apprised of the general nature of the *evangelical catechesis* to understand that our approach to the Acts narrative must be that of discovering and discounting whatever has been introduced for the purpose of maintaining the catechetical corpus, thus reducing it to elements from which it may to some extent be possible to reconstruct history. This is not an easy task but we now have the clues to what is needed for its performance.

4. *The Galatians Question: A Parenthesis*

Before reviewing the Acts narrative, it is desirable (for the sake of those who still consider that the question can have more than one answer) to say something about the much disputed question of the date of the letter to the Galatians. Millions of words have been printed on this subject, the issue being that if Galatians was written early in Paul's career he could have made the five visits to Jerusalem as described by Acts, but if it was late, then Paul's own statements in the letter allow for only three. In other words, the two visits that in Galatians he declares were the only ones he had made after his conversion could have been supplemented by three more *after* this letter was written, provided it was written early. In addition, we could accept (if we ignored other objections) the Acts version of the Council of Jerusalem in which the Jewish-Gentile conflict was settled by the edict of James, going on to believe, as Acts would have us do, that there was very little trouble afterward. (That is, we could do so to the extent we think that other factors permit it.) On the other hand, if Galatians was written late, the Acts story is incorrect so far as two of the visits are concerned and the Council story is a fabrication. This in turn confirms the view that Paul was deeply engaged in the struggle with the Judaizers even when he came to Jerusalem for the last time and was arrested.

Those who contend for the early date must also contend that the letter was not really written to the Galatians, since Paul did not go to them in his first campaigns, but to the communities in Pisidia and Lycaonia that Paul and Barnabas had founded during the "first missionary journey," the basis of the contention being that Pisidia and Lycaonia were included within the administrative Roman province of Galatia. Thus Pisidians and Lycaonians could properly be called Galatians!

Few theories have been more beloved than this, especially by the older scholars. And indeed, it does require a lot of cherishing if it is to appear as robust as its supporters wish! Originally the bandit kingdom of Galatia had occupied a small area in the middle northern part of Asia Minor, having been founded by Gauls who had migrated there from the west. Hence the name Galatia. In 189 B.C. the little nation, which had never ceased to rob and pillage its neighbors, was subjugated by Rome, and after a series of vicissitudes characteristic of the period was made into a Roman province in 25 B.C. Adjacent districts were added to this province until finally it included Pisidia, Lycaonia and a part of Phrygia in the south, the area in which Paul and Barnabas had worked in the so-called "first missionary journey."

Administratively, this southern area was undoubtedly a part of the Roman province of Galatia. But that its inhabitants would adopt the name "Galatians" is believable only by those who are very eager to believe it. Why would Pisidians call themselves Gauls? Do the Scottish, who live in the northern part of an island administered from London, call themselves English? Would anyone speaking of churches in Dumbarton, Paisley and Kilmarnock refer to them as being located anywhere else than in Scotland? Would he write to them as the "Great British"? Why then should Paul, if he was writing to Pisidians and Lycaonians, address them as "Galatians"?

Moreover, in Acts itself it is twice explicitly stated that Paul visited Galatia and *the adjacent Phrygia,* which surely points to Galatia proper. In the sixteenth chapter we are told that he "went through the region of Phrygia and Galatia" (xvi, 6), and in the eighteenth that "he went through the region of Galatia and Phrygia *in order, establishing all the disciples"* (xviii, 23). It is true that Acts tells us nothing further about these campaigns but this is equally so of other matters. There is nothing in Acts about the three shipwrecks that Paul tells us he suffered or about his being five times beaten by the Jews (II Cor. xi, 24, 25). Moreover, if there was trouble with Judaizers in Galatia, and if it arose late in Paul's missionary work, the composer of Acts would have every reason for suppressing all knowledge of it. Was it not his purpose to show that when Paul came to Jerusalem on his final visit there was perfect agreement between himself and the Jerusalem community and a comparable harmony between the Judaic and Gentile believers?

The fact is, however, that this was far from being the case either then, before then, or afterward. Undoubtedly, what happened was that the controversy became ever more strident during the course of Paul's work and that in the communities of Galatia, which he had founded during the middle period of his career or perhaps later, it had flared up about two years before his final visit to Jerusalem. The letter to the Galatians would thus have been written from one of the cities of the Aegean Sea while Paul was raising the collection for the Jerusalem believers.

In further corroboration of this thesis, it may be mentioned that it supports the natural and most probable interpretation of Paul's sickness that took him to Galatia for his first visit. Galatia is high country. Paul had been hastened thither from the malarial lowlands to increase his chances of recovery. When his health was partly restored he began to preach his "good news" and in spite of his "infirmity of the flesh" he was received as "an angel of God" (iv, 13, 14). None of which has any plausibility whatever if we relate it to the early campaign in Pisidia as described in Acts.

As to the internal evidence of the letter, it is too large a topic for brief discussion but few will dispute the close affinities with the letter to the Romans which, by universal admission, was written late. Galatians, then, we shall consider to have been written in about 52 A.D., not long before the final visit to Jerusalem, its destination being the communities founded by Paul in the true Galatia. This is what we would understand about Galatians if we had never read Acts or been deflected by the desire to bolster up its narrative. This is the view that increasingly prevails among modern scholars, reflecting the more realistic attitude that is now being taken toward the book of Acts.[43]

5. *The Narrative Reviewed*

Down to now, we have said little about the "authorship" of Acts since it is a problem better understood when we know something of the questions raised by a study of the book itself. Traditionally, Acts is said to have been written by Loukas, or Luke, known to have been a companion of Paul during the later years of his activity. There is, however, no attribution of the authorship to Luke in the New Testament, and the wording of the Muratorian fragment, which reports the testimony of some of the church fathers (Irenaeus, Tertullian, Clement of Alexandria, Origen, Eusebius and Jerome) is not clear as to whether it is Acts as a whole that Luke is supposed to have written or a part of it, perhaps one of its sources.*

Here we need not go into the matter at length. A companion of Paul's, unless he was extraordinarily young when he became such, could not have lived long enough to compose Acts. Nor would anyone who had really known Paul have caused Peter to say that by his (Peter's) mouth "the Gentiles should hear the word of the gospel and believe" (Acts xv, 7). Paul is quite clear that at the time Peter is supposed to have said this he was charged only with "the gospel of the circumcision" while it was Paul who was "intrusted with the gospel of the uncircumcision" (Gal. ii, 7, 8). This division of authority was vital to Paul's whole outlook on the Judaic-Gentile question, even though he expected Peter to recognize Gentile believers as being in full communion with the movement (Gal. ii, 11 ff.).

A further and (to the present writer) conclusive consideration is that the composer of Acts does not know—or if he knows, does not credit—Paul's claim to have seen Jesus. To Paul this was a matter of quite crucial importance. It was the seal and warrant of his apostleship (I Cor. ix; xv, 8). But in Acts, three times Paul has an experience of the presence of Jesus but does not see him. On the contrary, he is stricken blind. But then, this is only one more aspect of the fact that the writer of Acts repeatedly contradicts Paul's own testimony to his words and deeds. Luke

* This testimony is in execrable Latin, appropriately translated by Cadbury in Jackson and Lake, Vol. 2, p. 211 (See Bibliography).

could not have done this; he would have been too much identified with Paul's viewpoint to have wanted to do it. The most we can assume, therefore, is that Luke may have written one of the sources.

Of the latter, scholars have identified a varying number, some of them supposing that Acts is really two "books" (the first ends with xv, 35) combined into one. Schonfield believes that the first "book" is dependent "on Hebrew or Aramaic material, at least indirectly"; Torrey goes further and concludes that it was written in Aramaic and that we have a direct translation.[44] There is also a widely held opinion that in addition to a Judean source (whether in Aramaic or in Greek) there is a source (or sources) traceable to Antioch. There are also passages written in the first person plural, the so-called "we" passages, which either come from an eyewitness or are written as though they did.[*]

What we must suppose is that early in the second century an editor collected the sources, including possibly a diary of one of Paul's companions, and amended them as he saw fit for the purpose in hand, skillfully weaving them into the Acts narrative. Why he left the first person plural in the "we" passages we can only conjecture. Perhaps they were the only fragments he had of this material; perhaps he was stricken by a disabling sickness before he could make his final draft. We are not, however, entitled to suppose that because these passages remain in the first person he had left them *entirely* unaltered (or even, according to some scholars, that he had not composed them). It is also possible that this and any other source material that he had collected was already revised to some extent. In any case, it is this editor who contrived the book into the form it

---

[*] Acts xvi, 10-17; xx, 5-15; xxi, 1-18; xxvii, 1—xxviii, 16. The point at which the "we" sections end cannot be fixed with certainty since the first person plural may be absent from a few further sentences because the construction does not call for it, not because the source is no longer being quoted.

took for first publication, possibly about 105 A.D., though some scholars would say considerably later. Then, finally, came the redactor who inserted the clauses that speak of the Holy Spirit, as illustrated in a previous section,* and whose changes in other respects we cannot identify.

It is the 105 A.D. editor, however, that we have had chiefly in mind when heretofore we have spoken of the "composer of Acts," this term having been selected to keep the reader warned that there were reasons why we could not say "author." His later redactor was not a composer but a reviser and there is not much that can be done about him except to remember that his revisions at certain points have corrupted the text. It is this same 105 A.D. editor—or composer: he is as much the one as the other—who is meant when modern scholars speak of "Luke." This, admittedly, is a rather awkward usage from the standpoint of the general reader, at least until he has been informed of the special meaning, but it has the advantage of maintaining the identity of the composer of Acts with that of the composer of Luke's gospel—which has borne this name immemorially and will certainly continue to bear it. And so, although neither Acts nor Luke's gospel was composed by Loukas, the companion of Paul, it is convenient, when a sufficient explanation has been made, to continue to speak of "Luke."

Glancing back now over the narrative that we have outlined, together with some of its problems, in the two preceding chapters, we see that we were not dealing with history, either true or falsified in the ordinary meaning of these terms, but with Luke's *catechesis* of the apostolic period, written from a very special point of view. For the beginnings at Jerusalem he undoubtedly had an excellent source which provided details of the life of the early community and described the way in which it was organized. Occasionally, as we shall see when this community is dis-

* Pages 75-7.

cussed more fully,* material from the source can be identified. But what we are not permitted to see and are quite
unable to discover is the story that the source contained
about the episode of Stephen. All that is clear is that it
must have been in conflict with the *catechesis*. It was
therefore suitably revised to fit Luke's purpose, but with a
result which, from the historical standpoint, is obscuring
and confusing.

Whether the same source is still being used when we
reach the story of Paul's conversion cannot be determined.
Paul was not a hero in Judea and anything recorded about
him there is likely to have been hostile. It is possible that
Luke knew no more than that Paul's conversion was associated with Damascus and that his preaching to the Gentiles began either there or in connection with an experience
that came to him in the Temple at Jerusalem. In the first
chapter we attempted a reconstruction of the Damascus
journey which may at that point have seemed to the reader
rather radical. If he has followed our subsequent discussion he may now appraise it as too conservative. Many
scholars dismiss the story of the "journey" completely.
Goguel says that its evidence has little value and that "the
only feature which can be retained is the localization of
the [conversion] in the neighborhood of Damascus."45
Knox complains that the story is contradicted by "the clear
meaning of Paul's own words [in Galatians], and [we]
therefore must reject [it] out of hand."46

Yet there may be a basis for the story. It is true that Paul
says in Galatians that the Judean believers did not know
him by sight. But it was not the Judean believers whom he
persecuted. It was the Hellenists. If the persecution lasted
only a few days the Judean believers may well have heard
about Paul without actually seeing him. This, precarious
as admittedly it is, does allow a reconstruction of the story.

Turning to two other incidents which may never have oc-

* Part III, Chapter 1.

curred, Gamaliel, the famous Jewish rabbi highly esteemed in the Pharisaic party, is depicted as intervening with the Sanhedrin on behalf of Peter and the apostles, saying that it is better to leave them alone lest the Sanhedrin "be found even to be fighting against God" (v, 39), while later, Gallio, the Roman proconsul at Corinth, refuses to try Paul's case on the ground that he has not offended against Roman law and the matter is a mere dispute between rival sects among the Jews (xviii, 12-17).

Unfortunately for the first of these manifestations of tolerance, Luke's Gamaliel mentions the rebellion of Theudas, *which would not occur until ten or twelve years after the supposed speech he was making,* and then says that the revolt of Judas of Galilee *followed* that of Theudas, whereas it occurred *almost forty years earlier,* in 6 A.D.! Do we not have here another speech composed by our editor, a little uncertain this time about his dates, and is it not aimed at the Jews of much later days? Is he not saying in effect, "See how the great Jewish doctor, Gamaliel, treated the believers in Jesus! Why do you not do the same?"

As to Gallio, this incident has been given much greater credence, chiefly it would seem because of the inscription that was found which proves that he really was the proconsul in Corinth during a period when Paul was also there.[47] But even if Paul was brought before him, did Gallio express his impatience at Jewish quarrels and say, "I am not minded to be a judge of these matters"? Or is this not an idealized picture of how a Roman magistrate should treat Christians? Judaism was a legally recognized religion in the Roman Empire; since Christianity as such was not, it was highly desirable to have it regarded by the authorities as a branch of Judaism—indeed as the true Judaism—and at the same time to make the more orthodox Jews seem like renegades—or at least troublemakers. Gallio fits into this picture very well, lending the support of his official prestige to this aspect of the *catechesis.* What we are seeing in the Acts narrative—*and must constantly remember that we are seeing*—is not events as they would have appeared to those who participated in them but a narrative that met the doctrinal and practical needs of the nascent church at the end of the century. Thus Gamaliel and Gallio are cast in the parts that in Luke's view they should have played and therefore to all intents and purposes *did* play. What faith required, it projected into history.

Understanding in this way the methods of the Acts editor, we see perhaps what may have been suppressed in the story of Peter's departing from Jerusalem and "going to another place" (xii, 17). Herod Agrippa had ordered a persecution of "certain of the community" in which James the disciple (not "the brother of the Lord") perished. No doubt his brother, John, perished with him, but our editor cannot admit this since he knows of the tradition that John went to Ephesus and wrote the book of Revelation. Seeing that the execution of James and John "pleased the Jews," Agrippa decided to behead Peter also but the latter (here we disregard the miracle story of his escape from prison in xii, 4-19), being warned of it, made his escape.

But why does Luke tell us only that he went to "another place"? This is precisely a point on which it would have been natural to be explicit. Evidently the *catechesis* required that the locality be left obscure. Why? Was it not because Peter went to Antioch? And are we wrong in assuming that Luke wanted this erased from the record so that no one would be reminded of Peter's long association with Antioch after his quarrel with Paul which made the apostle to the Gentiles thereafter unwelcome in that city? Many scholars believe that Peter, working out from Antioch, "took over" the communities Paul had founded in southern Asia Minor and even extended his activities as far as Galatia.[48] At any rate, we may be sure that our editor had a good reason for not permitting us to know where Peter went.

Another example of meeting the requirements of the *catechesis* is found in the story of Apollos, a learned Alexandrian preacher who came to Ephesus, "knowing only the baptism of John" (xviii, 24-28). Here the Acts editor loses no time in having Apollos instructed by Aquila and his wife Prisca or Priscilla so that he immediately revises his "gospel" to make it accord with that of Paul. But we know that he did nothing of the kind. In his first letter to the Corinthians, Paul mentions the parties of Apollos (and Peter) as causing contentions in the Corinthian community (I Cor. i, 11, 12). It is a very curious passage since it also mentions a party of "Christ," and we shall consider it more fully in a later chapter. But at least we see that Apollos was preaching—and continued to preach—a different evangel from Paul's. What it was, our editor unintentionally lets us perceive. Apollos was an apostle of John the Baptist! As we have several times stated, the followers of John were very active not only in the first centuries but long afterward and survived in the sects of the Hemerobaptists and Mandeans.[49] But in Acts the intense early rivalry between the followers of John and of Jesus is covered up. This is because the rivalry still continued at the time Acts was composed and the John disciples of this later period must be given to understand that their brilliant protagonist, the famous Apollos, did not remain an apostle of John the Baptist but surrendered to Paul!

In the light of what we have learned of Luke's methods, it now also becomes clear to us that he arranges for the Jerusalem Council and James's edict of tolerance to the Gentiles at an early stage in Paul's career because he does not want the later stages clouded by evidence of the Judaic-Gentile conflict. Actually, although Paul may have subdued this conflict in the Aegean cities and in Galatia, it was still raging elsewhere. Indeed, his success in subduing it had inflamed Judaic hostility toward him that much the more. But Luke does not want his readers to know this and so produces the settlement which Galatians contradicts. The same consideration obliges him to omit all mention of the collection that Paul is taking to Jerusalem. No doubt it had been widely (and correctly) stated that this was a peace offering; but Luke wants it to appear that there was no tension and therefore no need to seek peace.

When we come to the story of Paul's trials before the Sanhedrin and the Roman procurators the narrative becomes, in Goguel's words, "obscure and on some points almost unintelligible."[50] The real question is undoubtedly as to whether Paul, in view of what was known about him, could still be counted a Jew or had become an apostate. He had been found in the court of the Temple from which Gentiles were excluded upon pain of death. Had he a right to be there? Was he of the Jewish faith or was he not? That this was a substantial issue is apparent from Paul's letters. But Luke wants him to appear as a missionary to the Gentiles who nevertheless remained true to the faith of his fathers, an apostle of Jesus who was also a loyal Jew.

And thus we have the key to the Acts narrative: Christianity is not an innovation (*advena*) but a development of Judaism, a legal religion (*religio licit*), and should be so recognized by the empire; indeed, it is the true Judaism, the Messianic visitation predicted in the scriptures which came first to the Jewish people, who for the most part rejected it, and which now has come to the Gentiles (just as the older Judaism was extended to its proselytes) and the Gentiles are accepting it; between the believing Jews and the believing Gentiles there was never any serious controversy: such questions as arose were amicably settled by the Council of Jerusalem after Peter and James had conferred with Paul and a decision had been reached in the presence of the entire congregation. Paul was a recognized emissary to the Gentiles and had the endorsement of the Jerusalem patriarchate. The Gentile churches are in every way legitimately descended from the first believers. Jesus himself had told his apostles that they must be his witnesses "unto the uttermost parts of the earth" (Acts i, 8).

To the Roman authorities Christianity had never caused any trouble. Pilate had found "no fault" in Jesus and would have freed him. The procurators would have been glad to free Paul. Gallio had refused jurisdiction when charges against Paul had been brought before him. It was the unbelieving Jews who had tried to suppress the new movement, just as it was they who had hounded Jesus to his death. It was the unbelieving Jews who were causing trouble now.

Such was the thesis of the Acts narrative, the *motif* of its *catechesis*. Nevertheless, here and there the true shape of events reveals itself, as we have occasionally seen. We shall now go on to equip ourselves to see more clearly.

PART TWO

THE SOURCES OF PAULINE CHRISTIANITY

CHAPTER I

IN THE CONTEXT OF HISTORY

1. *A World in Transition*

The story of Christian origins, as it is traditionally told, may be likened to a narrow river flowing through a wide stretch of sandy desert. On the surface of the river may be seen all the incidents recorded in the New Testament but in the surrounding desert nothing is visible but empty sand. It is almost as though, during this period in history, nothing was happening *except* as told in the New Testament. Only in this slender watercourse are there signs of life.

Now and again, it is true, a little pasteboard city is erected on the river banks so that the Apostle Paul may step off his raft and found a church. But the only thing that is real about the pasteboard city is the church just founded. Apart from the New Testament story, nothing worth noticing is going on.

The actual situation, of course, was vastly different. Instead of a desert we should envisage a luxuriantly fertile area, abounding with life. Instead of one narrow river we should see more streams than we can count, most of them eventually flowing together. For in the true story of Christian origins, the events chronicled in the New Testament form only one such stream. Indeed, it would scarcely overstate the matter were we to say that in every city and village in the Roman Empire there were activities at this time—customs, rituals, cultist practices—that would have an eventual part in the molding of Christianity.

93

Already, long before the apostles foregathered in Jerusalem or Paul set out on his missionary campaigns, worship was being offered in Rome itself—on the very site where the Basilica of St. Peter now stands in the Vatican—to a god who had died and risen again. Here at the appointed seasons a bull was slain and the sins of the initiates were washed away in his blood. This we know from inscriptions that were uncovered when the cathedral was being enlarged in 1608 and 1609.[1] Not far from the Vatican, where Cybele was the "great mother" and Attis, her son, the savior, was the shrine of Isis, whose son, Horus-Osiris, was adored as "risen lord." At Antioch, the Syrian capital where Paul and Barnabas preached their "good news," each spring when the river rose, the women wailed on its banks as they watched "the blood of Adonis," the dying savior, go flowing down to the sea.[2]*

In other cities where Paul gathered congregations there were annual pageants of the death of a redeemer, patterned upon the ancient drama of sacrificing a king. Prominent everywhere were the temples of Rhea (under one or other of her names) whose priests danced to wild music and in their frenzy gashed their arms to draw blood for the sacrifice, the blood that was the life. In sharp contrast with this orgiastic worship were the sermons of Stoics and Hermetics, preached at places of concourse, and the disputations of philosophers in some hall of quiet resort.

In Alexandria, in the great Jewish quarter, Philo, the allegorizer and adventurous theologian who had pressed Greek mentality into the service of Hebrew religion, was completing his work. After a while, much of it would be absorbed into Christianity. In the imperial palace in Rome, Caesar himself was trying an innovation—by making the worship of the empire an obligation of its subject peoples,

---

* At Byblos, the Adonis River was red with soil carried down from the mountains. The Orontes River at Antioch would be less dramatically discolored.

with the emperor as a demigod, the imperial divine lord.

In Judea, Pharisee was debating with Sadducee, and no doubt both with Essenes. The Zealots were awaiting the day when the signal for revolt would come and the people would arise and throw off the hated yoke of Rome. Contrary to the usual picture of the place and period, there were in Palestine many Greek-speaking cities, where pagan cults were practiced. To know of these despised rituals it was not necessary for a Jew to go abroad. Except for the pious minority, the Jews almost as much as the pagans had sunk to a low level of morality. When Jesus spoke of "an adulterous generation" he was not using a metaphor; nor was John the Baptist's rugged preaching unduly harsh.

Everywhere throughout the empire there was the sense of something missing, something lost. As the official religions of the city-states declined in authority, cults of salvation arose to take their place. The stars were worshiped, even by the highly educated; legions of demons infested both earth and sky. Never before had there been so wide a currency for such a vast profusion of beliefs and disbeliefs. East and West had met and mingled and the result was a miscegenous, unruly brood of faiths and fears that kept the empire inwardly disoriented no matter how tightly organized or how orderly its external form.

The world of the first century was a world in transition, though to most of its people all changes were expected to be for the worse. The Roman rulers had tried to stem this tide of pessimism and to present the empire itself as a basis for hope. Briefly, at least in Latium, there had been a short interval of optimism stemming from the achievements of Augustus; but even there it did not last. Elsewhere there was no such sense of promise. The individual might be saved through his communion with his mystery cult redeemer; this, however, was salvation for a future life and in another world. What could be done to save society? What hope was there for the world of the empire?

That the answer to this question had anything to do with a little company of Messianic believers who had themselves given up hope of the present world and were waiting for a supernatural deliverance, no one could conceivably have had the slightest premonition. Nor could anyone have known that the form the answer took would be affected by beliefs that shaped themselves within the restless mind of a Greek-speaking Jew from Tarsus.

How it came to pass will always remain one of the marvels—some would say miracles—of history. Yet we can partly understand it if we know something of the forces that were at work and can connect the links in the chain of events that marked the great transition and prepared the way for Christianity.

2. Judaism: The Political Background— A Rapid Survey

The infiltration of Palestine by Hebrew tribesmen from the desert began in about the fifteenth century B.C. First the northern area was occupied, although for the most part without displacing the Canaanite population of the cities; then the southern section, after an invasion by tribes the nucleus of which were Hebrews who had escaped from slavery in Egypt. Although there was frequent fighting between the Hebrews and the Canaanites, there was also intermingling, so much so that the Hebrews took over the Canaanite civilization including its laws and its art of writing.[3]

The tribes were first united under Saul (c. 1020), and more effectually under David (c. 1004 king in the south, c. 998 king of all Israel), but divided into two kingdoms in c. 926 and were never reunited. In 721 the northern kingdom, known as Israel, was ended by the Assyrians and many of its inhabitants were deported and dispersed. In 586 the southern kingdom, known as Judah, was conquered by the Babylonians and its leading citizens taken into exile. While in exile scribes began the work of compiling and editing the Hebrew Scriptures to religious and moral standards which by that time had become well established. Earlier, the people of both kingdoms had worshiped Canaanitish gods at least as much as they had worshiped their national God, Jehovah, but from the eighth century on there had been a trend toward monotheism.

With the rise of Persian power and the decline of Babylon, an opportunity was afforded to the exiles and their children to return to Judea. Many preferred to remain in Babylon, but those who went back did so out of an intense belief that God had chosen the Judeans to be his own "peculiar people." In this belief they imposed severe regulations, designed to maintain Jewish exclusiveness, and made the "Law of Moses," which, together with its official interpretation, was known as the Torah, strictly binding upon all Jews. Between 520 and 516 the Second Temple (the first had been built by King Solomon, c. 950) was erected by Zerubbabel who was crowned king and hailed as Messiah—the first, so far as we know, to receive this title, though with reduced significance it could be used of any high priest or king. The Persian emperor, Darius, soon put an end to the Judean kingdom and Zerubbabel was executed as a rebel. Nevertheless, Darius maintained his liberal policy in all matters of religion and national culture and continued to permit considerable freedom to the Jews.

In about 400 B.C. the final edition of the "Law of Moses"* was promulgated and Hebrew religion had become Judaism, opening the way to the synagogue and the transformation of an ethnic cult into a national church.

In 333 the all-conquering Alexander arrived at Jerusa-

---

* The Pentateuch, or first five books of the Bible: Genesis, Exodus, Leviticus, Numbers, Deuteronomy. *Pentateuch* is merely Greek for five books and derives from the Septuagint (Greek translation of the Old Testament) usage. Aramaic-speaking Jews referred to the "five-fifths of the Law."

lem, having inflicted crushing defeats upon the Persians from which they never recovered. With this event a new era dawned for all the Mediterranean countries, since Alexander was not merely a subjugator but a civilizer who was determined to spread Greek culture throughout all his domains. He lived only long enough (d. 323) to see this process barely begun. At his death, his empire was divided into four parts, ruled by Antipater, then Cassander (Greece and Macedonia), Lysimachus (Thrace), Seleucus (Babylonia and Syria) and Ptolemy (Egypt). Between the Seleucids and the Ptolemies Palestine became a buffer state.

In the second century the Hellenized Mediterranean world began to feel the increasing power of Rome. In 190 the Seleucid monarch, Antiochus III, who had recovered Palestine from the Ptolemies of Egypt, was disastrously defeated by Lucius Cornelius Scipio at Magnesia on the west coast of Asia Minor and the Roman exacted a huge tribute. To pay this tribute Antiochus had to plunder the temple treasuries of his dominions and died while engaged in this sacrilegious and unpopular pursuit. His son, Seleucus IV, sent his deputy, Heliodorus, to levy a tax to satisfy the Roman rapacity but Heliodorus assassinated Seleucus. And thus we come to Seleucus' brother, Antiochus IV, who called himself Epiphanes, which means "manifestation" but with the implication in this case that what is manifested is the glory of God! It was Antiochus Epiphanes who brought Jewish affairs to a crisis and affected profoundly the future course of Judean history.

The details of the story vary considerably according to who is telling it, Tacitus, Diodorus, Josephus or the books of Maccabees.[4] But we can be sure both that Antiochus sold the high priesthood at Jerusalem to the applicant who offered him the largest bribe and that he demanded the enforced Hellenization of Jewish religion and culture. The two indeed went together, for it was the high priest who was to do the enforcing. Had Antiochus been less impatient the possibility must be entertained that Judea, like all the rest of the Mediterranean countries, would eventually have accepted Greek culture. Already Hellenization had gone a long way. In Samaria the temple was dedicated to Zeus. In Galilee faithful Jews were so small a minority that when trouble broke out and they had to be brought to Judea for safety, it was a maneuver made easy by their insignificant numbers.

Under the high priest Joshua, who assumed the Greek name Jason, a gymnasium was built in which young Jewish noblemen competed in the games, bathed and took exercise entirely unclothed as was the Greek custom. According to the first book of Maccabees* some of them even "made themselves uncircumcised" (I Macc. i, 15) which most scholars take to mean that they had disguised their circumcision by some sort of surgical operation. Conservative Jews protested bitterly at the Hellenizing program and some of them formed a party of the pious, the Chasidim, from which (according to most scholars) came the Pharisees of the New Testament.

Jason's successor, Menelaus, who outbid him for the office of high priest, allowed Antiochus to plunder the Temple treasury, carry away articles made of precious metals, and even to strip off the gold facing from the front of the Temple itself. But Antiochus' fortunes were waning. Egypt had outmaneuvered him in diplomacy and had persuaded the Romans to send him a warning. Looking angrily at his shrunken realm and noting once more that it contained the troublesome and obdurate Judea he sent an army which entered Jerusalem on the Sabbath Day, slaughtered many of the men, sold women and children into slavery, and enforced a drastic prohibition of the observances of Judaism. In December 168, an altar to Zeus was

* The first two books of Maccabees, which record the history of this period from the orthodox Jewish viewpoint are in the Old Testament Apocrypha. The remaining two (three if we count one in Arabic) are later and not historically connected with this period.

erected above the altar of Jehovah and a pig was sacrificed—the ultimate in sacrilege and insult. Antiochus had
gone too far! This was the signal for revolt.

Mattathias, an aging priest, when he saw a Jew obeying
Antiochus' command to sacrifice to a heathen god on the
altar at Modein, not far from Jerusalem, killed him then
and there and laid him on the altar. He followed this by
killing the king's agent who was there to see that the anti-
Judaic decrees were complied with. This was the sign for
a general rising, ushering in a reign of terror in which Hellenistic Jews were butchered and the usages of Judaism
forcibly restored. Before the Syrians could regain control
Antiochus died, leaving civil unrest. The sons of Mattathias, later to be called the Maccabees (hammers), raised
armies of patriots and, aided greatly by the civil wars in
Syria, scored some surprising victories and survived some
shattering defeats. Eventually, however, it was necessary
to appeal for help to Rome, an appeal that was successful.
We cannot in a brief outline follow the fantastically complicated story of the Maccabees. Suffice it to say that first
religious liberty, then political independence were in large
measure achieved.

At the end of this period the office of high priest had become also *de facto* the office of civil ruler. Hyrcanus, the
son of Simon Maccabeus, occupied this dual office for
thirty years (135-105) and his campaigns of conquest in-
creased the Jewish domain until memories began to be
revived of the proud reign of Solomon. He tore down the
temple to Zeus at Samaria, forced circumcision upon the
Idumeans, was almost as intolerantly Judaic as Antiochus
had been impatiently Hellenistic.

Hyrcanus was succeeded by his son, Aristobulus (104-
103), whose father had intended him to be high priest but
not civil ruler, the latter role having been reserved for his
mother. But Aristobulus placed his mother and his brothers
in prison and made himself not only high priest but king.

During the one year of his reign he took full advantage of conditions in Syria, where the Seleucid dynasty was now disintegrating, and extended the borders of his kingdom farther north.

Upon the death of Aristobulus, his widow, Alexandra, freed his brothers from prison and married the oldest of them, Alexander Janneus (103-76). This high priest and monarch, a thoroughgoing militarist, enlarged the territory under Jewish rule until it was nothing less than a small though restless empire, but many of his people, led by the Pharisees, revolted against him. For six years civil war raged but in the end Alexander's subjects decided that they preferred him to the only alternative in sight: a Syrian overlord. Upon regaining control of the situation he had eight hundred leaders of his opposition crucified while he disported himself with his concubines. While these wretched men, presumably Pharisees, were dying, their wives and children were slaughtered before their eyes, and the next day a large number of terror-stricken Judeans fled the country.

Alexander Janneus is the hierarch and king most likely to have been the "wicked priest" mentioned in the *Habakkuk Commentary*, one of the famous Dead Sea Scrolls.[5] Undoubtedly he deeply antagonized the war-weary and the spiritual-minded who were repelled by seeing a man with so much blood on his hands serving at Jehovah's altar. These included the Pharisees, who were at times pacifists but were willing to engage in politics, and the ascetic Essenes who withdrew from political life, taking the full consequence of their conviction that Israel's destiny would be served neither "by might nor by power but by my spirit, saith the Lord" (Zech. iv, 6).

Alexander was survived by his widow, Alexandra (76-67), in whose reign the Pharisees were largely in control. Her son, Hyrcanus II, was appointed high priest, but upon his mother's death at seventy-three both the crown and the Temple office were soon seized by Aristobulus (67-63), his more energetic younger brother. At this point, however, the brilliant politician, Antipater of Idumea, enters the scene and it is his unobtrusive power that henceforth will mold events. If Hyrcanus I, half a century earlier, could have foreseen this consequence of circumcising the Idumeans, thus qualifying them for a place in Jewish political life, he might have hesitated. In any case, largely through the intrigues of Antipater, Hyrcanus II was restored to the high priesthood though not to the crown by Pompey, who entered Jerusalem in 63. Thereafter Judea, whether ruled by native princes or imperial procurators, was a subject-state of Rome.

Antipater's son, Herod, whom he had made governor of Galilee (which, it is worth remembering, was more Hellenist than Jewish), showed a marked talent for ingratiating himself with Roman leaders whether it was Pompey, Julius Caesar, Mark Anthony or Octavian, later to be called Augustus. The last two, being deeply impressed with Herod's ability and confident of his loyalty to Rome, recommended him to the Senate which thereupon appointed him king of the Jews (40 B.C.). It took Herod three years of fighting before he could lend substance to this title, but finally he made his way into Jerusalem and in 37 ascended his throne. He was without doubt the ablest of Jewish rulers (37-4) but in spite of his never-ceasing efforts to please and placate his subjects, he remained heartily disliked. As an Idumean, he perhaps never had a chance.

To read the list of those he executed or assassinated, including his Hasmonean* wife, Mariamne, is to wonder whether we are not dealing with an ogre. Yet, grotesque as it may seem, Herod was probably forced to commit these murders to stay in power—indeed to stay alive! Nor could

---

* The Maccabees were *B'nai Hashmonai,* children of *Hashmon,* hence this name was given to the dynasty which began with the sons of Mattathias (the Maccabees) and ended with Antigonus, who at Herod's request was executed by Mark Anthony.

he afford the one crime the Romans would never overlook in a ruler: failure to keep order. There is no doubt that he loved his wife, Mariamne, but despairingly since she detested him. When he had her killed he fully believed that she had been unfaithful to him, and if historians were not so prejudiced against him so might they. If the kings of this world with their bloody hands and uneasy consciences ever deserve the appellation, Herod too should be called "the Great."

At almost the end of Herod's reign, Jesus was born in 6 B.C.

After Herod's death his sons were obliged to go to Rome to have their father's will approved by Caesar and while they were away rebellion broke out in Jericho, Galilee, Idumea and Perea. Many of the people were sure that this was the prelude to the Messianic age which they believed would begin with violent deeds. The revolt was put down, however, and Augustus appointed Archelaus to be ethnarch (ruler of a nation but without the title of king) of Judea (4 B.C.-6 A.D.), Herod Antipas to be tetrarch (literally, ruler of a fourth part but by custom of any partitioned area) of Galilee (4 B.C.-39 A.D.), and Philip to be tetrarch of the northeastern parts of Herod's kingdom, the exact borders of which are not known (4 B.C.-34 A.D.). Archelaus was unsatisfactory to Rome and was replaced by a series of procurators (6-41 A.D.).

In 6 A.D., Judas the Galilean raised an armed revolt against the Romans and their kingling, Herod Antipas, which was swiftly suppressed and Judas was executed. This may have marked the beginning of the party called Zealots. Local rule under the procurators was largely assumed by the Jewish Council, the Sanhedrin, which had the responsibility of keeping order but which was always under observation by Roman agents who reported to the procurator. The latter generally lived at Caesarea, the port built by Herod, visiting Jerusalem only during festivals, at which time the crowded city was likely to suffer riots and disorders.

John the Baptist, whose view of the Messianic reign differed from that of the Zealots, his belief being that it was repentance and righteousness rather than revolt that would hasten the coming of the Messiah, probably began his preaching some time between 20 and 25 A.D. Herod Antipas, not at all sure that the distinction between John's Messianism and Judas the Galilean's would continue to be observed, took no chances and had John beheaded.

Similarly, in about 29 A.D. the Roman procurator, Pontius Pilate, upon the recommendation of the Sanhedrin, had Jesus crucified.

When the third Roman emperor, Caligula, followed Tiberius on the throne, he gave Herod Agrippa the tetrarchy of his father, Philip, and the title of king. Through trickery Agrippa managed to absorb the territory of his uncle, Herod Antipas, and presently it suited Roman policy to make him king of all Palestine (41-44). But he dallied with the thought of independence and when he conveniently died, Rome reverted to procurators. Agrippa II was never really a king but was given first the rule of Chalcis then of some Galilean cities and a measure of control over the Temple. So that from 44 A.D. all Palestine was a Roman province.

At about this time the prophet Theudas called his following together to watch him cross the Jordan dry-shod, but the procurator had him executed. James and Simon, sons of Judas the Galilean, then raised a revolt and were promptly crucified. The Zealots by now were openly advocating war against Rome, and the Sicarii, a fanatical band of assassins, were putting Romans and their supporters to death. While Paul was in Caesarea, waiting to be sent to Rome, the Jewish residents of that city tried to curtail the civil rights of the Gentiles and riots broke out. Swiftly the situation deteriorated—riot and rebellion, repression and massacre—resulting in the inevitable but useless war that began in 67 and brought destruction to Jerusalem (70). All over the empire Judaism was restless. There would soon be revolt in Cyrene, in Egypt (where already there had been a pogrom in the mid-century) and in Mesopotamia.

In 130 Hadrian ordered the rebuilding of Jerusalem as Aelia Capitolina with a temple to Jupiter where Jehovah's Temple had once stood. In 132, Simon bar Kozibah raised a rebellion and the Rabbi Akiba proclaimed him "Bar Kochba" (*son of a star*—"the Star out of Jacob"—Num. xxiv, 17) and thus the Messiah! But his rebellion failed. The Colonia Aelia Capitolina was built, the temple to Jupiter erected, and no Jew was allowed within the city limits— except eventually once a year, to weep where Jehovah's Temple had once stood.[6]

3. *The Legacy of Alexander*

Whether Alexander truly deserves to be called "the Great" will always be debated. There can be no such debate, however, about the stature of his father, Philip of Macedon, who unfortunately has not been given this title. It was Philip who saw that the Greek states, once unified, could carry Greek civilization to the entire Mediterranean world. Not only did he devote his own life to this purpose but, as no other ruler had ever done before (and as very few would do afterward) he painstakingly prepared his successor for the task of carrying it on. If Alexander was vainglorious and at times cruel and vengeful, it was not from his father but from his superstitious and hate-ridden mother that he took these repellent traits. Yet the scheming and malevolent Olympias, although she marred her son's character, was not able to defeat Philip in his determination that Alexander must be well equipped for the work he would do.

When the time came, Alexander was fully equal to his opportunity. That he squandered his resources in a foolish extension of his original campaign did not affect the marvelous success of the campaign itself. Nor did his untimely death destroy his achievement, although it did, of course, end all possibility of a Hellenic Mediterranean empire. Unification would be left for the Romans. But they would be Romans who spoke Greek! For Alexander had indeed carried Hellenistic* civilization to the entire Mediterranean world.

As has often been pointed out, the achievement of the Athenians was not produced by the populace but by the singularly gifted few. Nonetheless, as Gilbert Murray emphasizes, there were unusual characteristics in the populace, too. They were not a mob, he says, like the populace of Rome; they were artistic, intellectual, and if in the main they were at a very low level they could have flashes of very high inspiration. In many ways primitive, they were yet capable of an astonishing upsurge of mentality; as compared with other populations they were "more indecent but less lascivious, more capable of atrocious misconduct [but] more capable of idealism," and in any case, no matter how it happened "human thought got free."[7]

It was this freedom that made possible not only Greek philosophy and political experimentation but also Greek drama and art. As Plato had noted, in Egyptian art "the forms of excellence were long since fixed" so that "no painter or artist is allowed to innovate on the traditional forms or invent new ones."[8] In Athens the new liberty permitted the innovations that resulted in a perfection that has made it the standard by which all subsequent work is judged. It is art in which the human spirit is fully, freely and fearlessly expressed as it cannot be in Oriental art.

* The word *Hellenic* is used of the original Greek culture of the city-states, especially Athens. For the diffused and later Hellenism of the wider area the word *Hellenistic* is used.

Divinities are represented, not as in the animal-faced or many-armed symbolical figures of the East, nor even as in the multiple-breasted mother-goddesses of nearby Asia, but in the idealized beauty of the natural human form.

It is freedom that is also basic to the Socratic method of inquiry. All things may be called in question, though for Socrates—in contrast to some of his disciples who were corrupted by his method because they adopted his rationality without absorbing his virtue—all questions are pointed toward discovering the goodness that should be manifest in human life. There is, of course, no such thing as *the* Greek philosophy but only the many schools of thought that *freedom to think* without hieratical restrictions had encouraged and which a high degree of freedom of discussion had submitted to critical analysis and refined through unlimited debate.

To Athens also must be traced the advent of the scientific spirit—and even for that matter foreshadowings of scientific method. Here Alexander had an important part. For Aristotle was no solitary worker: he had a large company of research assistants at his disposal paid for by the hundreds of talents (a talent = about $1,800) which Alexander had made available so that want of money should not handicap his work.

Perhaps the greatest memorial to Alexander was the city he founded in Egypt to supply the place of Tyre, the Phoenician maritime metropolis which he had destroyed. This city, called in his honor Alexandria, was doubtless for a time the most important city of the ancient world. Besides its commerce, from which came its wealth, it had the first university, organized as such, which history had brought forth. Its fabulous library embraced every department of knowledge, its medical school and department of the sciences were unrivaled for more than a century anywhere in the ancient world. In Alexandria there were more Jews than there were in Jerusalem, some from Palestine but more from colonies that had long since been established in Egypt, and shortly, whether their language had been Aramaic or Egyptian, it would be forgotten. Like nearly all of the Mediterranean world, they would speak Greek.

This latter fact is of more consequence than most writers on Christian origins have assigned to it. The extent to which Paul and the early Christian theologians had absorbed Greek philosophy, the ethics of the Stoics or the system of the Hermetics can always be argued, but not their use of Greek. Here what we need to understand and keep constantly in remembrance is that it is *impossible to think in Greek and avoid Greek concepts*. Paul, like any Hellenistic Jew, differed and could not help differing *in the very way in which he did his thinking* from Jews who thought in Aramaic. We speak lightly of translating from one language to another. Actually we never really translate; we *render*. And nowhere is this more true than in the attempt to turn Aramaic into Greek.

The Semitic languages are primarily languages of volition and emotion; they express most easily what is willed and done and what is felt. But Greek is a *mental* language: with an immense capacity for precise communication it conveys what is *thought*. It is only to the extent that modern languages have absorbed the Greek vocabulary that they can equal Greek as tools for thinking. In ancient Hebrew or in Aramaic this kind of thinking is impossible.

Dodd, in his admirable study of Old Testament terms in Hebrew and Greek—in which he says that "translation is an impossible art, for the words of one language seldom or never convey precisely the same ideas as the corresponding words of another language" because of the "differences in the associations which the words have acquired in different contexts of thought and experience"—examines such words as "God," "Law," "Sin," "Atonement," "Faith," and shows how the meaning was affected when Hebrew was exchanged for Greek.[9] Here we have space for only one example. When the name for the Hebrew God (which was written in the Hebrew text but was not allowed to be spoken) was read in that language the reader was constantly reminded of the personal nature of the deity even though he said "Lord" instead of "Yahweh," but this ceased to be true when he read the same passage in Greek. Similarly, when *'Elohim,* the more general Hebrew name for God, became *theos* in Greek, a more fluid concept was introduced, permitting Hellenistic interpretation, so that Paul or Philo of Alexandria, while still thinking of God in a personal relationship, did not think of him as they would have done in Aramaic.* Illustrations might be multiplied but to the reader who knows no Greek or Hebrew they would be tedious, while the reader acquainted with these languages can easily consult the more technical works.

The point, however, is important. As well as what Paul took from Hellenistic culture as concepts that he consciously adopted, he was thinking *with* Greek concepts of which he need not have been conscious but which subtly and yet substantially affected his view of sin and redeemership and everything that entered into his theology. Even the *Torah,* the Jewish Law of Moses, which he said was superceded by the "gospel," takes on additional meaning, including the natural law of all creation, when it becomes *nomos* in Greek. This, moreover, was a process that would continue long after Paul, for Christian theology was *thought out* in Greek.

When we think, then, of the legacy of Alexander we must have in mind not merely that Hellenistic elements such as Greek philosophy had become part of the common heritage of all in the Mediterranean area in the first Christian century, to be appropriated or set aside, but that Hellenistic concepts and the Greek way of thinking were quite inseparable from the minds of all who spoke Greek.

* יהוה (*Yahweh*) for which אֲדֹנָי (*Adonai*) is substituted becomes κύριος (*kurios*) usually, but sometimes δεσπότης (*despotēs*); אֱלֹהִים (Elohim) becomes θεός (*theos*), a much more abstract term.

4. *The Judaism of the Diaspora*

The mobility of the peoples of the ancient world is seldom sufficiently recognized. We are prone to think, for instance, of the Greeks and the Persians meeting only in battle, whereas there were settlements of both in each other's territory. (For that matter, there were even Greek mercenaries in the Persian armies.) We are also prone to think of Palestine as being occupied almost wholly by Jews at the time of Jesus and the apostles, but as mentioned earlier there were Greek cities in Galilee when Jesus preached and it is possible that the Jewish Galileans were a minority, as we know them to have been two centuries earlier.

Certainly, there were far more Jews in the rest of the world during this period than there were in Judea. Some— a small proportion—had been forcibly removed from their homeland, as, for example, when certain of the inhabitants of Judea were carried off into Babylon (586 B.C.) or in later days when after a rebellion the families of the insurrectionaries were sold as slaves. The idea, however, that the *Diaspora* (Greek word for *dispersion*) was an "Exile" is completely false. Most of the Jews who went abroad did so because they hoped for a more prosperous—or at least more peaceful—life in countries with better prospects than their own. So that from about the sixth century B.C. on, first in Babylon and Egypt, then in Syria, Asia Minor, Cyprus, Libya, Ethiopia, North Africa, and finally in Europe too, there were large numbers of Jews.

According to the letter of Agrippa I to the Emperor Gaius Caligula, all countries that had "any advantages whatsoever of soil and climate [had] Jews settled in them."[10] Strabo, the Greek geographer, said that they were to be found in all cities so that "it is hard to find a place in the habitable earth that hath not admitted this tribe of men and is not possessed by them."[11] Hence, Paul could be sure, no matter to what city he went, that he would find a Jewish colony there.

In most cases it was a "colony" by choice, not through enforced segregation, with its own magistrates (*archontēs*) and often with its own "ruler of the people" (*ethnarchēs*). Although in at least one city, Leontopolis in Lower Egypt, there was a temple modeled upon that in Jerusalem—a rather surprising fact in view of the exclusive claims of the latter—the religious center was characteristically the synagogue. The origin of the synagogue is hidden in obscurity but it is not improbable that during the Babylonian captivity, when Jerusalem was far off and its Temple in any case in ruins, the *sopherim* or "doctors of the Law," (later the New Testament "scribes") formed the custom of calling the people together to hear their Scriptures read and to be instructed in the practices enjoined by their religion.

The word *synagogue* is Greek, as is also *sabbateion,* the alternative word for the same institution.* As the use of Hebrew and Aramaic lapsed in the colonies in Greek-speaking centers, it became necessary to provide Greek translations of the Scriptures of which the Septuagint, already described, was the foremost example, and the exposition, of course, was also in Greek. There was no priest or "minister" in charge of the synagogue. The resident rabbi, as a "doctor of Law," was the respected teacher who performed regular duties but anyone who had sufficient learning and the necessary self-confidence was encouraged to speak at the synagogue services. It might truly be said that here for the first time democracy was practiced in an institution of religion.

Besides Jews who were such by birth, the synagogue

---

* συναγωγή (*sunagōgē*) means a *bringing together* or assembly; σαββατεῖον (*sabbateion*) (used by Josephus but not in the New Testament) means a *sabbath-keeping* assembly. In Palestine, the name in Aramaic was *kenēsheth* (כְּנִישְׁתָּא), in Hebrew, *edah* (עֵדָה).

welcomed converts, but in the case of men circumcision was required as well as baptism. Klausner thinks that this may have been one of the reasons why there were more women proselytes than men.[12] The synagogues were all—or nearly all—of the Pharisaic tradition. This means that they were relatively liberal in interpreting the Mosaic Law, for it was the object of the Pharisees to adapt the regulations to contemporary conditions. The Sadducees, a much smaller party, was confined largely to Judea and its interest was centered in the Temple. An important difference between the two parties was that the Pharisees believed in resurrection and immortality whereas the Sadducees, correctly holding that no such doctrine is contained in the Law of Moses, were opposed to the belief.

It should also be emphasized that the Pharisees were tolerant of differences of belief within rather wide limits, provided the essentials of the Law were not forsaken. This was true even in Palestine, and our gospels, written considerably after the events they describe, are misleading to the uninformed reader in this respect. Outside of Palestine there must have been more latitude still. No picture is more mistaken than that of a synagogue congregation narrowly holding to stereotyped views. The Jews of this period as of all others enjoyed disputation and there was never any lack of debate. It was only when extremes were reached, as they were (from the Judaic standpoint) in the preaching of Paul, that new ideas were met with hostility. Between the rabbis there was always difference of opinion, sometimes quite sharp, as may easily be discovered from the Talmud.

We must be careful, moreover, to avoid any assumption that all Jews were pious or even that all were attached to the synagogue. There were Jews who subscribed funds to the Dionysiac festivals, Jews serving as guards in the temple of the god Serapis at Oxyrhynchus, Jews who swore by "Divine Caesar," and Klausner describes an inscription recording the gratitude of two Jews who had survived shipwreck which was found in a temple of the god Pan![13] According to Juster, there was a community of Jews in Media "so ignorant that they had never even heard of the Halakah [traditional oral law which interpreted the written Law] and who found the stories of the Flood and of Job, as recounted to them by Akiba, fascinatingly new."[14] It must also be remembered that the great Jewish theologian and philosopher, Philo of Alexandria, spoke of Jews who did not speak Greek as "barbarians" and that he revered Plato as much as he did Moses. He also adopted the pagan veneration of the stars.[15]

We are not to imagine then that the Diaspora was without variety. Nor must we forget that all Jews, even the most pious, lived in fear of evil spirits. Particularly prevalent was the notion that the earth was infested with the ghosts of those who were supposed to have drowned in the Great Flood. To these indigenous superstitions were added all the elements in pagan folk-fantasy that were assimilable to them. Nevertheless, fidelity to Judaic faith and practice was strongly marked throughout the Diaspora and made a deep impression on the Hellenistic world.

Many Gentiles who were unwilling to become proselytes, partly because of the requirement of circumcision, partly because they did not wish to join the Jewish nation (which the adoption of the Jewish faith carried with it), were constant in their attendance at the synagogue and were called "God-fearers." They believed, that is, in the one true God, revealed to the Jews, and had forsaken all others. Here we see the tremendous attractiveness of Judaism to Gentiles who had lost faith in the gods they had been serving and who had come to feel, like the Jews, that such deities were nothing but insensate idols. This was a theme the synagogues were always stressing; the pagan gods were no gods at all, even the noblest and most benevolent of them, and as for the animal-headed deities of Egypt, they were the butt of mocking jests and their worshipers were treated with contempt. To all this the "God-fearers" who stood in the back of the synagogue could readily assent, just as they could take an eager interest in the Jewish Scriptures, but they would not obey the Mosaic regulations or accept the Jewish "sign."

It was these "God-fearers" who were so easily converted by Paul. His message was exactly suited to their needs. Here was Judaic monotheism without Jewish nationalism, the Judaic morality without the Jewish dietary laws, the inheritance of the Judaic covenant, together with its Scriptures, without the hated rite of circumcision. As for the belief in Jesus as Messiah and Redeemer, it brought no serious difficulty. As we shall see in the next chapter, they were prepared for it by their pagan experience just as the synagogue had prepared them to become the people of the New Covenant, the true and faithful children of Abraham, the Christian Judaism.

5. *The Domain of Divus Caesar*

Almost anything that is said about the Roman Empire is in some degree true. It was oppressive, brutal, rapacious, ruthless, bloody—such adjectives might be multiplied indefinitely. Nor is there any difficulty in citing cases of cruel persecution, degrading spectacles of human suffering, senseless acts of dictatorial caprice. Yet, in a fair appraisal, these were the disfigurements of the Roman system, not its really definitive features.

By comparison with anything the world had known before, Roman rule was intelligent and efficient and on the whole benevolent. If the empire had been gained by force, it was administered in justice. If the *Pax Romana* was an imposed peace, hateful to rebels and a hindrance to political adventurers, it was nevertheless peace and a boon to the masses. Never until then had so vast a populace been given so large a measure of security. Never had there been so wide a freedom. By any realistic standard, Roman rule was the best the ancient world had known.

When abuses of power are pointed out, such as those of Roman procurators in Judea, it is only fair to remember the excesses of the native Jewish rulers, as, for instance, the crucifixion of hundreds of Pharisees by Alexander Janneus. Nor were these native rulers lenient conquerors: they liquidated without mercy and did not hesitate to impose circumcision upon subject populations. Indeed, the Romans came to Judea at the urging of no small part of the Jewish people who were weary of their high-priest kings. It should also be recalled that in the war of 67 A.D. which resulted in the fall of Jerusalem and the destruction of the Temple (70 A.D.), it is a question whether civil strife did not annihilate more Jews than did the armies of the Romans.

It is a notable fact, moreover, that Rome recognized Judaism as a *licit* (permitted) religion even though it meant that Jews could not be impressed into the imperial armies (because armed service would have required them to break the Sabbath) and special indulgence was repeatedly necessary as in the case of restraining the Roman legions from setting up their standards within the walls of Jerusalem. It was, it is true, a very uneasy "permission" and some of the emperors were inclined to curtail it, as was Caligula who wanted his statue placed in the Temple. But Herod Agrippa I was able to dissuade him from this (at least temporarily), a truly remarkable bit of intervention.

As we have several times seen, the Gentile believers in Jesus who eventually formed the Christian Church tried to gain for themselves the legal status that had been given to Jewish religion by claiming that it was they, not the unbelieving Jews, who were the true Judaism, a claim that was at first bewildering to Roman magistrates. After a while, however, the latter began to see—quite correctly—that

Christian intolerance was a threat to the empire such as Jewish nationalism had never been—a threat which was in fact made good when the Church took over the empire.

It had been the hope of Roman rulers that the empire itself might generate a universal religion, and thus Christianity, when it began to spread widely, had to be viewed as a serious rival. Yet there was never any real possibility that the imperial cult could have succeeded. Rome had awed the world by her conquests, won praise for her administration, respect for her justice, applause for her splendor, but had inspired no hope for the human future. Despite all its benefits—which most of the Mediterranean world freely recognized—the empire had not reached the hearts of men. As a political system it could and did attract loyalty; but as the promise of a good society to which men could give themselves in spiritual allegiance it could not break through the all-prevailing despair.

It was not believed that Rome could build a good society for the simple reason that it was not believed that society could be good. Something superhuman must enter terrestrial affairs before there could be any ground for optimism. There was need, said the poet Horace, for a new God. Human capacity was exhausted, man must look beyond himself and his former divinities, made in his own image. But where might he look? Where might the new God be found?

Not that there was any lack of religions or that they did not quicken faith in their devout. As we shall see in the following chapter, never since the dawn of history had there been so many cults to choose from. But, as indicated earlier, they did nothing for the empire, nothing for a good society of any kind; their concern was with a future life. It was true that they introduced a superhuman element, powerful saviors and redeemers, but the salvation they brought was through forsaking the world rather than renewing it. Where was the faith that could create the good society on earth—and create it within the fabric of the Roman Empire?

The fact was that the popular religions had abandoned the empire and were wholly engrossed with the redemption of the individual. The spiritual intoxication of *thiasos,* ecstatic communion with the divine savior who endowed the soul with immortality, had replaced the religion of *polis,* which reinforced one's duty to society. The old city-state religions had provided the inner cohesive force which had made social motivation dominant. But they had been decaying since before the time of Socrates. What was there that could take their place?

Roman rulers knew that what was needed was the old city-state religion but with a broader—indeed a universal—base. But how could they invoke it? The only answer they could find was in the worship of Rome itself. The Roman *genius* (mind-spirit) was incarnate, they said, in the emperor and he therefore would be the missing god. Not that at first the emperor claimed to be an actual deity—a God, so to speak, with a capital G. Augustus would not allow himself to be worshiped except as *"Rome and* Augustus," hoping in this way to stress the limits of his claim. The Emperor Claudius, when the citizens of Alexandria flatteringly offered to build a temple for his worship, wrote them that he could not allow "the appointment of a high priest to me and the erection of temples, for I do not wish to offend my contemporaries and my view is that temples . . . are the prerogative only of the gods."[16] This is clarity itself, but unfortunately it is a clarity that in the minds of later emperors got lost.

Nevertheless, no matter what the pretensions of the Caesars they were never really worshiped as God. For the most part the ritual in their honor was scarcely more than a gesture of submission, a salute to the Roman majesty. The empire had not solved its problem; it could not fill the emptiness in human hearts. What it did do, unintentionally but magnificently, was to open the way for Christianity. Its good highways, its large and well-ordered seaborne traffic, its organization of the Mediterranean world as a unified area within which communication was easy and new ideas freely transmissible, and above all its common language, the immensely articulate *koiné* Greek, made possible the swift spread of a religion that Rome would resist in vain.

At first, this too was a religion of a future world, either on earth when its Messiah arrived or beyond the skies where its believers joined their Risen Lord. But gradually, without ever forsaking these beliefs, the new faith would establish itself within the fabric of the empire as a ruler of this world, a terrestrial catholic church. It was this that was now beginning in the reign of the second of the emperors, the capable, unpopular Tiberius. Yet it was so unlikely a beginning that no contemporary, however prescient, could have foreseen what would come of it. Nor is it likely that events would have turned out as they did if at this time there had not appeared on the scene the Greek-speaking Jew who would reshape the faith of the early believers into a gospel for the Gentiles—Paul, the first Christian.

CHAPTER II

PAUL AND THE PAGAN REDEEMERS

1. *The World of Gnostic Theology*

When we read Paul's letters it is natural to assume that the terms he uses had the same meaning for him that they do for us, but this is frequently not so. When he writes, for instance, of "principalities and powers" (Rom. viii, 38; Col. ii, 16), he does not have in mind the kingdoms of this world but supernatural forces that have rebelled against God and which, according to his faith, have been made impotent by the crucifixion and resurrection of Jesus. That is to say, they have been made impotent in the case of those who are united with the Risen Jesus through having become a part of his "body," the word "body" being used in a special sense of which the modern reader has no notion until he acquaints himself with Paul's special terminology.

This, unfortunately, is possible to only a very limited extent without prolonged study and a knowledge of ancient languages. This section must therefore be restricted to conveying to the reader a very general impression of the difference between Paul's intellectual world and his own and to showing that Paul took many of his thought forms from his Hellenistic environment.

This does not mean that he merely appropriated them and left them unchanged. On the contrary, he drew them into his Judaic thinking and so molded and adapted them that they formed a new and distinctive system. One of the most important elements that he treated in this way was the group of "mytho-theologies" which, collectively, we call Gnosticism. It was believed until recently that Gnosticism was a Christian heresy which developed in the late first or early second century but it is now known that it existed considerably before that time and that Christianity absorbed some of its features and then came into severe conflict with sects that had retained others. In fact, for a while Christianity in many of its aspects was a part of the general Gnostic movement over which in the end it emerged victorious.[17]

The word *gnosis* is Greek for *knowledge* but it is a quite flexible word with many shades of meaning. For Gnosticism it meant a specially imparted knowledge akin to a revelation. When we read in Matthew's gospel (xi, 27) "No one knoweth the Son save the Father; neither doth any know the Father save the Son, and he to whomsoever the Son willeth to reveal him," we are dealing with a *gnosis*. Only those favored with the special revelation can possess this knowledge and only to them will it be the key to salvation.

The Gnostic myth took many forms, some of them exceedingly elaborate. Here we shall describe only the basic pattern. The Supreme God was far above terrestrial life and had taken no interest in it. There had been, before the beginning of time, a prototypal heavenly man composed wholly of light. Demonic powers of darkness (or a creator god, or *aeon,* or combination of *aeons*) had conquered this original man and broken him up into millions of tiny particles of light which they (or he) had used as magnetic forces with which the world had been created out of the chaos of darkness. It was necessary, however, that the sparks of light be closely guarded since if they were removed and reunited the world would go back to chaos; so myriads of demons kept watch over them.

In the case of earthly man the particle of light was his innermost self (it would be incorrect to say "soul") and it kept him more or less troubled, longing to return to heaven, which was his home. To keep this longing subdued the demons drugged and stupefied man so that sometimes he forgot heaven but at other times (or with certain individuals) his memory of it would be sharp and he would yearn for deliverance from his earthly prison.

Eventually, the Supreme God becomes aware of what the demons have done and, being moved by compassion at the sad plight of man, sends down his Son to save him. The Son is carefully disguised in an earthly body so that the demons will not recognize him.* He preaches and heals but his chief mission is to give to the elect ("his own" in John's gospel) the sacred passwords which will be needed in the journey through space as they proceed from planet to planet where the demonic powers have outposts. He goes before them to mark the way for them, passing through a series of "heavens" until he reaches his Father. (In John's gospel, "I go to prepare a place for you"—Jn. xiv, 2). There he waits while each of "his own" at death ascends to meet him. Finally, all the sparks of light will be reassembled to restore the heavenly man and the material world will fall back into chaos.

Here, it is plain, we have the main outline of a system of salvation through the Redeemership of the Son of God, even though some of its features are very different from those in the Christian *gnosis*. To Paul the Gnostic systems, or at least some of them, were thoroughly familiar. They were known all over the Mediterranean world. They must, as Professor Gilbert Murray tells us, "have been established in Antioch and probably in Tarsus well before the days of Paul or Apollos. Their Saviour," he continues, "like the Jewish Messiah, was established in men's minds before the Saviour of the Christians."[18]

---

* He may also be born of a virgin so that the demons will not know of his conception. This reason for a virgin birth is easily understood within the framework of Gnostic theology.

It was thus in Gnostic terms, though with reserve, that Paul thought through his soteriology.* It was even in these terms that he defined his apostleship. Jesus had appeared to him, he says, as to "one born out of due time," or, to translate literally, as to "the abortion"** (I Cor. xv, 8). This phrase is incomprehensible until we know that according to the Gnostic cosmogony the "abortion" is the surplus of crude matter which had been cast out of the cosmos when it was created but which was used later by the Gnostic Savior to form a perfect "Aeon" or (very roughly) "world-soul." What Paul is saying then is not merely that his apostleship came to him late or under humbler conditions than in the case of the earlier apostles but that his Savior, Jesus, had especially "formed" him out of the "material" rejected when creating other apostleships to make him the *perfect* apostle of the fully redemptive gospel.

Perhaps inconsistently with this, at least superficially, he uses the Gnostic term *pleroma**** or completeness of creative resource embodied in the cosmos to describe, first the creative supremacy of Christ, then the condition of believers "in Christ," an exceedingly difficult concept for the modern mind to grasp but unquestionably Gnostic (Col. i, 15-20; ii, 8-12).[19] He speaks of being "caught up into the third heaven" (II Cor. xii, 1), which is a reference to the series of Gnostic heavens (although there are Jewish counterparts to this), one above the other, and goes on to say that he "heard unspeakable words, which it is not lawful for a man to utter." This is a reference to the Gnostic obligation to keep secret the sacred formulas of the *gnosis,* especially those that are imparted only at the highest level.

Bible readers are familiar with the Pauline reference to

---

* From the Greek σωτήρ (*sōtēr*) = *savior* or *deliverer.*

** τῷ 'εκτρώματι (*tō ektrōmati*) *to a child untimely born.*

*** πλήρωμα (*plērōma*) *that which fills up,* as for example, the crew that "fills up" a ship, but in Gnostic usage (mystical) a *plenitude* as described in the text.

Jesus taking upon himself "the form of a slave, being made in the likeness of men" (Phil. ii, 7). This is generally understood as meaning that he accepted a humble station in his earthly life. Actually, the meaning is that by assuming sinful flesh (*sarx*) he became a slave (*doulos*) to the demonic powers and like all other men who are prisoners of the flesh came under the dominion of death. It was in this way that he overcame death.[20]

In I Corinthians, Paul tells us that he is speaking God's wisdom in a mystery, a *gnosis* that has been hidden, "which God foreordained before the worlds unto our glory, which none of the rulers of this world knoweth: for had they known it, they would not have crucified the Lord of glory" (ii, 7, 8). By "rulers of this world" he does not mean the Roman procurator or the Jewish king but the supernatural rulers of "the age," the demonic powers that have mankind in their grasp. It is the purpose of Jesus (as Paul views it) to be crucified in the flesh so as to defeat these demonic powers. Evil lives on by returning evil for evil; Jesus will allow evil to inflict its ravages upon him without resistance, absorbing all the damage it can do without returning evil for evil. In the end there will be nothing more that evil can do except kill him. This will merely strip him of his flesh and he will arise triumphant, evil having no further power over him. But if the demonic powers *had known* that this was what they were doing when they had Jesus crucified (through the agency of the evil men they controlled), they would never have done it since they would have seen at once that they were sealing their own doom.

This is what Paul means when he says that they "would not have crucified the Lord of glory" if they had realized who it was that they were nailing to a cross. Here again, the framework of his thought is Gnostic. The Son of God must outwit the demonic forces by not allowing them to recognize him. Otherwise they will not take the part required of them in the drama of salvation.

Efforts have been made—and are still being made—to equate these elements in Paul's thinking with Judaic concepts but such efforts can never succeed. As W. D. Davies admits in his *Paul and Rabbinic Judaism,* the very terms Paul uses in speaking of the *flesh* that is crucified (as well as related terms for *psyche* and *spirit*) have no Judaic equivalents.[21] This is not to say that Paul was thinking *otherwise than as a Jew.* No one who was *not* a Jew could have thought as he did, as we shall see later. But he was a Jew thinking in Greek, and just as he drew Rabbinic concepts from his Jewish background so did he draw Hellenistic concepts from his Greek background, fitting both to his needs.*

2. *The Mystery Religions*

The close similarity between the mystery cults and Christianity was acutely embarrassing to the early church. Since it was known that the mystery cults were older it was impossible to claim that they had borrowed from the Christian ritual—yet how could it be admitted that there had been any borrowing in the opposite direction? So the church fathers, vexed but resourceful, set forth an argument that Satan had foreseen what the Christian ritual would be and had caricatured it in advance, expecting by this stratagem to entrap the unwary and confuse the true believers. Tertullian called it "the zeal of the devil rivaling the things of God," and asked how the similarity could be genuine when "the unclean cleanses."[22] Justin Martyr made the same point, bitterly complaining that demons had counterfeited the sacraments, including the Supper of the Lord with its bread and wine.[23]

* The reader who desires a better understanding of Pauline theology in relation to the Gnostic salvation drama, which in these pages it has been barely possible to introduce, cannot do better (if he is not afraid of a little concentrated study) than to read John A. T. Robinson's *The Body,* in the Studies in Biblical Theology Series, Henry Regnery Co., Chicago, 1952.

Evidently then, there was a relationship between the mystery cults and Christianity which the church fathers deplored and wanted to hide. To the modern mind it may not seem deplorable but a natural process of history. Just as Christianity took much of its substance from Judaism, a fact which has long been familiar and which no one wants to cover up, so also has it drawn upon pagan sources, and with equal innocence.

What were the mystery cults? In origin they went a long way back, each having its individual history.[24] There were important differences between them, not only in myth and ritual but in moral standards. Nevertheless, psychologically they belong together as varying manifestations of a single phenomenon, the root of which was the desire to be saved from death and from all evil through being united with a divine redeemer. Common to all the cults was (1) a rite of initiation signifying purification and new birth, (2) a sacrament or sacraments through which unity with the redeemer was achieved or maintained, (3) a promise of happy life beyond the grave in a world into which the believer would be admitted through his savior.[25]

The basis of the salvation-god myth was the vegetation cycle: the death of earth's flora in winter, its resurrection in spring, its fruitfulness in summer and autumn, and then the repetition of the cycle. Originally the salvation-god was a *chthonic* (earth or beneath the earth) deity and was always associated with a goddess who represented the earth itself or the food-providing soil that covers it. To understand the myth we must keep always in mind that *its deities were impersonations of natural forces*. Later, the redeemer-gods were *also deified human heroes* who had become *associated mythologically* with these natural forces.

What was the "reasoning"? The earth is fertile. The earth is the mother of life. This fertility is represented by the wife-mother-goddess (Cybele, Isis, etc.). But fertility is a thing the earth can lose. It must be constantly renewed. It must be seeded for the crops that are desired. This renewing of fertility and seeding of the soil is represented by the dying god (Attis, Osiris, etc.), the redeemer whose blood must be poured into the soil and who will "rise again" in the new harvest. He is also the seed from last year's harvest which, although "dead," will come to life in the new crop. This is the crude basis upon which the mystery religions were elaborated.

As Frazer has so clearly shown in his *Golden Bough*,[26] the slain redeemer was once an earthly king, or his son, or a surrogate for his son, sometimes a criminal, but in any case an actual person who was ritually murdered as a sacrifice to promote the fertility of the soil. Later, an effigy was substituted, though in some places the slaughter of a human victim may have persisted well into our era. As will be described in the next section, the body of the victim was sometimes embedded with seeds which, after interment, would sprout and thus very vividly signify the resurrected life which was growing from the god through his human representative.

The reasoning behind the mystery cults was homological: the divine power of life that so miraculously arose from the dead in the seed planted in the soil could equally arise in a human being provided he could know the formula and become invested with the divine power. This he attempted to do through union with the earth-god who himself had died and risen again and who now, besides being a fertility god, was man's divine-human redeemer.

Initiation into the cult was very elaborate but always involved some kind of "new birth," either through being buried in soil or baptized in blood or water. From either element (and sometimes by passing through fire) the candidate emerged as a "new person" whose life was united with the redeemer's. Through sacraments (described in the next section) this union was maintained and enhanced so that, when the believer died, his personal self or soul went on into the redeemer's paradise.

Sometimes the ceremonies were grossly sexual and this has led to indiscriminate condemnation. But it is a question whether even in the cults that did have sexual symbols and sacramental practices the significance was what it would be to a modern mind. Generative power was thought of as dramatic evidence of the potency of the life-power itself, which potency was not sought for sexual purposes but as the means of living beyond death. Along the same lines, sexual ecstasy was doubtless considered a form of god-possession, as was exhilaration through wine, or ritual dancing, or frenzied bloodletting. It is therefore somewhat doubtful whether in our sex-dominated modern culture we are able to understand what the mystery cultists were conveying in their ritual. But on any rendering, as Ramsay puts it, these cults "remain one of the most instructive and strange attempts to frame a religion, containing many germs of high conceptions expressed in the rudest and grossest symbolism, deifying the natural processes of life in their primitive nakedness."[27]

The fact is, however—and it should be emphasized—that obscene symbolism and licentiousness were *not* characteristic of *all* the mystery cults, some of which were actually ascetic. As Enslin appropriately points out, "the beautiful *Odes* of Pindar were penned by a devotee to the Orphic rites,"[28] and Apuleius has left us eloquent testimony to the refined delicacy of his initiation into the cult of Isis.[29]

One of the better-known ritual dramas is that of Attis and the earth-mother Cybele. On a day in March known as the Day of Blood (corresponding to the Christian Good Friday), Attis in effigy and no longer impersonated by a human representative is fastened to a tree where he "bleeds" to death. The real blood is provided by his priests who strike knives into their arms during a frenzied dance. Sometimes, apparently, some of them emasculated themselves, a practice which was well known to Paul who, in his letter to the Galatians, tauntingly recommended that extremists in that community do the same (Gal. v, 12). At the end of the day the effigy is buried, either in the ground or (for example, in Rome) in a sepulchre. (Where a sepulchre is used instead of the soil itself the symbolism is that of the cave beneath the earth from which new life emerges in the springtime, impersonated by the fertility gods and goddesses who have become redeemers.)

When the days of mourning are passed it is announced that Attis has risen from the dead, and his effigy is brought from the sepulchre. Now comes a time of great rejoicing, corresponding to the Christian Easter but with wild and often orgiastic celebration.[30] This ritual, which had reached Rome before the beginning of the Christian era, came from Phrygia in Asia Minor and its affinities with the story of the death and resurrection of Jesus were as obvious to the early Christians as they are to the modern reader and were deeply resented.

In the Attis mystery, Cybele (the wife-mother) seems to fade somewhat into the background, at least in the West, but this is not true of the cult of Isis. Of Egyptian origin, the worship of Isis, whose tears annually raised the life-giving waters of the Nile, had spread far and wide throughout the empire. The myth, which had many variants, is basically as follows: Osiris, the savior-god who is the husband of Isis, is killed by Set (or a demonic power of darkness) and his body, broken into fragments, is buried in widely separated places (or planted like seed in the soil). Isis, like all the *mater dolorosas* mourning for the dying redeemers, bitterly laments his death and tries to find his body and revive it. At this point the myth takes many forms but in any case Osiris is resurrected and becomes the ruler of the world beyond death while his son, Horus, born to Isis, becomes in effect a renewed Osiris.[31] Images of Isis and her son, Horus, are indistinguishable from those of

Mary and Jesus. The birth stories of Horus also have him born in a cave, but this was true of other redeemers and at a much earlier time, as the great classical scholar, Jane Harrison, has shown.[32]

The resurrection of Osiris was celebrated in a number of different ways but in essence corresponded to the ritual of Attis—or of Dionysos, Tammuz, Adonis, or any other of the redeemers. The joyful shout rang out, "He is risen," and in the cult ritual the initiate identified himself with the god's resurrection, the priest reciting, "As truly as Osiris lives, he shall live also; as truly as Osiris is not dead, he shall not die; as truly as Osiris is not extinguished, he shall not be extinguished," which reminds us inevitably of the words used by Paul about those who are resurrected "in Christ."[33]

To describe the remainder of the mystery cults is beyond our scope. It is important, however, to realize that they did not remain apart but were constantly affecting each other and intermingling. It should also be kept in mind that a member of a mystery cult could be a Gnostic in theology, could believe in astrology, could be attached to one school or another of Greek philosophy. It was possible, moreover, to belong to more than one mystery cult; they were not exclusive.

When it comes to the influence of the mystery religions and how widespread it was, we must acknowledge that at least at certain times and among some elements in the population it was not unknown even in Judea. In the prophet Ezekiel we read of Jewish women weeping for the slain redeemer, Tammuz (viii, 14), and Frazer believes he sees Adonis worship in Bethlehem itself and even in the name, which means "House of Bread."[34] So that while, as we shall see, the main current of Judaism was sharply resistant to the mystery religions, we can by no means be sure that there were not Jewish factions which were considerably affected by them. To such Jews as Paul, living in the Greek-speaking Diaspora, no amount of resistance could produce immunity. To this, however, we shall come after we have considered the mystery-religion sacraments.

3. *Sacraments of Bread and Wine*

Like other religious practices, the bread and wine sacrament goes back to crude beginnings. As Frazer has shown, the corn spirit was originally embodied in a human representative who was ritually killed and eaten.[35] Later an animal was substituted. Decorated to represent the god, the unfortunate beast was torn to pieces, its flesh devoured and its blood drunk by devotees in a state of frenzy. In this way it was believed that the god became one with his worshipers.

We have already mentioned the Egyptian custom based upon the burial of the life-giving corn god in the soil. Seed corn (the word "corn" used in this context means such cereals as wheat and barley, not maize) was embedded in the corpse of the victim who represented the god and this in time sprouted, grew into ripened corn and was harvested. Bread made from this corn was almost literally the body of the god, i.e., of his representative. To eat this bread was to absorb the god into oneself.

The eventual connection of this ritual with the hope of immortality is well attested by effigies found in Egyptian tombs. Images of Osiris were made of layers of linen within which was vegetable mold, barley seeds and a sticky moistening agent. When the barley sprouted, the life-force given to it by the god was conveyed to the dead person with whom it was entombed. Smaller effigies were frequently placed between the legs of mummies, these also being sown with corn. The location chosen was due, no doubt, to the association of life-force with the generative organs.[36]

The transition from a sacramental meal of flesh to one

of bread is not difficult to understand against this background. The bread was the body of the god just as was the flesh of his animal representative. In a similar way, wine was the blood of the grape created by the life-force of the deity. In areas where there were no vineyards and thus no wine, other fermented beverages were used. It had been noticed that water in which cereals had been placed would sometimes acquire strange qualities. This was the work of the god. The chemistry of fermentation was of course not understood and the change that had taken place in the liquid was therefore unaccountable on any natural basis. When the liquid was imbibed it was self-evident that the power of the god was in it because of its effect upon those who drank it! Hence the worshipers were said to be *enthused,* the literal meaning of which is *filled with the god.*

When the original crudities had faded into the past—which did not happen everywhere but did in some of the mystery religions—the meaning became more elaborate while the ritual grew more refined. But it was *not symbolical* in our sense of the term. Difficult as it is for a modern mind to grasp, the intention of the sacrament was not to signify a spiritual union between the worshipers and their redeemer but a *material* participation in his *body.* This does not mean the body in which his earthly life was lived. There were considered to be what Paul calls "bodies terrestrial and bodies celestial" (I Cor. xv, 40) but the celestial body was definitely material. Here we are dealing with meanings quite unfamiliar to us, particularly the meaning of the Greek word *soma* which in some of its uses is quite untranslatable.[37]

When the flesh (*sarx*) perished, the body (*soma*) of the redeemer in its "form" and "organized aliveness" had endured beyond death as the locus of his "soul" (psūche) and spirit (pneuma) which, however, were not limited by it. If the reader finds this too difficult to comprehend he may be comforted by knowing that those familiar with these concepts do not entirely comprehend them either. To the modern mind they are unreal; but this does not mean that they were unreal to the mystery cultists or to Paul. They were so real to the early Christians that they accepted martyrdom in complete reliance upon them. They were a part of the *church* which was "the *body* (*soma*) of Christ" (I Cor. xii, 27, etc.). As such they would pass into the celestial world leaving their flesh (*sarx*) in the world of "corruption."

We emphasize this matter because it is the basic principle of sacramentalism both in the mystery cults and in the New Testament and it is *not Judaic*. To Paul as to the mystery cultist the ear of corn is the key to life beyond death. In the initiation ceremonies we know that ears of corn were given a prominent, often a climactic, place in the proceedings. It is to this ritual that Paul is referring when he reminds the Corinthians that they do not sow a whole ear of corn in the ground to get an ear of corn in the harvest but just a "dead" seed. To this seed God "giveth a body even as it pleased him" (I Cor. xv, 35ff.), and God will do the same thing in giving the believer a "spiritual body" after his death. The miracle of the sprouting of the corn from a "dead" seed is the basis of the belief that man too can have life out of death but only if he is joined to the body of the already resurrected redeemer. This redeemer, let us be reminded, is not only the deified human hero but the personification of the life-force that raises the earth out of the death of winter.

What the believer did, then, in partaking of the sacramental meal was *to participate in the substance* of the redeemer-god. It was because this was his view of "the Lord's Supper" that Paul so sternly warned the Corinthians that if they ate and drank of this meal unworthily they were "guilty of the body and blood of the Lord," which would cause severe sickness and sometimes death ("For this cause many among you are weak and sickly and not a few sleep" I Cor. xi, 30). As one scholar comments, "his comparison of the Christian meal with those in honor of pagan divinities is pointless unless it be conceded that both were capable of bringing about a distinct mystic union—in the one case with Christ, in the other with the demon."[38] Here Paul has invested a mystery cult usage with a Judaic exclusiveness, a matter of no small import for the future Christian Church. To partake of the body and blood of the Risen Jesus, he says, and then to partake of the body and blood of a pagan redeemer is to set up a violent *physical* conflict within the body which will cause sickness and may cause death.

In its sacramentalism the Pauline movement may thus be seen to be a mystery religion with a Gnostic theology. For, as Bultmann has expressed it, "Christian sacramental theology differs little from Gnosticism, if at all."[39] This judgment is equally valid if we have ascribed to Paul a greater share in the development of the sacraments than he actually took—a subject, of course, of perennial debate. Scholars such as Loisy do not credit the Pauline authorship of the passage in Corinthians (I Cor. xi) in which Paul sets forth the ritual of the Lord's Supper.[40] Some scholars would place it as much as a century later. In this event we would need to suppose that, in Schweitzer's words, "as though by a pre-established harmony in the history of religion, it came about that [the Pauline mysticism] was able to find complete representation in the language of the mystery religions, and found there ready to hand conceptions and expressions which facilitated, suggested, and in some cases were even indispensable to its fuller development."[41]

Upon this basis, although Paul's part was less than we have been imagining, it was still a vital part. It was he more than all others who *prepared* the new movement for its absorption of the mystery religion sacramentalism. In our view, however, his role was the larger one that we have been describing. The Corinthians passage that many scholars do not accept as Paul's has nothing against its authenticity except the supposed improbability of the sacramental meal being so highly developed so soon. The emphasis was still upon the reappearance of Jesus in his *parousia*. How then could there have been so institutionalized a ritual as though the eschatological expectation had sunk out of sight? This is a disturbing question and not easy to answer. Yet the passage concerned (I Cor. xi, 23ff.) sounds as Pauline as any in the New Testament. The ritual of the Supper did not come to Paul from tradition but had been "received of the Lord"—the very way in which he describes everything else that came to him by inward revelation!

May we not suppose that this is the way the sacrament *was* established? Paul knew of the much simpler Last Supper of Jesus with an intimate few of his disciples in which Jesus had given thanks and broken bread and perhaps had even used a familiar Essenic ritual. This would have been a *Jewish* ceremony—unless like Maurenbrecher and Gunkel and a number of other scholars[42] we are willing to believe that the Galilee of Jesus' time had been strongly influenced even as to its Jewish elements by an invasion of the mystery religions. Setting aside this last hypothesis as improbable (but not impossible) and allowing that the Jewish ceremony observed by Jesus was also observed in some manner by the Palestinian early believers, what reason is there why Paul, audacious in other matters, was not equally bold in this?

Knowing that there *had* been a Last Supper but that it did not have the sacramental features that were essential to the sacred meals familiar to his Gentile converts, he saw that these features could be supplied. They were already represented in his Gnostic-influenced theology. They could be provided in a way that would completely satisfy those in his movement who belonged—or had at one time belonged—to a mystery religion. Indeed, did it not seem to Paul that what was claimed for other saviors *by right be-*

longed to Jesus? So he "received of the Lord" what the sacrament should be and thereupon instituted it. Then, when the gospels eventually were written—or during a later editing as seems to be the case with Mark[43]—the institution of the body and blood sacrament was attributed to Jesus.

This at least is one possible way by which the mystery religion sacrament came into the Christian Church. The details we shall never know. Nor can we know how many varieties of sacred meals there once were. We do know that wine was not always used even in the mystery religions. We know of the use of fishes (which is reflected in the stories of the feedings of a multitude with barley loaves and fishes in the gospels). We also know of the use of "barley-water," which presumably was fermented. There were indeed many variations but always on the single theme of salvation from evil and from death through sacramental union with a redeemer.

4. *The Rise of Mithraism*

Christianity's most serious rival, even into the fourth century, was unquestionably Mithraism. The origin of this religion, although it goes back many centuries before the Christian era into India and Persia, cannot be traced with any certainty. Perhaps it was in part the cult that Zoroaster tried to put down in his reforms and which re-emerged later, changed and with a secret ritual. In any case, beginning in the first century B.C. it swept through the Roman Empire as a mystery cult, carried chiefly by soldiers but also by slaves, until it became the religion of most of officialdom and of the military, and was found everywhere from Persia in the East to Britain in the West.

The central act in the drama of Mithras is the slaying of a bull, a scene which is depicted in relief in all places of his worship or *Mithraea*. While the god stands with his left knee on the back of the bull, his left hand dragging its head up by the horn or the muzzle and his right hand plunging a knife or dagger into its throat, a scorpion has fastened itself upon the bull's scrotum and a dog and a serpent (the latter usually but not always present) drink the blood from the wound. A crow is often seen perched somewhere on the god's mantle and the bull's tail terminates in ears of corn. Sometimes corn sprouts from the wound.

Whatever may be obscure about this scene it is clear that it represents a fertility myth and its attendant ritual. The blood of the bull is the life-force of the god restoring the soil and producing the corn. In Persian mythology it was from the bull slain by Ahriman that all vegetable and animal life took their rise and from his blood that the grapevine was created. The scorpion and the serpent try to arrest this creative process but the potency of the bull's blood and his great generative power frustrate them. This, however, was the creation myth. At the end of the world order another bull would be slain, this time by a redeemer, and new life would flow from the blood of his sacrifice.

Mithras was undoubtedly this redeemer, and besides his redeemership undertook most of the other active functions of the deities, the highest god, Ahura-Mazda, being far removed from human affairs. He was also the all-conquering Sun, giver of light and life to the earth, and the leader of the hosts of righteousness in the struggle against the powers of evil and darkness. Here we see an eschatology which reminds us of the Jewish Messianic eschatology which undoubtedly owed something to it, just as Judaic religion in other ways was indebted to Persian influence.

The initiate into the Mithraic cult passed through seven grades or degrees and was finally handed a garland pierced by a sword which he placed briefly on his head, then rested it on his shoulder, saying, "Mithras is my crown!" He was thereupon branded in the forehead with a red-hot iron.

There was also baptism by immersion, an ordeal of passage through flames, a drama of death and rebirth into new life, and a sacrament of bread and wine. In addition, there were sometimes special tests of courage such as leaping from a cliff.[44]

In the Mithraic liturgy of initiation there was a long invocation which has been preserved in a papyrus now in Paris (#574) part of which reads as follows: "O Lord, hail, mighty in power, king majestic in sovereignty, highest of gods, Helios, Lord of heaven and earth . . . if it please thee, make announcement of me to the highest God, who hath begotten and made thee; for I am a man, [name], the son of my mother, [name], born of the mortal body of [mother's name] and of seed that gives life, and [begotten again] by thee this day who hast made so many myriads immortal. . . . [For I am] a man who wills and prays that he may worship thee according to a man's power." Then, continues the ritual, "when you have prayed thus, he [Mithras] will come into the vault of heaven and you will see him walking."[45] Which must refer, as in the case of similar "theophanies" in the initiation dramas of other mystery cults, to an impressive impersonation.

The ethical standards of Mithraism were undoubtedly high and to its devotees it was evidently a deeply satisfying religion. But it was a religion for men. The much larger place accorded to women by Christianity would alone be enough to account for its triumph over Mithraism; and it was a less austere religion. Yet it was a triumph that yielded something to the defeated. It is not without significance that the birthday of Jesus had to be moved to the 25th of December, the birthday of Mithras, the Invincible Sun; and in English (and German) the first day of the week, the Lord's Day, is still called after Mithras, Sunday.

The full indebtedness of Christianity to Mithraism may never be known; its indebtedness to the mystery religions as a whole is also hard to measure. But certainly it was great. As Dean Inge estimates it, the Christian Church owes to the mysteries "the notions of secrecy, of symbolism, of mystical brotherhood, of sacramental grace, and above all, of the three stages in the spiritual life: ascetic purification, illumination and epopteia"* (vision of the deity leading to blessedness).[46]

5. *The Beginnings of a Synthesis*

One of the worst pitfalls in reconstructing the New Testament period is that of overemphasis. The Semitic specialist finds Judaic concepts everywhere, even when they are plainly Greek; the student of Gnosticism discovers that Paul is a Gnostic, even when he is quoting the Old Testament; the writer on mystery religions treats Christianity as though it were a mystery cult almost solely. The fact is, of course, that each of these emphases is *partly* correct, none wholly so, and they need to be kept in proportion. Nor should we neglect factors less prominent than those mentioned, such as the teaching which became embodied in the Hermetic literature at about the same time the gospels were being written. This teaching we shall now briefly describe.

Hermes Trismegistus (Thrice-Greatest-Hermes) is the Greek name of the Egyptian god, Thoth, who had revealed an evangel which it was the duty of his worshipers to preach far and wide. Unlike the mystery cults, which it nonetheless must have influenced, Hermetic religion was not sacramental but appealed to man to subdue his earthly nature and, through knowledge from God, to set free his higher or celestial nature.

---

*'εποπτεύω (epoptevō), *to look over or watch over*, took on a special meaning in the mystery cults. The final and culminating experience of the initiation was the appearance of the god or goddess in bright light which led to the extreme happiness of becoming an 'επόπτης (epoptēs), one initiated into the highest mystery. In Christianity this became the blessedness of the mystic through less literal vision.

In the *Poimandres,* the most important of the tractates,[47] God is portrayed as Mind (*nous*) and the Word (*logos*) as the Son of God, reminding us of the beginning of John's gospel. After a description of the fall of archetypal man, which recalls Paul's description of the "first Adam," man is described as he is and as he shall be in his ascent toward God. Finally, the prophet who receives the revelation vows to "enlighten with his grace those of the human race who are in ignorance, my brothers, thy sons," and prays that he may share in God's holiness.

This unquestionably is a high level of religion and the Hermetic preachers must have had influence. It is furthermore notable that they were preaching when Paul and the apostles were conducting their missionary work and that in both cases the movement was westward.

Meanwhile, for some centuries Stoicism, a philosophy that was almost a religion, had been widely proclaimed. God, for the Stoic, was Mind and the Soul of the Cosmos, reaching out in all directions and filling the universe with his creative "seed-concepts" (*logoi spermatikoi*) and powers (*dunameis*). As is well known, the ethical precepts of Stoicism were exceedingly high and it is beyond doubt that they were, so to speak, pace makers for Christian ethics.

There were also such sects as the Therapeutae of Alexandria, monastics and scholars somewhat similar to the Essenes, whom later church fathers mistook for Christian monks. The fact that the literature of these sects has perished and that they are known to us only through brief descriptions (in the case of the Therapeutae, by Philo)[48] does not mean that they were without considerable influence or even that they were not eventually absorbed into the Christian Church.

What we must see in the New Testament period is immense vitality creating and mingling a large variety of religious ideas and practices and, through extreme mobility, spreading most of them far and wide. No movement stood apart; each affected the others. Even monastic movements absorbed something from outside themselves, as did the Therapeutae and Essenes. As Angus illustrates it, "the Persian Mithra-cult was at least partly egyptianized; the Egyptian Isiac cult largely hellenized. Stoicism exerted an immense modifying influence upon Gnosticism. The Hermetic literature is such a blend that scholars are not agreed as to the relative proportion of Egyptian, Babylonian, Stoic, Platonic, Neo-Pythagorean, and even Christian ingredients. We often cannot tell from sepulchral inscriptions to which cult the deceased belonged; the language would sometimes point equally to membership in the Christian Church or in a mystery-cult."[49]

In such a world it was impossible for the original Judaic Messiah to be preached abroad without becoming swiftly changed in his significance and characteristics. Even the New Testament book of Revelation, an apocalypse entirely in the Jewish manner, portrays Jesus as a luminous being on a white horse "and his eyes are a flame of fire and upon his head are many diadems . . . and he is arrayed in a garment sprinkled with blood" (xix, 11ff.)—which is a portrait not of Jesus but of Mithras! Whence too in the same book came the references to "the blood of the Lamb?" The baptism in blood ("And they washed their robes and made them white in the blood of the Lamb"—vii, 14) belonged to the Attis cult and its variants where the initiates stood beneath a grating while an animal (usually a bull) was killed above them and they became covered with his blood.[50]

That Paul borrowed from the mystery religions we have already shown. But he was also in conflict with them as the New Testament itself evidences in a passage which has been obscured for us by the difficulties of translation (Col. ii, 18). "Let no man rob you" (this verse should read) "on the pretext of humility and [by belonging to] the [approved?] cult of angels, which he has seen at the initiation."* Which is to say, "Do not allow yourself to be impressed by well-behaved members of a highly esteemed mystery religion who have seen the divine vision at their initiation." Here the real world of New Testament times comes to life and we see Paul contending for his own Judaic-Hellenistic cult against those that *sacramentally* are akin to it. These cults, he continues, are the body (*soma*) separated from the Head, which must always be Jesus, and although they have a "show of wisdom" are actually worthless (Col. ii, 19).

It is time, however, that we said something about those who in this period were disenchanted with all religions. There was skepticism—and even cynicism—as well as an abundance of interactive religious faiths. Carved on some tombs would be found such words as "I was not, I became: I am not and I care not"; and "Hold all a mockery, reader; nothing is our own."[52] Against those who believed in the immortality conferred by the cults and, presently, by Christianity were arrayed those who disbelieved not only in immortality but in God, goodness, the reality of the moral struggle, and the entire meaning of life. We must never forget that this was a time when despair was widespread, or in Gilbert Murray's words, a time of "failure of nerve."[53]

To those who believed in nothing and expected to go on believing in nothing, Christianity can have made no greater appeal than the mystery religions. But to those who still hoped, and for whom the philosophical teachings of Stoicism were beyond their grasp and the Hermetic gospel too austere, both the mystery religions and Christianity must have had attractions. It was not merely—and not chiefly—that these religions could inspire faith. The better of the mystery religions, and certainly Christianity, evoked

---

* Loisy points out that 'εμβατεύων (*embateuōn*) is the mystery cult term for the first step of the initiation.[51]

love. The redeemer of the cult *loved* his worshipers and they were admonished to love one another. In the case of Jesus this love was no small part of the reason for Christianity's triumph. It was not that benevolence was absent from the Hellenistic philosophies and cults; but the religion of which Paul was an apostle gave it an impulse which, so far as we can see, was not found in the same intensity elsewhere.

In the opinion of many scholars, one of the chief reasons for the change in the status of Jesus from Jewish Messiah to universal Redeemer lay in the simple fact of the use of the term "Lord."* In Hebrew this word (*Adonai*) could only have meant Jehovah, the one and only God, and Jesus could not have been hailed as Lord. In Aramaic (*Maran*) there already begins to be a change. The Syrian redeemers were *lords*. In Greek (*kurios*), however, the term would definitely identify Jesus as a redeemer-god just like the other lords of the mystery religions. It is not that the word *kurios* was reserved for this use alone. One could say "kurios" as in English one says "sir." But when one used the word of Caesar or of a redeemer-god its meaning became exalted.

The word was in fact one which would inescapably be used of Jesus in this higher sense as soon as he was preached to the Gentiles, since without it he would be diminished to a lower dignity than Attis, Tammuz or Osiris. Yet, as soon as the word was applied to him he took on some of the features of these redeemer-gods and it could not have been otherwise.

Even the idea of the redeemer as the Son of God was already present before Paul began his mission, as for example, in Gnosticism, in the Hermetic movement and for that matter in Hellenic religion several centuries before.[54] And of course the concept of the Mother of God, which presently would be applied to Mary, the mother of Jesus,

* See also pp. 108-9.

was already highly developed in Isis, Cybele, and innumerable other *mater dolorosas*.

To Paul, as we have already suggested, all these redeemer-concepts, salvation dramas, sacraments and rituals, while unacceptable in themselves to one of Judaic faith nevertheless *prefigured* the one true Christ. What the salvation cults set forth as myth and drama Jesus, as Paul saw it, had *lived into history*. Attis was an effigy nailed to a tree, Jesus was the Son of God nailed to a cross. What Judaism had prophesied plainly and paganism had previsaged darkly, God had actually brought to pass and Jesus was Lord and Savior!

We need not suppose that this perception came only vaguely to Paul or that he was not fully aware of its import. This is to do the boldness of his mind injustice. He had worked it out with great thoroughness. It was to him a complete *gnosis* of human destiny. Surely it was what he saw in his vision! Just as the mystery cult initiate saw his redeemer at the climactic moment of the sacred ritual, so Paul saw Jesus! What the nature of the vision was, objectively considered, we need not ask. It is enough that to Paul it was the very essence of reality. Jesus had shown him who he was and had made him his apostle.

And thus began the great synthesis.

CHAPTER III

HOW MUCH CAME FROM JUDAISM?

1. "Are They Israelites? So Am I!"

Even by writers who should know better, the claim has sometimes been made that Paul was not Jewish. It is a claim supported more by wishes than by evidence, the wish on the part of Gentile writers being to divest him of Jewish religion, of which they would like to make Christianity more independent, and on the part of Jewish writers to expel him from their nation, which they think he betrayed. Paul himself (even if we leave out the testimony of Acts) insisted that he was a Jew and the last thing in the world he ever thought of doing was to betray either Judaic religion or the Jewish people.

"I advanced," he tells us, "in the Jewish religion beyond many of mine own age among my race, being more exceedingly zealous for the traditions of my fathers" (Gal. i, 14). "Are they Hebrews?" he asks (having in mind the Judaizers who had harassed his work). "So am I! Are they Israelites? So am I. Are they the seed of Abraham? So am I" (II Cor. xi, 22). In another place he tells us he was "circumcised the eighth day, of the stock of Israel, of the tribe of Benjamin, a Hebrew of Hebrews, as touching the Law, a Pharisee" (Phil. iii, 5).

None of this need we doubt. Paul's knowledge of the Old Testament was extensive and indicates close study. While he mostly uses the Greek version (the Septuagint) he several times translates from the Hebrew.* Sometimes he seems to use a version not known to us but similar perhaps to some of the documents and fragments found in 1947 in the Dead Sea caves. At other times he appears to rely upon his memory and his quotations are quite inexact.[55] Certainly, Paul had been schooled by the doctors of Law, the synagogue scribes of Tarsus.

His manner of expounding Scripture is rabbinical, so much so that many scholars think he must have been trained to be a rabbi. This, however, does not necessarily follow; he could have heard this kind of exegesis for long enough to become familiar with it. As to the use to which he puts the rabbinical method—for instance in Galatians where he transforms the Jews who have not accepted Jesus into children of Ishmael, Abraham's son by a slave woman, while the Gentile believers become the true children of Isaac and hence of Israel—there can have been few rabbis indeed who would have ventured upon so outrageous an exposition! (Gal. iv).

Yet even in this Paul remained Jewish. It was through the Jews that God had given both the Law that condemned and the Christ who saved. Between God and Israel there had always been a special relationship. If the Jews had rejected the Messiah it was God's way of bringing salvation to the Gentiles; moreover, in Paul's expectation the Jews would at last accept Jesus (though, inconsistently, as we shall see later, he could sometimes condemn "his nation").

While Paul saw no reason why Gentiles should submit to circumcision and the regulations of Mosaic Law it seems likely (even if again we leave out the testimony of Acts) that he believed that Jews could not be exempted from these obligations. This may be the explanation of the perplexing passages in Galatians where, after defending himself vigorously for his abrogation of the Law, he turns

* E.g., Rom. ix, 17; xi, 4; xii, 19; I Cor. iii, 19.

about and defends himself for his insistence upon obeying it (Gal. v, 11-12). But we cannot be sure; this is the angry passage in which he makes the taunting suggestion already noted: that those who are demanding that his Gentile converts be circumcised might well do a more thorough job and castrate themselves like the priests of Attis.*

We have noticed earlier that in formulating his theology Paul uses Gnostic concepts. We must now add that in doing so he adapts them to Judaic doctrine. The prototypal man is the First Adam, who already in the apocryphal books of the Old Testament is blamed for the Fall of Man. In IV Ezra, for instance, we read, "O thou Adam, what hast thou done! For though it was thou that sinned, the fall was not thine alone but ours also who are thy descendants!" (vii, 119). In innumerable other ways which it is beyond the range of our study to take up, Paul concerns himself with Old Testament and rabbinical ideas. It is as a Jew that he thinks, using Jewish resources in a Jewish way—and yet, as we have earlier emphasized, he thought in Greek.

Millions of controversial words have been printed on the extent to which Paul's theology was derived from Judaism. Attempts have been made to derive virtually the whole of it from this source,[56] but it is equally possible to make out a case that the greater part of it was Hellenistic. Here we must recall to mind that much of the Judaic thought of Paul's time is unknown to us. It was the rabbinical tradition that survived and thus became the normative Judaism of later thinking but how can we tell what other traditions there might have been? We have learned from the recent discovery of the Dead Sea Scrolls that there was a vigorous

---

* ἀποκόπτω (apokoptō) = to amputate. (The same verb is used in Mark ix, 43: "And if thy hand cause thee to stumble, cut it off.") Paul seems to have had in mind that circumcision originated as a "token" sacrifice, the severed foreskin taking the place of the *testes* which previously were surrendered to the deity in the fertility cults. A complete discussion will be found in ERE, Vol. 3, pp. 659 ff.

Essenic Judaism with marked differences from the Pharisaic and rabbinical and there were undoubtedly other sects, not necessarily so monastic. Within Pharisaism itself there may have been variations wider than those revealed to us in the Talmud—and even these are by no means narrow.*

It is thus quite possible that there were correspondences between schools of Judaic thinking and their Hellenistic counterparts which were more extensive than we have been supposing. In this event, Paul may not have been as lonely in his general viewpoint as is usually imagined. After all, Philo in a different way had Hellenized his Judaism. There must have been others. Very little of the literature of this period is available to us and there is much that we can never know.

We shall have but little understanding of the matter, however, if, like some of the more traditional scholars, we make Paul think with *our* mentalities instead of projecting *our* minds into *his*. Paul did not have to identify *this* idea as Judaic, *that* as Hellenistic, as we do. Thinking of himself always as a Jew, whatever he absorbed into his thought became for him Judaic. This process might be illustrated perhaps by noticing the extent to which modern psychology has been absorbed into contemporary religion. A sermon even by a fairly conventional preacher may owe a good deal to Freud which is nonetheless attributed to the Bible. The preacher is not aware of the extent to which he has absorbed Freudian insights and carried them into his exposition of traditional Scripture. He preaches, not as a

---

* There are really two Talmuds, the Palestinian and the Babylonian, the second being much the larger. The Palestinian Talmud dates from about the middle of the fifth century A.D., the Babylonian—which is the one indicated when we say *the* Talmud—about half a century later. The Talmud is composed of immensely variegated material which for a long time was known only as oral tradition. The core of the book is the *Mishna* ("repetition") which attempts to explain the Mosaic Law; the Mishna in turn is explained by the *Gemara* ("completion"). There is also material from the *Tosephta* ("supplement").

Freudian but as a Christian. Nevertheless, he *is* a Freudian to the extent that his insights stem from Freud. In the same way, many of the Hellenistic concepts absorbed by Paul became Judaic so far as he was concerned although he had derived them from Hellenistic sources. Yet, as in the case of the contemporary preacher and Freud, Paul is so deeply indebted to Hellenism that it is fair to call him Gnostic or mystery cultist or even to say that his thinking had been paganized.

Sometimes of course the process would be conscious and deliberate, as it is today when Protestant theologians relate the depth psychology to their theological doctrines. In a similar way Paul saw relationships between Jewish and Hellenistic ideas which he thereupon developed in original ways though all the time supposing that he was merely enriching his Judaism from his Gentile environment. The modern theologians follow the same pattern: to them the depth psychology enriches the traditional theology. They do not regard themselves as depth psychologists but as theologians, and Paul, on a like basis, does not think of himself as a Greek but as a Jew.

Provided we do not carry it too far, or allow ourselves to forget that Paul's conceptual world and ours are radically different, this comparison can give us a better understanding of how Paul transformed his Jewish faith into a Jewish-Gentile religion while insisting that he remained a devout and faithful Jew. That there were other Jewish thinkers who went some part of the way in Paul's direction we may well suppose. There were, for instance, as Klausner has shown, a minority of rabbis who believed, as Paul did, that when the Messiah came he would change the Mosaic Law and perhaps abolish the ceremonial regulations.[57] But this would only be when the Messiah came in his *parousia* to establish his reign, not while his believers were awaiting him. It is the same with all the other cases in which Paul is found to share a new departure with rabbis of his period.

The similarities are entirely real; but so is Paul's greater and distinctive outreach. The Judaic thought, Messianic and otherwise, that entered into Paul's theology, was of large proportions, but within the workings of his mind it was changed and transmuted, sometimes subtly, sometimes violently, into what his enemies were quite right in recognizing as *not* Judaic.

But to Paul, it was! This is the paradox that we must unconditionally accept. To Paul the crucifixion and resurrection of Jesus were absolutely transforming events which had affected Judaism even as they had affected the entire world—the cosmos itself—and this remained true no matter how resistant the majority of Jews might be to understanding what had happened. So that, as Paul saw himself, he was a completely faithful Jew who had recognized what other Jews had failed to recognize: that their religion had culminated in the Messianic era which even then in its beginnings was already present. The Law had fulfilled its purpose, the world had been brought under judgment; the Messiah-Redeemer had conquered the powers of evil through his death and resurrection, he would soon reappear to rule the earth in righteousness. This was the Judaism of *the present and the future* to which the faithful Jew must give unqualified devotion.

As Schweitzer states it, for Paul "there was only one religion: that of Judaism. It was concerned with God, faith, promise, hope and law. In consequence of the coming, the death, and the resurrection of Jesus Christ, it became its duty to adjust its teachings and demands to the new era thus introduced, and in the process many things were moved from the shadow into the light and others from the light into the shadow. 'Christianity' is for Paul no new religion, but simply Judaism with the center of gravity shifted in consequence of the new era."[58] Yet, as it turned out, Christianity *was* a new religion, and beyond all others it was Paul who made it such.

2. Jewish Messiahs and Pagan Redeemers

Christians define the Messiah by reference to their view of Jesus. They think that what Jesus is said to have done and to have become is what was expected of the Jewish Messiah. This is far from true. The Christian portrait is a paganized one, which is natural since so much of the New Testament was written under pagan influence. The differences between the expected Jewish Messiah and the pagan redeemers are in fact so great that it is marvelous that the two were blended together so comparatively easily.

This is a matter not only of function and characteristics; it is a matter of the psychology that formed the two contrasting concepts. The Jews were never as pessimistic as the Greeks or Romans. Their God, Jehovah, had not faded away as Zeus and Jupiter had done. They thought the human situation was bad but not hopeless; and so, although they needed a kind of leadership that ordinary humanity was not able to provide, they did not feel the need of superhuman leadership. Their Messiah was not a Son of God or supernatural personage; he was merely a man of heroic stature, endowed with more than ordinary powers. At least, this was the typical expectation, though it may have been exceeded by the followers of Jesus and some of the Essenes.

This psychological difference is important. It has sometimes been expressed by saying that God said to the Jews, "Fulfill my purpose," and they answered, "We will." To the Gentiles also, God gave the same command. But the Gentiles came back and said, "We have tried, Lord, and we have failed. You will have to fulfill your purpose yourself or it will not be fulfilled." This probably overstates the matter but the point it stresses is valid: Jewish religion, although it recognized man's limitations, did not admit his incapacity. Man would sin and God would have to forgive him. But then God *would* forgive him, provided he repented sincerely and did the best he could. But to the Gentiles of this period—as to the apostle whose Judaism had been so greatly influenced by his Hellenistic thought—man was wholly under the sway of sin, and a divine deliverer was needed to redeem him.*

With this distinction in mind, let us look at the Jewish idea of the Messiah.[59] It was widely varied. In the Old Testament prophets, who speak of the coming "Day of the Lord," Jehovah himself is usually his own Messiah, or he may be represented by a hoped-for king of Israel of heroic stature. The idea of a King-Messiah was in fact very persistent. The word *Messiah* means "one anointed," and in Israel this was always true of a king. Christian scholars have made much of the term "Son of Man" in the book of Daniel, seeing in this concept something superhuman, but as Jewish scholars have repeatedly pointed out, it means only the same thing as Man, for which it is a poetic periphrasis.[60] In fact, what the writer of this remarkable book is saying is that Israel itself will be the deliverer. The other nations of the earth are signified by animals, some of them devouring beasts, but Israel is a "child of man" or a human being, and will establish a humane world order under Israelite dominion.

In the Prophets, it is frequently—one might say characteristically—a "collective Messiah" that is expected, either Israel itself or an Israelite elite. Because of its righteousness and undeviating devotion, God will endow the faithful nation or elite with special powers so that it will be able to repulse all enemies and establish the people of God in security and peace.

Yet there was also the idea of an individual Messiah. He

---

* There were Gentiles, of course, to whom this did not apply and to whom even the idea of the Jewish Messiah was quite irrelevant. But they were philosophers to whose thinking ordinary people could not attain, and thus a permanent minority.

would be preceded by a prophet who would prepare his way—often thought of as a resurrected Elijah. There would be terrible wars, possibly a withering away of the natural world. The stars might fall out of heaven, the moon turn into blood. It is in the books not included in the Bible that we get this more developed idea of the Jewish Messiah fairly clearly presented. But by the time these books were written (as is the case also with the book of Daniel), Persian and even Greek influence had been playing a part. Nonetheless, the concepts must be counted Jewish since it is still the Jewish Messiah who is being described, and by and for the Jews who were expecting him.

What we have in this later development is far more elaborate. There will be signs that will warn that the advent of the Messiah is near. There will be pain and travail throughout the earth. Elijah will come to prepare the way. A trumpet will blow, the Jews of the Diaspora will be gathered home, proselytes will be received in large numbers, there will be a great war with the forces of evil, the armies of Gog and Magog. Then the Messiah will arrive, the failing earth will be renewed, there will be a Day of Judgment, a resurrection of the dead, and at last the long-awaited new world order. Not that any of this fits a consistent pattern or is imagined always in the same way. It is poetry, allegory—at any rate in form—and yet it refers to expected realities.

What we are dealing with, however, from first to last, is a *human* Messiah even though surrounded by events that are surely preternatural. Admittedly, he has taken on some awesome characteristics; but he is still a man of flesh and blood. We must remember that as late as 135 A.D., when the Jews revolted for the second time against Roman rule under the warrior Bar Kochba, the Rabbi Akiba, the most revered and famous rabbi of his time, proclaimed Bar Kochba the Messiah, for which after Bar Kochba's defeat he was decapitated. So a very human man indeed could be the Messiah even in the opinion of an exalted rabbi of the second Christian century.

By this time (and undoubtedly earlier), there is talk of two Messiahs, one the Messiah of Joseph (signifying the former northern kingdom) who will fall in battle when his work is accomplished, the other the Messiah of David (Judean) in whose reign there will be remarkable miracles. Fruit trees will produce tenfold their ordinary yield, trees that were never supposed to bear fruit will nonetheless do so. Human height will increase to twice the height of Adam, and there will be many other such marvels. This, be it noted, is the concept of the Messiah pictured in the Talmud and is much later than the time of Jesus; and yet it throws light on Christian concepts. For evidently the Jewish development of the Messianic idea continued on its own way independently of Christianity and *with entirely different features*.

To sum up, in the words of Klausner, the foremost Jewish authority on this subject, "the Jewish Messiah is a redeemer strong in physical power and in spirit, who in the final days will bring complete redemption, economic and spiritual, to the Jewish people—and along with this eternal peace, material prosperity, and ethical perfection to the whole human race." The Jewish Messiah, he concludes, "is truly human in origin, of flesh and blood like all mortals."[61] And he quotes the Jew, Trypho, into whose mouth the church father, Justin Martyr, puts the words: "We Jews all expect that the Messiah will be a man of purely human origin."*

The Christian view of the Messiah diverged from this even from the beginning, before it can properly be called Christian. This may be because the community at Jerusalem to which the followers of Jesus belonged had a differently developed concept than those of other Jews, especially perhaps in emphasizing that the Messiah must suffer

---

* ἄνθρωπον ἐξ ἀνθρώπων (anthrōpon ex anthrōpōn) = a man from men.

and die before he could be manifested in triumph. Some scholars see strong indications that the Messiah was expected to suffer before his *parousia* (or perhaps had already suffered) in the Qumran Scrolls.[62] In any case, the disciples of Jesus, once they came to believe in his resurrection, were not deterred by his sufferings or even by his crucifixion from hailing him as the Messiah. To other Jews this was an impossible belief. The Messiah would come *once* and would be unmistakably the Messiah: his coming was in the future. To the followers of Jesus he had come already and soon would come again.

When Gentile believers were added, as they may have been quite early in Jerusalem and as they certainly were in Antioch in Syria, it was easy in their case to think of the Jewish part of Jesus' Messiahship as having already been fulfilled. His earthly ministry had discharged it. He was now no more a Jew but a universal man—and more than a man—who belonged both to Jews and Gentiles. No one needs to be a specialist in these matters to see that Gentile believers would have little use for a Messiah who was going to establish a new world order presided over by the Jews. So that even before Paul, the concept was being changed, and what more certain than that it would be changed still further?

Upon the basis of this delineation, how can it be possible (as some still argue) that the Messiah-Redeemer of Paul was a Jewish development? To Paul the crucifixion was indispensable to the redemption wrought by Jesus: on the cross the powers of evil had done their utmost to destroy him and had destroyed only his flesh (*sarx*); since according to Paul's doctrine the sins of all mankind were represented in the flesh of Jesus that was destroyed, Jesus had triumphed over the powers of evil once and for all and on behalf of the entire human race, and had risen in the body (*soma* not *sarx*), which risen body would be shared by all the redeemed who believed and were baptized. This, as we have already noted, is Gnostic in theology (modified to meet Paul's thinking) and mystery religion in its sacramental modus of salvation. In contrast with it, we can only note with Gilbert Murray that to ordinary Jews who tried to see Jesus as the Messiah, the crucifixion, instead of being the means of salvation, was an insurmountable obstacle. "One who failed, it seemed obvious, could not be the Messiah." It was not the Jews but "the common people of the Hellenistic world [who] knew that the Savior must die; to die and be re-born was [to them] the course of his normal history."[63]

Thus, while doubtless a Jewish Messianic believer to begin with, Paul absorbed into the Judaic concept so much that belonged to pagan redeemership that he changed the concept completely. Yet—we will remind ourselves once more—it was as one who still regarded himself as a loyal Jew that he wrought this transformation.

3. *Jewish and Pauline Theology*

A full comparison of Pauline with Jewish theology would require a large volume; even a brief comparison, if it dealt with all the main questions, would take up more pages than there are in this book. Since our inquiry, however, is more concerned with history than with matters of doctrine (except as the two are interwoven), it will be sufficient if in this section we take note of some salient features.

Being a Jew, Paul was a monotheist. This belief in only one God was an important element in attracting Gentile believers. If it had not been for the dietary laws and circumcision it would have attracted far more converts than it did to Judaism. Even as it was, it drew to the synagogue the numerous "God-fearers" (not proselytes but loosely affiliated worshipers) many of whom Paul so easily converted. As Jane Harrison has remarked, amid the crosscurrents and confusions of this era, "the whole tendency of theology, of philosophy and of poetry was towards mono-theism."[64] This had resulted in the fusion of many of the gods of similar function and sometimes in the attitude that regarded all deities as merely aspects of one ultimate Di-vinity. Jewish monotheism had a strong appeal for minds turning in this direction, for it was more than a tendency, no matter how strong: it was a historical achievement—one that belonged not to the philosophical minority but to all the people. Moreover, it had a sacred literature, fasci-nating ancient scriptures which were monotheistically in-terpreted.

Paul doubtless never realized that in turning the Jewish Messiah into a Redeemer who could replace Osiris, Attis, Tammuz and the rest, he was modifying his Jewish mono-theism. But he most assuredly was. It is true that there had been a Jewish school of thought which regarded wisdom as a sort of daughter-goddess, similar to the *logos* in Hel-lenistic thought.* Still, Jewish theology had stopped short of deification; but the acclaiming of Jesus as Lord would never be able to stop short of it. Paul himself was not able to stop short of it. Although believing himself to be a de-vout Jewish monotheist, he regarded Jesus as *God the Redeemer*, and—strangely as it seems to the modern mind —without perceiving that it was affecting his monotheism. Yet it could not fail to do so. As Bultmann states it, "The Kyrios (Lord) Jesus Christos is conceived as a mystery deity, in whose death and resurrection the faithful partici-pate through the sacraments."[65] This could not possibly be harmonized with Jewish monotheism.

From Judaism Paul took his view that the world was God's world, created and ruled by him, yet somehow a world in the power of Satan. This logical inconsistency was never resolved by Paul (nor by anyone else) and did not

* See the Old Testament apocryphal books of Wisdom (of "Solomon") and Ecclesiasticus (The Wisdom of Jesus, the son of Sirach); cf., the first chapter of John's gospel, where the *logos* is called "the Word."

seem to bother him. He went further than Judaism ever did, however, in adopting the Gnostic view of the role of Satan as "the god of this world" (II Cor. iv, 4) and in accepting some (but by no means all) of the Gnostic elaborations of the Satanic conspiracy.

In making *will* rather than *reason* primary, Paul was a Jew, not a Greek. In Hellenistic thought, faithful in this to the great days of Athens, man would always will to do right provided he clearly understood what it was that *is* right. Otherwise, he would be willing harm against himself, for what is not right is bound to be harmful—and what man would knowingly do himself damage? Therefore, if reason could make plain what is right and what is wrong the will to do right would necessarily follow. In the Judaic view this was not so. Man could know the Law (which was by revelation rather than from reason but nevertheless reasonable) and not do it. Wrong-doing was sin, and sin was disobedience to God. In this context a man *is* his will and must be judged accordingly. Paul assumed this without question and to that extent his doctrine of sin was Judaic.

But not his doctrine of what must be done about sin. In Jewish theology a man repented of his sins and offered sacrifice; God forgave him if his repentance was genuine, and as for his being unable to avoid further sins, he could balance these up with good works and in the end come out fairly well. Paul's view was quite different. Sin gained possession of a man and ruled him through his flesh (*sarx*), which was under the control of "the god of this world," who was Sin *personalized*. Only through the intervention of Jesus as Redeemer could there be salvation from (and forgiveness for) sin. Man must surrender himself completely to the *grace* (*charis*) of God manifested in Jesus and, after losing his *flesh* (*sarx*) sacramentally, be united with the risen body (*soma*) of Jesus. He was then not his former self (which in Judaic thought he always continued to be) but "in Christ, a new creation." This was a drastic departure from Jewish theology.

Paul's Messianic thinking began with his acceptance of Judaic eschatology. It was the period of "last things" and the Messiah was at hand. From this beginning he went on, as we have seen, to transform the concept of the Jewish Messiah into that of a mystery cult Redeemer. Yet he retained a great deal of the original concept too. How he was able to do this is thoroughly perplexing and has led to endless debate. Some scholars deny that it was possible and therefore assign those parts of his letters that deal with Jesus as Redeemer to a later writer and thus entirely recast the scope and character of his work. But this will not do. There is a unity of the two concepts—Jesus as Messiah and as Redeemer—within the letters themselves that indicates quite plainly that what may be a psychological impossibility for us was not at all impossible for Paul. In a way that we can glimpse but not clearly see, Paul believed that Jesus was the Redeemer through whom the "saved" would be given a happy life in the hereafter and at the same time the Messiah who would establish a new world order in the here-and-now.

No matter how many thousands of words are added to those already printed on this remarkable conflation of concepts, there will still be questions and we may well remind ourselves of the second-century writer of the letter called II Peter who, as we noted earlier, complains that there are "some things hard to be understood" in the writings of "brother Paul" (II Pet. iii, 16).

Proceeding then with what is more comprehensible, in Jewish theology as in Pauline, there is a *people of God*. In the one case, however, it is the Jewish people of the Covenant; in the other, all who are "in Christ." From Judaism, too, for the most part, Paul takes his idea of *the spirit* (but translates it into Greek—*pneuma*). The Hebrew prophets were inspired by the spirit, the earlier ones to frenzy, the later to prophecy (preaching). The first believers are said to have had an ecstatic visitation of the spirit at Pentecost a few weeks after the resurrection of Jesus (Acts ii, 1-4). The result is a *glossolalia,* an excited and incomprehensible mouthing of sounds, *not* a speaking of foreign languages. Paul is somewhat concerned about these frenzies, and although he says he surpasses others in his gift for becoming "possessed" in this way, he thinks it unserviceable unless someone "interprets": on the whole, it is better to preach straightforwardly (I Cor. xiv).

Spirit-possession, like demon possession, was regarded as being literally possessed—inhabited—by a particular spirit, and the words spoken (or the ecstatic sounds vocalized) were those of the particular spirit. This is not a phenomenon peculiar to Hebraic religion, of course, but was familiar in the Hellenistic cults (for example, Dionysiac). However, there was also a more exalted level in which God was thought of as spirit (*pneuma*) and it was by *the spirit of Jesus* that Paul felt himself guided in his mission. The Greek word *pneuma* which we translate *spirit* is, in its literal meaning, breath, and we might roughly describe the idea of *holy spirit* as being the breath that God is constantly breathing into his creation, or the communicable aliveness of God. This was Judaic but also, in Paul's thinking, Gnostic, and in relation to flesh (*sarx*), body (*soma*), mind or rationality (*nous*), organized-life-of-the-body-mind (psūche), took on a uniquely Pauline meaning.

Further aspects of Paul's theology will be seen as we proceed with our study. This section, however, must be concluded with an emphatic word of warning. We can gain *some insight* into Paul's theology but we *cannot understand it in the significance it had for him.* His intellectual world is not ours. Paul would not have understood our modern theologians any more than they have understood him. Systematic theologies built upon Paul's letters are not and cannot be Pauline. *Paul was not systematic, he was not consistent, he did not write for theologians.* His letters are addressed to practical situations, to doctrinal questions that have arisen, to disturbances, to controversies and conflicts. We do not have all of Paul's letters. It is quite ridiculous to build up a rigid system out of what we find in the fortuitously salvaged Pauline *corpus*.

Again, we have mentioned with a fair amount of confidence such concepts of Paul's as *the body of Christ*, to which, as we have shown, he gives a special meaning. But we must not suppose that even here he is consistent. He can speak of the *spirit* when we would expect him to go on speaking of the *body*. He can do similar things with other terms. We repeat therefore: we can gain insight into Paul's thinking but never fully understand it or possess it.

4. *Paul and Jewish Morality*

Morally, Paul was an ascetic Jew. His conversion changed the sanctions of his morality but not the morality itself. If the Mosaic Law was superseded by Jesus the Messiah, its ethical provisions were nonetheless to be carried out on the new basis just as they had been on the old. If the Mosaic Law had brought only judgment and condemnation to the world, from which Jesus the Savior had redeemed it, nevertheless the *grace* of Jesus should maintain ethical standards that were at least equal to the Mosaic ones.

When Paul found that some of his converts, believing that their sacramental union with Jesus had set them above the Law (whether Mosaic, Noachian* or natural) and that they could therefore behave licentiously without sin or penalty, he was horrified. Although he still insisted upon his theological position ("All things are lawful for me"— I Cor. vi, 12), he added that what was theologically not prohibited was still morally repugnant (I Cor. v) and prudentially unwise ("Not all things are expedient"—I Cor. vi,

---

* It was a Jewish belief that part of the Law was binding upon all men since all were descended from Noah. This part of the Law (which is variously given as seven or thirty or some other number of laws) is called Noachian.[66]

12). Moreover, immorality is sacrilege against the body of Jesus of which the believers had become a part.

What Paul wants is good behavior not because the Law demands it but because the spirit of Jesus impels it. But it was not an easy principle to maintain. If the Jews had become hair-splitters in interpreting their Law, Christians were likely to have so fluid an ethic that there would be no definite standards at all. What was there to go by if you had no moral code? The Jews were never slow to point out immorality among Christians and attributed it, quite naturally, to abandoning the Law. What Paul wanted—free and spontaneous goodness through the prompting of the spirit of Jesus—was a lot to ask of ordinary people.

It is sometimes said that the mystery religions encouraged the idea of sacramental salvation with no moral obligations attached. Some of them did. Persons influenced by these cults would be difficult for Paul to convince. But in others of the mystery religions ethical standards were very high. Judaic morality was not the only high morality; it was at least equaled in some of the mystery religions and was perhaps surpassed by the morality of the Stoics. Nor is it true to suppose that among pagans there was no kindness. Pliny's famous letter to a slave's master, appealing to him to forgive and receive back an offending slave, was not the only one of its kind,* and Paul had abundant resources in pagan ethics with which to reinforce his Jewish morality.

As to the latter, it must not be imagined (though all too often it is) that it was negative and oppressive and had no place for the love and compassion of Christianity. The late Jewish writings in particular, especially the *Didachē* (as translated in the *Doctrina*) and the *Testaments of the Twelve Patriarchs* have the same ethical attitude that we find in the New Testament. "You shall hate nobody; some

---

* "Concede something to his youth, to his tears, to your own natural mildness of temper; do not make him uneasy any longer, and, I will add, do not make yourself so, for a man of your kindness of heart cannot be angry without feeling great uneasiness."[67]

you shall love more than your own soul" (Doctrina ii, 7); "Be meek, for the meek will possess the holy land. Be long-suffering and upright in your business" (iii, 7-8); "Associate with upright and humble men" (iii, 10)—these are examples. Of the *Testaments* Canon Charles remarked more than forty years ago that "the Sermon on the Mount reflects in several instances the spirit and even reproduces the very phrases" of this Jewish writing. He adds that "St. Paul seems to have used this book as a *vade mecum*."[68]

The Rabbi Hillel, when asked for a summary of the Law that could be recited while a man stood on one foot, replied as follows: "What is hateful to thyself do not to thy neighbor; this is the whole Law, the rest is commentary." The Rabbi Akiba's summary was, "Thou shalt love thy neighbor as thyself; this is the greatest principle of the Law." Ben Azzai felt that there was a more fundamental principle still: man's likeness to God. "When God created Adam he made him in the likeness of God; this is a greater principle than [Akiba's]"—by which he meant what Jesus meant when he said, "Ye therefore shall be perfect as your heavenly Father is perfect" (Mt. v, 48).[69]

Paul's asceticism is represented in his views on marriage. It is definitely better not to be married, he says, and "not to touch a woman" (I Cor. vii, 1 ff); however, it is "better to marry than burn." In case marriage is chosen, the spouses must meet each other's sexual needs without denying one another except perhaps during a season of prayer. Here indeed is a strange agglomerate of ascetic renunciation and concessions to connubial expediency! Paul is as a matter of fact quite practical in his permissiveness but where did he get his principle of abstinence? It is not Pharisaic or normatively Jewish and there is no evidence that Paul was an Essene.*

* There is no evidence but there could be plausible conjectures. He is called a Nazarene (Nazorean) in Acts, which, if correct, indicates the improbability of his being a Pharisee and the probability of his belonging to an Essene-type community. Josephus describes himself as having once been an Essene although for most of his life he was a Pharisee.

In a curious passage which has been variously interpreted, he says that he has just as much right as Cephas (Peter) to "lead about a 'sister-wife,' "* from which, however, he refrains (I Cor. ix, 5). This has traditionally been explained as meaning that he was entitled to be married to a believer, a "sister" in the "church." But this makes him say something that is obvious and needless. The "sister-wife" was more probably a woman companion (legally married) with whom there was no sexual relationship. This is somewhat confirmed by what we know of Essenic practices (and tendencies) but gives an odd twist to the traditional view of communal life among the early Jerusalem believers.

In any case, Paul seems to have thought of women as "souls" to be saved, never as desirable companions in the intimate mutuality of family life. As wives, he thinks of them only sexually. If there is *libido* to be satisfied it is better for a man to have a wife and a woman a husband. Otherwise, there will be fornication. The notion that marriage has its daylight hours seems not to have occurred to Paul. This is a truly low view not only of marriage but of family life as a whole. Where do the children fit into this picture? Nor does the fact that Paul is expecting the *parousia* of Jesus and the inauguration of a new order explain or excuse this view. Truly, his own family life must have been pitifully unhappy (adopting here the diagnostic approach of modern psychologists). Fortunately, even fundamentalists who say that they follow the Scriptures literally (every word being inspired by God) do not seem to take this advice of Paul's too seriously. Perhaps he is not sure of it himself. He says he is speaking according to his own judgment but that he *thinks* it is also according to "the Spirit of God"! (I Cor. vii, 40) There is charm in his self-doubt even if there is none in his marriage counsel!

* ἀδελφὴν γυναῖκα (*adelphēn gunaika*) *sister wife,* not "wife that is a believer" as in RV. Here the RV interprets where it should translate.

As a whole, however, Paul's emphasis on high ethical standards and upon brotherly love, which he derived chiefly from Judaism and reinforced from Stoicism and other pagan sources, is the most ennobling element in his entire gospel. As Enslin well puts it, he required that "the Christian's life must conform to his new and exalted status of being 'in Christ.' "[70] Many of his converts preferred to believe that baptism and the sacraments in and of themselves ensured salvation and that matters of moral conduct had nothing to do with religion. This is what they had been conditioned to suppose, except where they had belonged to a sect or mystery cult in which there was encouragement for high ethical standards. But Paul insisted that as in the Judaism of his fathers, so in the new Judaism of the Messiah and Redeemer, religion and morality belonged inseparably together.

Nor must we forget—as it is all too easy to do when we are looking at the Pauline movement from the historical standpoint, trying to reconstruct it in its many-sided, complicated context—that at the heart of his religion was love. There is, he says, as though a little impatient for the moment with his own theology, a "more excellent way." It is the way of love. Without love eloquence is noise and clamor, knowledge is vanity, even faith that can "move mountains" is unavailing; it is the same with philanthropy, even with martyrdom itself! It is love alone that "never faileth" (I Cor. xiii).

There is a great deal in Paul which, as we have several times explained, we shall never understand. Even in this beautiful poem on love the scholar finds questions to be pondered. Nevertheless, in the thirteenth chapter of First Corinthians Paul is speaking a timeless and universal language.

PART THREE

THE SEARCH FOR HISTORY

CHAPTER I

THE NEW COVENANTERS
OF JERUSALEM

1. *What Was the "Church" of Jerusalem?*

The attentive reader who goes to the book of Acts without preconceptions is at once struck by the remarkable rapidity with which the Galilean movement centered in Jesus becomes a strongly established Jerusalem community. If he turns back from Acts to the gospels, hoping to find some clue to this astonishing transformation, he soon notes the perplexing inconsistency of the appearances of the Risen Jesus to his disciples in Galilee—whither they fled in panic at the time of his arrest at Gethsemane—with the immediacy and continuity of his appearances in and about Jerusalem—where the disciples seem to have remained, confidently expecting that he would soon join them. Panic and Galilee or confidence and Jerusalem—which was it? It cannot have been both.

The answer to this latter question, as we saw in a previous chapter,* is that the Galilean appearances belong to the older tradition, the Jerusalem stories to the creators of the later *catechesis*. But this only increases the difficulty of the first question: how did the Galilean believers become a Jerusalem community, well organized under James the "brother of Jesus," in such a short time? Even more extraordinary, how did the belief in Jesus so swiftly reach the Grecian Jews and their aggressive leader, Stephen?

* See p. 71 ff.

Moreover, it was Peter who was supposed to have been at the head of the movement; upon him, according to the gospel narrative, Jesus would build his "church." But as it turns out, it is James the "brother of Jesus" who is in charge of affairs at Jerusalem, and Peter takes second place.

The traditional answer, as we know, glosses over these disquieting questions and calmly refers to the original "Christians" who formed the Jerusalem "church." This, as the reader has been constantly reminded, is misinformation and a misuse of terms. The first believers were not Christians in any sense in which we use the word *Christian* and the Jerusalem society was a Jewish Messianic community and not a Christian church. We must now ask how and when this community came into being, and of whom and upon what basis it was composed. For clearly, the traditional answer will not do. It is not even in the true sense an answer: it is a mere unwillingness to face the questions.

That the disciples fled to Galilee at the time of Jesus' arrest is not to be doubted. Mark, the oldest gospel, says that it was there his disciples would see him (Mk. xvi, 7). Luke of course alters this to fit his own *catechesis* but the tradition still holds in the second century that (to quote Justin Martyr) the disciples "repented of their flight from [Jesus] when he was crucified, after he rose from the dead" (Dial. 106). It was in Galilee then, their homeland to which they had fled, that the dismay of the disciples was transformed—that is, in the case of some of them—into a belief that Jesus was still alive and would soon return. As Enslin puts it, "before the band of erstwhile followers returned to the nation's capital they had achieved a confidence that their leader had not been defeated by death which did not need to be bolstered up by the discovery of an empty tomb."[1]

But when the Galileans arrived in Jerusalem, how within so short a time as three or four years did they develop the quite impressive organization of which we catch glimpses in Acts? It may be answered, "Through the preaching of Peter and the apostles." But this is quite incredible. Peter's conversion of "five thousand souls" (Acts iv, 4) through such bold ventures as preaching in a porch of the Temple is contradicted by the way in which the first believers are left quietly untouched during the persecution following the stoning of Stephen. Neither the Jewish nor the Roman authorities would have allowed the large assemblies described in Acts. As Weiss expresses it, "the author [of Acts] seeks to show how the supreme council of Judaism (the Sanhedrin) made every effort to crush out the gospel concerning Jesus; but he cannot conceal the fact that the community continued its propaganda almost unhindered."[2] And he goes on to point out that for some time the entire company of believers was able to gather in one house (Acts iv, 23).

The solution of the problem can only be that there was at first a small group of *believers in the Risen Jesus* which was part of a much larger group of *believers in the coming of a Messiah without reference to Jesus*. The bond of the community was its *expectation* of a Messiah, which the followers of Jesus fully shared; but in *their* case and at first *only in theirs* it was believed that the coming Messiah would be the Risen Jesus.

This solution, fortunately, has been considerably reinforced by the discovery, in 1947, of the famous Dead Sea Scrolls.[3] Among these documents, which it is now almost universally agreed were produced within the two centuries before the time of Jesus, is one that describes the regulated life of the Qumran community in their monastery near the shores of the Dead Sea where the manuscripts were found ("Manual of Discipline"). This description, which greatly supplements and illumines what we already knew of the Jewish sect (or sects) of the Essenes, takes us right into the book of Acts.[4]

Professor Frank M. Cross, one of the scholars who has done important work on the Scrolls, tells us that "it is difficult to exaggerate the importance" of these documents "for the study of Christian origins" and refers to "intimate parallels" that are to be found "between the Essene and primitive Christian communities . . . in their theological language, in their theology of history, in their liturgical institutions and in their ecclesiastical organization."[5] Numerous other scholars confirm this testimony and the facts are now beyond dispute.*

Both the Essenic sects and the Jerusalem community call the congregation considered as a whole *the Many;* both have an executive committee called *the Twelve;* both have a superintendent or *episkopos* (translated by our word "bishop"). In both cases the communities have "all things in common," which means that the wealth of the members and their current wages must be contributed to a central treasury in charge of a steward who will make the necessary disbursements on behalf of the community. There are similar rules for the regulation of behavior and the trial of offenses, similar theological concepts, and a similar belief in the coming of a Messiah.

Both the Essenic sectarians and the Jerusalem community call themselves people of the *New Covenant* (which is exactly the same as *New Testament*); both practice baptism and have a sacred meal; both speak of themselves in such terms as the *Elect* or the *Poor* and speak of the truth of God as *Light* and themselves as *Sons of Light:* these are

---

* Dupont-Sommer's *The Jewish Sect of Qumran and the Essenes* (New York, 1956), John Allegro's *The Dead Sea Scrolls* (London, Penguin paperback, 1956), Duncan Howlett's *The Essenes and Christianity* (New York, 1957) are a few out of many available studies. Gaster's translation, *The Dead Sea Scriptures* (New York, 1956) is valuable but perhaps too free; it interprets where it should translate; Millar Burrows' translation, *The Dead Sea Scrolls* (New York, 1955) is much more literal. The present writer's *The Meaning of the Dead Sea Scrolls* (Signet-Key paperback, New York, 1956) discusses most of the questions raised by the Scrolls.

a few among the large number of identical practices and concepts.

Must we not see then that the Jerusalem community *as a whole* was an Essenic body which had existed considerably *before* the crucifixion of Jesus, perhaps for several generations before, and that it was in fact an urban and less monastic counterpart of the Qumran society fifteen miles away on the shores of the Dead Sea? We must remember that the Essenes probably never called themselves by that name (it may have meant "holy ones"*) but rather the *Elect, they that believe, they that are in Messiah* (Christ), the *Sons of Light*, the *Poor, they that are of the Way*, the *Brethren*, the *Saints*, etc., which are precisely the terms used of themselves by those who are called the "primitive Christians."

The word Nazorean (which usage changed into Nazarene) is also the name of an Essenic sect. There may not even have existed a city called Nazareth in the time of Jesus. It is not mentioned in the Old Testament, the Talmud or even by Josephus who minutely describes the war (67-70 A.D.) with the Romans in Galilee, he himself being the commander of the Jewish forces. If the word Nazareth at that time existed it most probably meant Galilee.[6] Or it could have been an encampment of Essenes broadly similar to that at Qumran (where it is believed that tents were used in connection with the caves). According to Loisy, *Nazorean* is derived from *notzer*** the orthography of which word he sees as pointing to "observer of a rite," the

---

* From the Greek ὁσιόω (hosio-ō) *to make holy*, but with a sense also of following natural law.

** נָצַר (notzār) is a word with many shades of meaning such as *to keep or observe a covenant*. נֵצֶר (netzer) (the same letters in ancient Hebrew: the vowel points seen beneath the line were not used until long after New Testament times) means a shoot or branch and meant the Messiah as a "branch of Jesse" (who was the father of David from whom the Messiah—or *a* Messiah if more than one was expected—must be descended).

rite in question being baptism as in the case of John.[7]
Bacon and many other modern scholars, without being as
confident as Loisy as to the exact meaning, follow Abbott
and Burkitt in believing that grammatical and textual difficulties (too technical to be discussed here) as well as historical considerations point away from *Nazorean* having
anything to do with a city called Nazareth and require
that we recognize that there was a Nazorean sect to which
the original disciples of Jesus (or some of them) and perhaps Jesus himself belonged.[8] It is almost certainly to such
a sect that Acts refers (xxiv, 5) when it speaks of the
Nazoreans,* *not* the Nazarenes.

What we are dealing with in the Jerusalem community
is thus not a primitive Christian church at all but a Jewish
sect of Essenes or Nazoreans (the terms may have been
interchangeable at this time), which, as Bultmann correctly judges, "did not split off from Judaism as though it
were conscious of itself as a new religious society. In the
eyes of their contemporaries they must have looked like a
Jewish sect, and for the historian they appear in that light
too."[9] Peter and his associates, the leading Galilean followers of Jesus, must either have belonged to this sect or
been closely related to it for some time before Jesus
preached in Galilee, and there are signs, as suggested
above, that Jesus also belonged to it.

Reconstructing the most probable course of events after
Peter had his vision of Jesus as Risen Lord soon after
the flight to Galilee, Peter must have persuaded some of
his friends that Jesus was still alive, a persuasion made
easier no doubt because they themselves saw Jesus in
dreams or under circumstances not known to us, where-
upon the little group returned to Jerusalem and joined (or
rejoined?) the Essenic or Nazorean community whose

---

* The Greek is τῶν Ναζωραίων αἱρέσεως (*tōn Nazōraiōn haireseōs*), literally: *of the Nazorean faction;* in this context, a sect in the sense of Jews
that have broken away discordantly from normative Judaism.

superintendent was James. In addition, they had their own house, probably the home of John Mark's mother, where the little company of first believers held their meetings and perhaps resided.

Gradually at first, then more rapidly, members of the larger group superintended by James accepted Peter's testimony and became believers in the Risen Jesus. After a while (though of this we cannot be entirely certain), James himself accepted the belief, bringing with him a large number of Essenic adherents. The survival of Jesus beyond death, which to the skeptical mind of our own times is difficult of belief, would not be doubted in the same way in the New Testament period. It would seem just as possible in the case of Jesus as in that of John the Baptist. Indeed, all the Messianists hoped for immortality in the reign of the Anointed One, and may have hoped for life beyond death quite apart from the Messianic expectation.[*][10]

The really great obstacle to belief in Jesus as the Messiah was his crucifixion. How could one who had failed— whose claims indeed had ended in the most shameful of deaths—nonetheless be the Messiah? Jesus could be received as such only where it was deeply believed that the Messiah must suffer before his *parousia*, which, however, seems to have been the expectation of the Qumran sectarians from whom we have the Dead Sea Scrolls.[12] It may therefore not have been too difficult to persuade the Jerusalem Essenic community—whose theology may have been further developed in this respect than the Qumran sect's— that Jesus had undergone this suffering in achieving his Messiahship.

At any rate, this general view of how the movement that

---

[*] According to Josephus, the Essenes believed, somewhat inconsistently with their eschatological expectation, "that there lies away across the ocean a habitation for the good souls . . . [and for the bad] a dark and tempestuous den full of never-ceasing punishments."[11]

is called "primitive Christianity" actually began explains much better than the traditional view not only the matter of how a highly organized and strongly established community could be in existence within a few years of the crucifixion but also how there could be a *Twelve* which were not the "twelve disciples" of Jesus in his lifetime and how "the chief apostles" could include James, Barnabas and others who were not appointed by Jesus. The community already existed and the Galileans were added to it. Its organization, including lesser apostleships or missionary messengers, had been complete for some time. Indeed, here too may be the explanation of the community that was thriving in Antioch so soon after the crucifixion—and apparently at Damascus and doubtless in a number of other places. They were originally offshoots of the Jerusalem Essenes or Nazoreans. The unifying basis of the movement was the anticipated *parousia* of the Messiah *who only later came to be identified with Jesus:* this and the theological and ethical elements held in common which were the eventual contribution of Essenic Judaism to Christianity.*

There are scholars, of course, who would go further than this in identifying the Essenes with the early believers in the Risen Jesus. Oscar Cullman, who is said by Bultmann to be "on perfectly good ground," holds that even the Dead Sea Essenes themselves "passed into Jewish Christianity,"[13] but the present writer doubts this since the Qumran excavations and the work on the Scrolls and fragments down to now yield no such indication. But that the Jerusalem

* The reader should perhaps be reminded at this point in our study that the canonical explanation of Christian beginnings to which he is accustomed is merely a tradition so frequently and impressively repeated that it is regarded as a standard view from which it is rather audacious to depart. Whatever it may be from the standpoint of dogma, historically this "standard view" has no better claim than any other: indeed, since it fails to explain the New Testament situation satisfactorily it is inferior to any view that sees a clearer solution to the problems. This must always be the approach of the seeker for truth as it is of the honest scholar.

community did so and those of Antioch, Damascus and possibly other cities within the Aramaic-speaking area seems virtually certain, and thus came the churches of the Nazarenes (Nazoreans) and Ebionites in the Middle East which are well known to church historians and occasion no dispute.

Meanwhile, whence came the Hellenistic movement led by Stephen? Here we are completely in the dark. There is no reason for supposing that there were Essenic colonies throughout the Diaspora. Yet if they existed at Damascus and Antioch they may also have existed in a few other places. It may be better, however, to suppose that Stephen's Hellenists were of the Pharisaic synagogue but with distinctive Grecian features that in some way permitted Stephen, after his conversion to the belief in Jesus, to mold this part of the movement to the cast of his own thought. This leaves us wondering, however, upon what basis the dispersed Hellenists, after the death of Stephen, were received in such communities as Damascus and Antioch, which presumably were more conservatively Jewish.

Was it these "Stephanists" and their Antioch converts (together with later converts) whom Paul was defending against Peter in their quarrel at Antioch? Had their movement really originated in Jerusalem as a result of Peter's message or did it perhaps go back, even as an organized society of New Covenanters, to before the time of Peter? Or should we in their case assume the more traditional explanation that conversion was a very rapid process and that everything began after the crucifixion and in Jerusalem? If so, why was the conversion of the Hellenists so swift and turbulent and that of the community under James so slow and quiet? Or again, the Hellenists were persecuted, Peter's group was not. How great was the difference between them? Where did the Hellenists get their gospel of the Risen Jesus if not from Peter? And how in so short a time did so much happen? Was it really the

Risen Jesus in whom Stephen believed? Was it he whom he meant when he spoke of the "Righteous One"? We cannot answer these questions with confidence but we can see how much that is obscure to us played an important part in the early development of what eventually would be the Christian church.

2. James "The Lord's Brother" and the Eclipse of Peter

In John's gospel we are told that the brothers of Jesus "did not believe on him" (vii, 5). But in Acts and in Paul's letters one of the brothers, James, is the superintendent of the Jerusalem community. What are we to make of this? We must remember that John's gospel was written much later than Paul's letters and somewhat later than Acts. It is impossible that its author did not know that James was a leading figure among the first believers. Why then did he make so unqualified a statement? If what he meant was that the brothers of Jesus did not believe on him during his "earthly ministry" it is nevertheless strange that his phraseology should make no allowance for the belief that came afterward.

We must therefore ask whether James was "the Lord's brother" in the sense of being a member of the same family or as a member of the Nazorean sect to which both belonged. It is Paul who is our earliest authority for the relationship: in Galatians he speaks of James "the Lord's brother" (i, 19). It is true that this is the only such reference in the New Testament but it is much corroborated by the apocryphal literature and the church fathers and we can hardly doubt that either physically or in an Essenic-type sect, James was the brother of Jesus.

The mention of the "brethren" of Jesus in Acts (i, 14) as being in the company of believers from the very beginning is in such sharp contrast to the gospel view of Jesus where he seems almost estranged from his family (Luke viii, 19 ff., based on Mark iii, 31 ff.; John vii, 5) that it tends to confirm the possibility that they were brethren in the Nazorean sect. This conjecture, however, is precisely that —a conjecture and no more. The traditional interpretations are also nothing but conjectures, for as Weiss truly says, we "have nothing upon which to base any hypothesis."[14] The fact that Mary, the mother of Jesus, is mentioned in connection with his "brethren" does not help us, unfortunately, since this is almost certainly a later substitution for Mary, the mother of John Mark, in whose home, it will be remembered, some of the believers were meeting, and perhaps living, in Jerusalem.*

Since a confident hypothesis concerning the meaning of the term "brethren" cannot be built up, let us see if there are hints of the status of James in the Acts narrative as revealed by details that tell us more about the composition of the community. Here we must try to see behind the editorial handiwork of the composer and catch a glimpse of his source material.** Going thus to the narrative we discover such facts as that Barnabas had belonged to the community for long enough to become an apostle although he is quite definitely not one of the *Twelve* appointed by Jesus. Evidently then, he was an apostle, at least originally, in the wider community ruled by James and of which Peter and his group were only a part. We find priests in the community, a very perplexing circumstance as long as we have in mind the priesthood of the Temple order but immediately comprehensible when we remember the priests of

---

* The story of Jesus'-mother being a witness of his crucifixion is found only in the late tradition (John xix, 25), not in the Synoptics. Historicity is on the side of estrangement from his family as reported in the earlier tradition. There was no need of presenting a close connection between Jesus and his mother while the former was regarded only as the Jewish Messiah, but when he became a Redeemer there had to be a *mater dolorosa* in substitution for Cybele, Isis, etc. Hence the rise of the close relationship tradition, which eventually made Mary "the Mother of God."

** The Judean Source. See p. 82.

the Essenic sects as described in the Dead Sea Scrolls.

That the *Twelve* of James and the *Twelve* of Jesus were different *twelves* we can scarcely doubt, though there may have been some overlapping in the membership. This brings us to what might be called "the confusion of the *twelves*." In Mark's gospel, the *Twelve* are sent to the Jewish people only (vi, 7 ff.). In Matthew they are first sent solely to the Jewish people (x, 5 ff.), then to all nations (xxviii, 19). Luke forgets the mission of the *Twelve* to the Jewish people and has them sent to all nations, beginning at Jerusalem (xxiv, 47), and in Acts (i, 8) they are to go to "the ends of the earth"—which they do not do! Justin Martyr (completing the *catechesis*) says that "from Jerusalem, men, twelve in number, went out into the world . . . to teach the word of God to all" (Apol. i, 39). So strong has the tradition become that the world was evangelized by a *Twelve* appointed by Jesus that, as one scholar remarks, their original task is forgotten; and not only so: "St. Paul is forgotten also."[15]

This *Twelve* of the *catechesis* was developed to meet the situation near the end of the first century and is based, no doubt, in part upon an original group of intimate disciples which Jesus did not in the least send out to evangelize the world since he expected his *parousia* as Messiah at the time of his sufferings in Jerusalem. The other part of its basis is the *Twelve* of James, which was the real *Twelve* of Jerusalem and which *stayed there* and did *not* go "to the ends of the earth" to preach Jesus.

The *Twelve* of James, we may confidently infer, were of Jewish faith and remained such. They had little to do with preaching missions. As Karl Kundsin succinctly states the matter, undoubtedly correctly, "We arrive at the conclusion that the circle about James, whatever may have been their importance in other respects, had little to do with the formulation of the gospel tradition."[16]

How then does James come to overshadow Peter? According to the *catechesis*, Peter's prominence was such that it could be said of him that he was the rock upon which the "church" would be built. It may be noted, however, that James (the disciple not "the Lord's brother") and John have a strong claim elsewhere in the *catechesis* (Mk. x, 35 ff.) and that in the gospel bearing his name it is John who is "the beloved disciple" (xiii, 23 & *passim*). The Petrine tradition thus has its difficulties; and yet it is strong. If on the whole we accept it, how can we explain the dominance of James ("the Lord's brother") over Peter? Clement of Alexandria explained it by saying that "Peter and James and John, after the ascension of the Savior, though they had been preferred by the Lord, did not contend for the honor, but chose James the Just as bishop of Jerusalem."[17] As we have seen, this will not do. James was not superintendent by permission of these three disciples of Jesus. He has unquestioned authority to which they must bow (Acts xv).

Indeed, the more we look at James the more it occurs to us that irrespective of our earlier assumptions we must ask a searching question. Was he truly a believer in the Risen Jesus? Paul says that Christ (Messiah) "appeared" to him (I Cor. xv, 7); and in Acts he certainly seems to be a believer. To be thoroughly objective, however, we must notice that the Epistle of James (it is truly an epistle rather than a letter like Paul's, its form being that of a carefully composed general communication) is addressed to "the Twelve Tribes of the Diaspora" and is Judaic rather than "Christian" from beginning to end. Scholars increasingly regard this epistle as coming genuinely from James and with an early date, say 45 A.D.[18] Apart from its salutation in which James appears as a "bondservant of the Lord Jesus Christ" and a similar reference at the opening of the second chapter, there are no specific references to Jesus, and these two, of course, could easily have been inserted by an editor. Moreover, if genuine they do not necessarily refer to the Jesus who was crucified by Pilate, as we shall see in the next section.

In content, the Epistle of James has close affinities with late Jewish scriptures such as the document that is translated in the *Doctrina* (*Didachē*) and especially with the *Manual of Discipline* and some of the *Psalms* in the Dead Sea Scrolls. In fact, as Gaster has suggested, James actually quotes the *Manual of Discipline*[19] when he asks, "Do ye think that the scripture saith in vain, 'The spirit which [God] made to dwell in us lusteth to envy'?" (iv, 5) There is no canonical passage to which this can have reference but we are told in the *Manual* of the "spirit of wrong-doing . . . that tends to greed . . . and arrogant zeal" (iv, 9 ff.). At the very least we must admit that James lived in the thought-world of the Qumran monastics; but what of his office? Was he not called "the Just," "the Righteous," "thou Righteous One," because he held an office that the Teacher of Righteousness had in effect created? In short, was James anything less than the leader of all the Essenic groups including the Nazoreans to which Peter and some of the disciples of Jesus belonged?

Not only is this exalted position implied by Hegesippus, the second century A.D. historian of the Jews, but he reports that the scribes *urged James to preach against Jesus,* from which we must infer their assumption that he was free to do so if he had so chosen.[20]

That the Epistle of James was circulated to counter the influence of Paul has long been maintained and with good reason. Paul's emphasis was salvation by faith; man could never be saved by good works but only by God's grace in Christ. James points out that faith without works is empty and ineffectual. "What doth it profit," he asks, "if a man say he hath faith but have not works? Can that faith save him?" (ii, 14) The devils themselves believe in God, he continues, but they "believe and shudder." Then know, "O vain man, that faith apart from works is barren" (ii, 19, 20).

Unquestionably, this is a strong Judaic argument (and in Essenic vein) against the excesses of salvationist religion as preached by Paul. But the greater part of the epistle is almost certainly not newly written by James but a selection of Essenic (and generally Judaic) precepts.

Whether James actually believed that Jesus (i.e., the Jesus who was crucified by Pilate) had risen from the dead and was the coming Messiah it is impossible to be absolutely certain. He may have gone no further than to count the belief permissible provided the requirements of the Mosaic Law and the Essenic New Covenant were carried out by Jewish believers. Gentile believers may for him have taken a very secondary place: this could account, as we suggested earlier, for his partial tolerance of the gospel of Paul (how much of it he tolerated is not clear). One thing, however, is plain: when emissaries from James arrived in Antioch, neither Peter nor Barnabas felt independent enough to go on eating their meals (or partaking in sacraments?) in common with the Gentile believers. They at once returned to Jewish regulations. Such was the dominance of James. Peter was—and doubtless had always been—his subordinate.

That James did believe in the Risen Jesus is best argued from the testimony of Paul. Jesus appeared, says the latter, first "to Cephas (Peter), then to the twelve; then he appeared to above five hundred brethren at once . . . then he appeared to James, then to all the apostles; and last of all . . . to me also" (I Cor. xv, 5-8). What sort of appearances these were (for example, to five hundred persons at once) we can scarcely even conjecture. But it is permissible to notice that the appearance to James was not among the first though it did come before the appearance to Paul. So that we might say (without being entirely sure of it) that James was in some way persuaded that Jesus was the coming Messiah some time within the first three or four years after the crucifixion.

At all events, James was the supreme leader of the Palestinian Essenic movement that came to accept Jesus as promised Messiah. That it did so accept Jesus, sooner or later, we may deduce from what is known of the tenets of the Nazarenes and their successor sects in the east Mediterranean region. Yet a doubt remains, for we cannot be entirely sure who is meant by Jesus; it is to this we must now turn, devoting to it a new and rather long section.

3. Was There a Messiah before Jesus?

In writing to the community he had founded in Corinth, Paul complains that he is being supplanted there by other apostles who preach "another Jesus, whom we did not preach" (II Cor. xi, 4). This passage is almost never taken as meaning what it says, largely no doubt because the traditional consensus regards it as settled that in the apostolic era only one Jesus was preached. We are therefore told that what Paul means is not another Jesus but the same Jesus wrongly presented, as, for example, with too great an emphasis on his earthly life. But what Paul says is "another Jesus." Why should he not be taken literally? The reason is, of course, that if there was "another Jesus" besides the one crucified by Pontius Pilate (and whom we shall call "the canonical Jesus") it is necessary to ask questions which from any standpoint, traditional, liberal or even fairly radical, it is disturbing to have to take up.

If, however, there is any possibility that there was indeed a second person in New Testament times who was preached as the Messiah in the apostolic communities, honest scholarship cannot ignore it, no matter how strong may be the wish to do so, but must make it a matter of unprejudiced inquiry. This, within the compass of the space available, we shall now proceed to do.

First, we can eliminate consideration of the "false Mes-

siahs," such as Theudas,* whose failure put an end to their
pretensions; their only relevancy for us is the witness they
bear to the number and variety of Messianic claimants. We
can also, without needing to dwell upon it, take note of the
fact that Jesus was a common name—Jesus, son of Ananus,
Jesus, son of Damneus, Jesus, son of Gamaliel, Jesus, son
of Sapphias, may be cited as examples.[21]

But the word *Jesus,* no matter how commonly it was
used as an ordinary name, could have a special meaning as
the title of an office. *Jesus (Iesus)* is the Latin form of
Iēsous, the Greek equivalent of the Hebrew *Yeshua*
(Joshua) which means "Yahweh (Jehovah) is salvation."**
Thus the word *Jesus* was used for a Savior, as indicated by
Matthew who says, "And thou shalt call his name JESUS
for it is he that shall save his people from their sins" (i, 21).
In other words, he is to be called *Iēsous* (Savior) because
he *is* an *Iēsous* (Savior).

In the oldest manuscripts of the Greek testament the
name is often written $\overline{\text{IC}}$, $\overline{\text{IY}}$, $\overline{\text{IN}}$, and occasionally $\overline{\text{IHY}}$.
Concerning the reason for these abbreviations, as also con-
cerning the entire question of the orthography and etymol-
ogy of the name *Iēsous* there has been long discussion and,
while little has been settled, it is abundantly evident that
as well as being a proper name it is a "mystery" word with
cryptic connotations clustered about the central meaning
of *Deliverer* or *Savior.*[22] Paul may therefore have used the
word in this functional sense so that when he says "another
Jesus" he means "another Savior-Messiah" who was being
preached instead of the canonical Jesus. In this event the
rival Messiah need not have borne the proper name of
Jesus.

Could there have been a predecessor of Jesus who was

* See p. 104.
** The Greek Ἰησοῦς (*ē-ā-sūs*) = Hebrew יֵשׁוּעַ (*yesh-ū-a*); or יְהוֹשֻׁעַ
(*y'hōsh-ŭ-a*).

regarded as a Messiah? Was it possible to conceive of more than one Messiah being authentically such? Answering the last question first, we know that two Messiahs, one called Messiah ben-Joseph and the other Messiah ben-David, were at one time expected,* and there is evidence of two Messiahs being anticipated in the Dead Sea Scrolls.[23] There could therefore very easily have been another Messiah, or as Paul puts it, "another Jesus," in New Testament times. As to his having been a predecessor of the canonical Jesus, there is not much difficulty with this either, since there are a number of indications that point strongly to the probability that the Teacher of Righteousness mentioned in the Dead Sea Scrolls was regarded as a Messiah and that he was done to death about a century (or a little more) before the crucifixion of the canonical Jesus.

Let us look at some of these indications, first in the apocryphal New Testament, second in the Talmud and other Jewish literature, then in the church fathers. In the Apocalypse of Peter (early second century and thus within the period when the New Testament Scriptures were still being written), we read: "And when they [Israel] shall perceive the wickedness of their deeds they shall turn away after them and deny him [whom our fathers did praise] even the first Christ whom they crucified and therein sinned a great sin. But this deceiver is not the Christ" (Eth. text).[24] M. R. James, in his translation of this Apocalypse, interpolates the following comment on this passage: "Something is wrong here: the sense required is that Israel perceives the wickedness of antichrist and does *not* follow him."[25] Perhaps so and perhaps not! It is a thoroughly perplexing passage. But what *is* plain is that a *first* Christ is mentioned, thus clearly implying the belief in a later Christ or Christs; and if the remainder of the text is taken as meaning what it says, then although it was a

* See p. 153.

great sin to kill this first Christ, he nevertheless must be regarded as a deceiver and not as *the* Christ.

Could this mean that although two Messiahs were preached by rival groups of apostles for most of the first century, by the beginning of the second century the first Messiah, the Teacher of Righteousness, was being repudiated as a "deceiver" (just as John the Baptist was being given a subordinate place*), an attitude that Paul had taken all along? If so, we see more clearly why, a little later, Irenaeus in his formulation of the faith insists upon "one only Christ" (Heresies, i, 10).

Before coming to the Talmud references something more must be said of the Teacher of Righteousness. In one of the Dead Sea Scrolls, the *Habakkuk Commentary*, a revered Teacher is mentioned seven times. In the *Damascus Document*, a related manuscript which comes from Cairo, not from the caves of the Dead Sea, he is called the Unique Teacher. This Teacher, wrote Solomon Schechter (who published the *Damascus Document* in 1910) "is identical with mâshiah [Messiah] . . . whose advent is expected by the [Essenic] sect." Some scholars, however, have doubted that the Teacher mentioned was regarded as the Messiah and others have doubted that a single individual was intended, preferring to believe that the Teacher's office was filled by a succession of individuals.[26] But the weight of evidence is in favor of the Teacher as a single individual, irrespective of whether there was a later office which took this title. (We think there was.) In the *Habakkuk Commentary* he is persecuted by a "wicked priest" and "man of the lie" (perhaps the same person). Would anyone contend that the Jews of this period had a succession of persons who were appointed to *this* office? The "wicked priest" is clearly a single individual and by the same token so is the original Teacher of Righteousness.

This argument has been strongly reinforced by How-

* See p. 62.

lett[27] who quotes the Psalms Scroll as referring to an individual person who was persecuted, one who was

"a banner for the righteous elect,
an interpreter of knowledge in wondrous mysteries.
The men of deceit roared against me
like the sound of the roar of many waters.
Devices of Belial were their plans;
they turned to the pit the life of a man
whom thou didst establish by my mouth
    and didst teach him;
understanding thou didst put in my heart
to open the fount of knowledge to all who understand."[28]

This and several others of the Psalms cannot but refer to one person, the Teacher of Righteousness who was killed by order of a wicked high priest. When did his death take place? Who was he? The most persuasive identification is with a leader of the Essenic New Covenanters who perished during, or shortly after, the reign of Alexander Janneus (103-76 B.C.).

What we now need to ask is whether there are references to one who came to be regarded as a Messiah or a *Jesus* (Savior-Deliverer) and who is connected with the reign of Alexander Janneus. The answer is that there are several such references. In the Talmud and in the Toldoth Yeschu (which will be explained later) there are references to a Jesus of the Alexander Janneus period that so perplexed G. R. S. Mead, a theosophical scholar, that he wrote a book attempting to answer the question as to whether Jesus (the canonical Jesus) had lived in 100 B.C.[29] He came to no definite conclusion since it was impossible to integrate the canonical evidence with the extra-canonical and he was unaware of there having been a Teacher of Righteousness (he wrote in 1903).*

---

* We are indebted to Mead for some of the suggestions followed up in this section. Had he known of the Teacher of Righteousness he would undoubtedly have followed them up himself.

The Talmud references to Jesus have suffered a great deal, unfortunately, from the exigencies of Jewish-Christian controversy and the evils of persecution. In many cases they are deliberately made unintelligible except to the initiated so that they would not be understood by the Christian ecclesiastics who collected and burned cartloads of Talmuds because of what they found "heretical" in the contents. Nevertheless, there are clear allusions.

In one of them in which Yeschu (Jesus) is excommunicated by Rabbi Joshua ben Perachiah, the time is definitely stated as the reign of Alexander Janneus (B. Sanhedrin 107b; repeated B. Sotah 47a). Goldstein, in his *Jesus in the Jewish Tradition*, makes the following comment on this (and a second related) reference: "If Jesus of Nazareth is truly meant in this passage, then it would seem that he lived about a hundred and fifteen years earlier than is generally accepted."[30] But, as we have seen, this is not necessary if the reference is to the Teacher of Righteousness, an earlier "Jesus."

The Talmudic allusions are too esoteric and require too lengthy an explanation for further examples to be given here but the suggestion is ventured that the perplexity that has always afflicted Talmudic scholars in their effort to reconcile the Talmudic and canonical portraits of Jesus would be much alleviated if they would consider that the Jesus of the gospels and the Yeschu of the Talmud are not the same person but that *both may have played a part* in the religious movement that evolved from Essenism into Christianity.

The Jesus of these Jewish writings is a man of great learning with influence in the Palace and the Temple ("his place was near those in power"—B. Sanhedrin 43a). He is either stoned or hanged, or first stoned and then hung from a tree after his death, reminding us of the references in Acts to "Jesus whom ye *slew and hanged* on a tree" (v, 30;

x, 39).* Here two traditions may very well have been con-
flated. In the Talmud, moreover, there is no mention of
Pilate; the entire matter is a quarrel between Jews. Why
should the rabbis absolve Pilate when they had every in-
centive for allowing him to bear the blame of the execution? And why is there a tone of regret about the treatment
meted out to the Talmudic Jesus? There can be only one
answer: the Talmudic Jesus was not the canonical Jesus
but may well have been the Essenic Teacher who died a
century earlier.

When we turn from the Talmud to the Toldoth Yeschu,
the impression created by the former is immediately deep-
ened. The Toldoth Yeschu or "Generations of Jesus" col-
lects and supplements the Talmud material and has long
been "suppressed" because of its offensiveness to Christians. Perhaps this is permissible so far as general circula-
tion is concerned, for it might not be remembered how
great the Christian provocation was in the days when it
was compiled. But the Toldoth should certainly receive
more attention from scholars. And it should be known to
all that in these ancient writings (there are several versions) we are given the startling information that Jesus
lived while Israel was ruled by Queen Helene. Indeed, it is
before her and not before Pilate that he is brought to
judgment.

There is a betrayal in the Toldoth, as there is in the
New Testament; also a crown of thorns, vinegar to drink,
and a number of other parallels with the gospels; but Jesus
is quite definitely hanged, not crucified, and is buried on a

---

* Acts does not say "slew *by* hanging on a tree" but seems to indicate
two separate actions. It is true that *xulon* (ξύλον) is used for *tree*, not
dendron (δένδρον) and that *xulon* can mean a piece of *timber;* nevertheless, it is *xulon* that is used for *"tree* of life" in Rev. ii, 7, just as *etz* (עֵץ)
which also can mean *timber* or a *stick* is used for *"tree* of life" in Gen.
ii, 9, as well as for *tree* in numerous other places. If crucifixion had been
meant *stauros* (σταυρός) is the word that should have been used for the
cross (literal meaning: a *stake*) not *xulon; stauros* is the word used for the
cross twenty-nine times in the New Testament.

Sunday, not a Friday, and not in a sepulchre but beneath a stream in a place that cannot be found. As to who this Queen Helene was, there have been various conjectures including the absurd one that she was the Christian Saint Helena! Only one explanation makes sense: Helene is a disguised rendering of Salina or Salome, the wife and later the reigning widow of Alexander Janneus.*

Putting the story together (to the extent this is possible) from the Jewish writings, what we have is a Jesus who fled to Egypt during the reign of Alexander Janneus (who crucified eight hundred Pharisees and we do not know what he may have done to the Essenes), returning to Judea after this king's death, and perishing during the reign of Queen Salome (Alexandra) at the hands of the wicked high priest —or if the stories are variants and cannot be harmonized then it is Alexander himself who may have been the wicked high priest.** It is also possible that a trial took place before Alexandra while Janneus was away from Jerusalem fighting one of his numerous wars but that he returned in time to be the wicked high priest who did the Teacher of Righteousness to death. We cannot expect to piece the narrative out in detail; all we can hope to discover is the probability of there having been a Jesus in this earlier period who could have been the Teacher of Righteousness of the Essenic New Covenanters.

To turn briefly to other testimony to the dual tradition before going to the church fathers, a fourteenth-century writer, Schemtob ibn Schaprut, in a little-known book, *The Touchstone*,[31] writes as follows: "Behold, you discover with [the Jews] many writings which recount [the wonders and miracles of Jesus]; for instance the document that was composed as a history of Jeschu ha-Nōtzri (Jesus the

* See p. 101.
** The reader will remember that the kings of this period were also the Temple high priests. See page 100. But Alexandra, being a woman, could not be high priest.

Nazōrean) and states that it all happened in the time of Queen Helene; further, in the document that was composed as a history of Jeschu ben Pandera, written in Aramaic, which places it in the time of Tiberius Caesar."

Or again, from the eleventh-century Spanish historian, Abraham ben Daūd, we have the following: "The Jewish history-writers say that Joshua ben Perachiah was the teacher of Jeschu ha-Nōtzri (Jesus the Nazorean), according to which the latter lived in the days of King Jannai (Alexander Janneus); the history-writers of the other nations, however, say that he was born in the days of Herod and was hanged in the days of his son Archelaus [sic]. This is a great difference, a difference of more than 110 years."[32]

Passing now to Christian writings, we will omit passages requiring lengthy explanations and pass at once to the most remarkable testimony to the dual tradition in all the pages of Patristic literature. Epiphanius, fourth-century bishop of Salamis (Constanta), in his famous *Panarion* (a refutation of all heresies!) develops an argument (Heresy XXIX, 3) that "the throne and royal altar* of David" are combined in the priestly office of the Church, the succession of David having continued until the time of Christ himself. This order of succession "ceased and ended," he continues, when Christ was "born in Bethlehem of Judea, in the days of Alexander, who was of high-priestly and kingly race; and after this Alexander this portion failed, from the times of himself and Salina, who is also called Alexandra, for the times of Herod the King and Augustus Emperor of the Romans; and this Alexander, one of the *Christoi* [anointed ones or Messiahs] and reigning princes placed the crown on his own head." After which he goes on to say that Herod, "an alien king and no longer of the line of David" assumed the diadem.[33]

---

* Translating ἕδρα (*hedra*) as *altar*, the less usual meaning, rather than *seat* which is tautological and does not fit the argument.

Θλεξμ τῆς Ἰουδαίας (1), ἐπὶ Ἀλεξάνδρου τοῦ ἀπὸ
γένους ἱερατικοῦ καὶ βασιλικοῦ. Ἀφ' οὗ Ἀλεξάνδρου
διέπεσεν οὗτος ὁ κλῆρος ἀπὸ χρόνων αὐτοῦ τε καὶ
Σααλίνας (2), τῆς καὶ Ἀλεξάνδρας καλουμένης, ἐπὶ
τοῖς χρόνοις Ἡρώδου τοῦ βασιλέως καὶ Αὐγούστου
τῶν Ῥωμαίων αὐτοκράτορος. · Ὃς καὶ διάδημα ἐπ-
έθετο ἑαυτῷ ὁ Ἀλέξανδρος οὗτος, εἷς τῶν χριστῶν
καὶ ἡγουμένων ὑπάρχων. Συναφθεισῶν γὰρ τῶν δύο

Reproduction of part of column 393, Lib. I, Tom. II, Haeres
XXIX, in the Migne Edition of Epiphanius, Paris, 1863. It is in
this column and again in Col. 930 (Haeres LI) that Epiphanius as-
serts that Christ was born in the reign of Alexander Janneus (104-
76 B.C.) but also in the reign of Herod the Great (37-4 B.C.).*

Here is a plain statement, though in a confused context,
that Jesus lived in the days of Alexander Janneus. But he
also lived, the passage continues, in the time of Herod and
Augustus! No wonder that Petavius, an able Jesuit scholar
of the seventeenth century, having exhausted his resources
in trying to rearrange this passage to make it support the
canonical tradition, wryly confesses his failure! ("Verum
huic conjecturae nostrae non admodum confidimus.") Besides, he points out, Epiphanius repeats the "anachronism"
in Heresy LI, 22. This he most certainly does, telling us
that in the days of "the anointed ruler Alexander and
Salina who was also Alexandra** in those days the proph-
esy of Jacob was fulfilled: 'A ruler shall not cease from
Judah and a leader from his loins until he come for whom
it is laid up, and he who is the expectation of the nations'—
that is, the Lord who was born."

* The preceding (and connecting) lines in column 392 of the page of
Epiphanius' "Panarion," part of which is reproduced above, are as follows: Ἔληξαν γὰρ ἐν τῇ τοῦ χριστοῦ παρουσίᾳ οἱ κατὰ διαδοχὴν ἐξ Ἰούδα
ἄρχοντες, ἕως αὐτοῦ τοῦ χριστοῦ ἡγούμενοι. Διέπεσε γὰρ ἡ τάξις, καὶ ἔστη,
ἐξότε αὐτὸς γεννᾶται ἐν Βη-
** And Salome and Helene!

Now whatever may be said of Epiphanius, such as that he was an intemperate controversialist, it certainly cannot be maintained that he would have invented or transmitted anything that he thought damaging to the claims of the Church. The only reasonable explanation of the foregoing passages is that they represent the combination of two traditions, each of which was so strong that even in the fourth century (at least in Cyprus) it could not entirely displace the other. Epiphanius knew there was an Anointed One (*Christos*) who lived in the time of Alexander Janneus; he also knew there was a *Christos* who was born in the reign of Herod. And he believed that these two were somehow one—perhaps through a theological unification or conflation.

Against this background it is necessary to take up anew the report of Seutonius that the Emperor Claudius (41-54 A.D.) expelled certain Jews from Rome because they "constantly made disturbances at the instigation of Chrestus" (*Chresto impulsore*).[34] Scholars have generally thought that "Chrestus" in this reference is a misspelling of "Christus" and that in any case the Jews who were expelled were believers in the canonical Jesus. But Seutonius may have *meant* Chrestus for this name also appears in other ancient writings and both Tertullian in the third century and Lactanius in the fourth make mention of it.[35] In this event the name could be derived from a Greek root with rather flexible meanings among which are a *prophet* and a *righteous one.** It could thus have been the Teacher of Righteousness who was signified, though even if the intended word was "Christus" it still could have meant only a Messiah and not necessarily the canonical Jesus.

Of course, in either case he cannot have been in Rome at about 50 A.D.! Concerning this, controversy has raged

---

* χρήστης (*chrēstēs*) = one who propounds oracles, a prophet; χρηστός (*chrēstos*) = upright, serviceable, conferring benefits; χρηστότης (*chrēs-totēs*) = uprightness, goodness, righteousness.

for many years, most scholars holding that the "Chrestus" or "Christos" in question was a spiritual presence only, a fact which may not have been clear to Seutonius who was not a contemporary, while a few have held that there was a pretender to the Messiahship in Rome (as there had been many in Judea) whose activities had caused riots and that it was he who was the "Chrestus." For ourselves we have no solution; our purpose in introducing the problem, as in this whole section, is to face the questions that have been concealed by preconceptions and to show the wide range of possible hypotheses. However, it is not without significance that the most ancient Christian inscription to which we can assign a date (318 A.D.) reads "The Lord and Savior Jesus the *Chrestos* (Righteous)" not *Christos* (Messiah).*

Turning now to the New Testament, we read in Paul's First Letter to the Corinthians (i, 12, 13): "Each of you saith, I am of Paul; and I of Apollos; and I of Cephas; and I of Christ. Is Christ divided?" The inclusion of followers of "Christ" in the parties which had arisen in the Corinthian community is, to say the least, remarkable, for Paul immediately follows by saying that none of them were baptized in the name of a party leader ("Were ye baptized into the name of Paul?") but in the name of Christ (not a party leader but inclusive of all parties) who was crucified for them all.

If, however, we suppose that later hands changed the original reading from "Chrestos" to "Christos," ("I am of Chrestos") the passage becomes more intelligible. Again, it could have been the party of the Righteous Teacher. Or of James "the Lord's brother" who was called "the Just" and "thou Righteous One" and who superintended a Messianic community that, like the Essenes of the Dead Sea monas-

---

* Legend over the door of a Marcionite Church.[36] Weiss thinks the original name of Christians was *Chrestians* meaning followers of Jesus the Good; Goerke says it was first a Latin name (Chrestiani) and originated in Rome.[37] Neither hypothesis can be sustained as plausibly as one that allows for two "Messiahs" within one general Messianic movement.

tery, may well have exalted the Teacher of Righteousness. Unless this is the explanation the best we can do with the passage is to join Goguel (and others) in considering "the words 'I am of Christ' to be a clumsy gloss."[38] But what could be the purpose of such a gloss? Surely the text was changed to eliminate the name of Chrestos.*

If our suggestion is correct, Paul is subordinating the claims of the Teacher of Righteousness to that of the Messiah who was crucified under Pontius Pilate, the one and only divine Savior according to his gospel; in this also there may be a hint of what he had in mind when he spoke of "another Jesus" being preached who was not the Jesus whom Paul was proclaiming.

An extended study would require us to examine some further New Testament passages. Who is the "Righteous One" of whom Stephen accuses the Sanhedrin of having become "betrayers and murderers"? (Acts vii, 52) Paul too speaks of the "Righteous One" (according to the composer of Acts) as having spoken to him in the Damascus road episode (xxii, 14). Presumably, but not certainly, these references are to the canonical Jesus. But it seems more than possible that by the time Luke wrote his Acts *catechesis*, the terminology that had been used of an earlier Messiah—the Teacher of Righteousness, the *Dikaios*, the Just One, the Righteous One—had begun to be applied to the canonical Jesus.

We may be sure that it was a gradual process. As Weiss points out,[39] according to the earliest theology, as revealed in the Judean source used by Luke in Acts, it was the resurrection, not the life mission, of Jesus that made him "Lord and Christ" to Peter and the first believers. What their eschatological beliefs were and whom they regarded as Messiah before they came to believe in the Risen Jesus we can only guess. If we knew the answers to these ques-

---

* The reader may be confused by the two spellings *Chrestus* and *Chrestos*. The first is Latin, the second Greek.

tions, as also to other questions raised in this section, not only might it revise the traditional view much more drastically than our own analysis has done, but it would doubtless to a considerable extent revise our analysis.

To this we would not object. Nor would we expect it to disturb the basic elements of religious belief. It is only unique and supernaturalistic claims that would be affected. Meanwhile, having introduced the reader to the problems and uncertainties that must be faced when the scope of inquiry is widened to its fullest dimensions, we shall now continue with our interpretation of the less adventurous explorations of modern scholarship.*

4. Did Paul Know Jesus "In the Flesh"?

In Second Corinthians (actually it should be called Fourth if the letters were restored to their most probable original arrangement),[40] Paul writes, "If we have known Christ after the flesh, yet now we know [him so] no more" (v, 16). The earthly life of Jesus he sees as irrelevant; a new era has begun and the believers are now "a new creation" through faith in the divine Messiah-Redeemer, the Risen Lord. Why does Paul dispose of the life-mission of Jesus in this summary fashion? Is it because he knew him before his death and realized that the Galilean as he really was did not fit the Pauline Christology? Or is it because, unlike the other chief apostles, he did *not* know him and therefore wants to discount earthly knowledge of Jesus so that he, Paul, can be equated with those who *did* know him?

It is a difficult and elusive question and there is little if any evidence upon which to base an answer. Neverthe-

---

* It is probable that this section will be harshly criticized, not because it sets up a thesis (it does not) but because it raises questions (and sometimes suggests answers) which traditionalists do not like to face. The reader who believes that all pertinent questions should be honestly stated and objectively examined will not be misled by this criticism.

less, many answers have been given. Sir William Ramsay, the conservative English scholar, is fully persuaded that Paul must have known Jesus "in the flesh" or he would not have recognized him when he appeared to him at the time of his conversion.[41] Weiss also believes that Paul knew Jesus "in the flesh." His "vision and conversion are psychologically inconceivable," he says, "except upon the supposition that he had been actually and vividly impressed by the human personality of Jesus."[42] The Jewish scholar, Klausner, fully agrees. "The vision on the road to Damascus," he feels, "would not have been possible at all if Paul had not seen Jesus one or more times during the latter's lifetime."[43] And he goes on to conjecture that Paul was present at the crucifixion of Jesus and that this, together with the sight of the stoning of Stephen, left him with haunting memories which "in conjunction with an involved psychological process" brought about his conversion.

The English literary critic, Robert Graves, insists that there was no vision but that Jesus, who had suffered only a coma on the cross, from which he had been revived while lying in the sepulchre, was physically present during the incident on the road to Damascus.[44] Paul, according to Graves, had gone to Damascus not to persecute believers but to recapture Jesus so that he could be crucified afresh. Jesus had received warning of this and, together with Peter, came upon Paul and his company while they were having their afternoon *siesta* in the shade by the side of the road. As a result of the interview, in which at first Paul expected that Peter would plunge a sword into him, Paul became "converted."

These are all interesting theories and none of them, even Graves's (which scholars have not seriously entertained) can be disproven. Yet, we must remember that the ministry of Jesus is not likely to have lasted more than a few months,[45] and took place mostly in Galilee where an en-

counter with Paul, though possible, is improbable.* As for
Paul's presence at the crucifixion, surely if he had been
there he would have mentioned it. We do not have all his
letters, it is true, but in those we have there are many
places where it would have been natural for Paul to mention that he was an eyewitness when Jesus died, if this
had actually been the case.

At the opposite extreme from the opinions just cited are
such views as Conybeare's who believes that Paul regarded
the "earthly career" of Jesus as "an awkward and unpleas-
ant topic,"[46] because Peter and the Jerusalem apostles (i.e.
some of them) had participated in this career, a privilege
which Paul had not shared and which therefore he dis-
esteemed. Hence, to the latter the ministry of Jesus was
nothing; everything began with "Christ crucified" who had
appointed him to his apostleship in a special vision. It is
this deficiency, thinks Conybeare, as compared with the
Jerusalem apostles, that leads Paul at times to sneer at the
latter ("those who were reputed to be somewhat—whatsoever they were, it maketh no matter to me"—Gal. ii, 6) and
draws him wholly to the Messiah-Savior who dwells with
God and will presently appear.

Schweitzer's explanation is eschatological.[47] To Paul a
new era had begun with the resurrection of Jesus, which
had "no link of connexion" with the previous "world-
period" in which Jesus had lived and taught. The earthly
mission of Jesus had been to the Jews alone and he went to
his death as the Jewish Messiah. In his resurrection God
had made him a universal Messiah-Savior, the deliverer of
both Jews and Gentiles. Similarly, Jesus in his earthly mission had been "under the Law" but when through his
death the power of sin (which was "personalized" in Paul's

* Against this view may be cited, for whatever it may be worth, the
rather slender tradition that Paul's parents came from Gischala in Galilee.
Jerome, who derived it from Origen, mentions this tradition (Commentary
on Philemon, 23).

thinking) had been destroyed, the Law was fulfilled and superseded. It was not necessary, not desirable, to know the earthly Jesus who was a limited person with a limited mission. It was the Lord Christ from whom these limitations had all been cast off that it was needful to know.

This sounds persuasive. And yet there are questions. What did Paul talk about when, as he admits, he went to Jerusalem to see Peter? Must there not have been some discussion of the life and teaching of Jesus? How could Paul have connected a universal purpose with Jesus if Jesus was as narrowly the Jewish Messiah as Schweitzer thinks? If there was none of the liberalism in Jesus that is indicated, for instance, in the Parable of the Good Samaritan, how could Paul argue that his gospel to the Gentiles found any sanction in Jesus? It is all very well to say that everything had been changed by the resurrection and that Paul had received his instructions from the Jesus of the vision, but so long as the man who lived an earthly life in Galilee and was crucified by Pilate in Jerusalem is the Jesus indicated, his life before and after assuming the Messiahship cannot be altogether separated.

Why did Paul (so to speak) choose Jesus the Nazorean as the Christ-Savior of the Gentiles if Jesus was utterly unconcerned with the Gentiles? The Pharisees were eager to make Gentile proselytes; why not Jesus? What ground was there for Paul to stand upon in his disputations with Peter and James if the latter could merely have said to him, "But Jesus was absolutely against what you want to do"? These questions do not rebut the explanations of Schweitzer and others and are not intended to do so. But do they not cast doubt upon them?

We do not have the evidence, we do not live in Paul's conceptual world and only in minor part are we able to reconstruct it; and thus, unhappily, much that we would dearly like to know must remain obscure. It may be that factors described in the previous section have relevancy to our problem: the Jesus whom Peter had known and partly understood, Paul (though knowing him only through others) may have understood much better; whereas the Jesus exalted by James may have been the Teacher of Righteousness (or he may have believed that the Teacher was reincarnated in the canonical Jesus). We by no means assert these things, but we are not in a position to dismiss them either. The sad fact is that we can discover more about Paul and the mystery religions or Paul and Gnostic theology than we can about Paul and Jesus. We can see from Paul's theology how his scheme of salvation required a Savior who was crucified. The sacrificial deaths of the pagan redeemers "on a tree" in myth and pageant became in the death of Jesus an actuality. This could be the reason for his selecting Jesus as the historical nexus of the cosmic drama. It could explain, if we press it hard enough, his eagerness to leave the earthly life of Jesus far behind. Not Jesus who taught in Galilee, no matter what his message, but Jesus on the cross inaugurating the new era was what Paul needed. So he took what he needed, setting aside the earthly life of Jesus as irrelevant. This at present is where the argument seems to rest.

Yet, it might be better to finish with a question. To Paul, too, the cross was at first a stumbling block. He persecuted the believers. Then something happened that revealed the crucifixion to him in a new light. It must have owed something to Jewish prophecy—to the picture of the "man of sorrows, acquainted with grief." It must also have owed something to a deep belief, similar to Peter's, in the continued aliveness of Jesus (not necessarily a physical resurrection). It was undoubtedly indebted to what Paul knew of Gnostic theology and of the mystery religions. The crucifixion fitted itself into a master design that was forming in Paul's thinking. Then there was an emotional crisis, a fervent conviction, a sudden and uncompromising dedication. The many elements in the mind of Paul came together in a single pattern of divine deliverance. It was a new era. His own vocation was plain before him. God had revealed to him his divine plan and Paul's crucial part in its performance.

This we may accept. But here is the question: could it have happened no matter who had died upon the cross? Or was there not something immense and indispensable that came from the life of Jesus?*

* An answer to this question could be attempted only in a full length study of Jesus. The present writer recognizes that the trend of recent scholarship is heavily in the direction of seeing Jesus as the Jewish Messiah rather than as a teacher of timeless and universal truth; but he is not persuaded that the latter concept has no place in a balanced interpretation of Jesus.

THE NARRATIVE RESUMED

1. *Paul Before Antioch*

Of Paul's boyhood in Tarsus, little is known. He tells us that he was brought up in the strict Jewish faith, instructed in the Law after the manner of the Pharisees. Eager to excel, he surpassed others of his own age and was "exceedingly zealous" for the traditions of his fathers.* That he attended the university at Tarsus may be doubted; his letters are not those of a man schooled in Greek philosophy but rather of one trained in the rabbinical manner—who nevertheless, whether in Tarsus or later, became well acquainted with the thought-forms of Gnostic theology and the rituals of the mystery cults.

If his upbringing was rigorously Jewish, Paul would not have been allowed to witness the processions of Baal-Tarz, the city deity of Tarsus, or to have any contact with Mithraism, which during his boyhood was spreading through Cilicia, or to visit the temples of salvationist religions. But he was certainly not insulated from these things any more than a modern Jew living in New York, however orthodox, is insulated from his cosmopolitan environment. Indeed, in Paul's case we shall have to suppose that at some point in his more impressionable years he learned enough about non-Jewish Hellenistic life to equip him for his mission to the Gentiles. His enthusiasm for this task may or may not

* The passages in which Paul refers to his upbringing are: Rom. xi, 1; II Cor. xi, 22; Gal. i, 14; Phil. iii, 5.

have been a sudden inspiration but his comprehension of what it required can only have been due to associations that had grown with the years. Perhaps it all began through knowing "God-fearers" at the synagogue, the Gentiles who revered the Jewish scriptures but would not submit to circumcision and the Jewish regulations.

It has been surmised that Paul's mother died when he was very young and that his father was a harsh disciplinarian. This could account in part for his emotional difficulties, his attitude to marriage and his morbid preoccupation with inability to keep the Law. Down to the thirteenth year the guilt for a Jewish boy's "sins" was borne by his father; thereafter he himself was responsible. This, no doubt, is what Paul alludes to when he writes that he was "alive apart from the Law once," but that when [at twelve years of age] he came under "the Commandment, sin came to life" (Rom. vii, 9). Out of a stormy and guilt-ridden adolescence Paul emerged into gloomy manhood, convinced that he was condemned under the Law and unable to find salvation.

It is difficult to believe that even at this time he gave no thought to the salvation that was offered by the mystery religions. Not that he ever considered joining such a cult, but the ideas that emanated from the mystery religions began to pose questions about the role of the Jewish Messiah. Was it to save his people from Roman tyranny or from the tyranny of sin? It is not to be doubted that the prolonged spiritual crisis that kept Paul chained to the Law that he could neither obey nor renounce forced his thinking far in all directions, pagan as well as Judaic, in the search for liberation.

It may have been this quest that took him to Jerusalem and possibly to the famed Rabbi Gamaliel. If so, he was disappointed in what was offered to him. The diverse interpretations of the Law—the school of Gamaliel on one side, that of Shammai on the other—no matter how edifying as ethical instruction, did not speak to his condition. The Law, no matter how it was expounded, still condemned him. So he went on seeking. The Jewish scholar, Schonfield, thinks that he found his way into "the mystical and esoteric aspect of Pharisaic Judaism,"[48] which had absorbed Gnostic-type concepts and seems also (if we credit the little that we are told about it) to have had affinities with the theology, if not the ritual, of the mystery cults.

If there was really a kind of Pharisaism that had been as much influenced as this by pagan religion, Paul, once he had discovered it, had only a few steps farther to go before his Jewish Messiah would be the counterpart and rival of Osiris and Attis, Mithras and Hermes, a universal Jewish-pagan salvationist redeemer. This, apparently, is Schonfield's view. Paul merely borrowed, he says, "as the Pharisees also borrowed, but only to reinforce the presentation to non-Jews of his own mystical Jewish tenets."[49]

However this may be, in one way or another Paul was moving from normative Judaism into ways of thought that would eventually be angrily repudiated by virtually all Jews and which therefore were not Judaic except to himself and to those who held, as he did, that the movement soon to be known as Christianity was the new and authentic Judaism. For ourselves, we think that Paul's doctrine of the Redeemer came later, when he had faced the crucifixion, and not in student days, whether at Tarsus or Jerusalem. For the present, it was a matter more of questions, of suggestions, than of formulations. Not until his conversion —and in its complete development not until his Aegean campaigns—did Paul arrive at the Saviorhood of Jesus as his letters define it. Yet he was groping toward it, helped a little perhaps by "mystical Jewish tenets" but mostly walking in darkness, longing for the light.

One possibility that may explain how Paul, though a Tarsian, had close associations with Jerusalem is the conjecture earlier mentioned: that he was one of the *apostoloi*

who carried the annual contribution from the Cilician syn-
agogues to the Temple treasury. The Greek word *apostolos*, which originally had to do with naval expeditions
seems eventually to have meant an ambassador. However,
the Hebrew word translated as *apostolos* meant only a
messenger.* In this event, Paul was an *apostolos* in one
sense before his conversion and in another afterward. The
ambiguity of meaning would thus have encouraged the
sort of play upon words which was so popular at this
period. Paul's first and lowlier apostleship under the Temple dispensation was a foreshadowing of his later and
plenary apostleship as an ambassador of Jesus. Similarly, as
under the one dispensation he had collected money for
the Jewish hierarchy, under the other he had made a collection for the Jerusalem patriarchate ruled by James.
Moreover, if this supposition is correct it makes it easy to
see how Paul may have gone to the synagogues of southeastern Asia Minor in his early campaigns as a man of
prestige, already known to the congregations; and it means
that from the beginning he was a seasoned traveler.

His first appearance in the New Testament narrative, at
the stoning of Stephen, we have sufficiently considered in
dealing with the traditional story.** But we see now that
the situation into which he entered was far more complex
and multifaceted than would appear from the chronicle in
Acts. Jerusalem as much as ever was in a ferment. How
many sects there were, each with its own emphasis, we
cannot even guess. Within the Essenic groups, as also
among the Pharisees, there was wide latitude, apparently,
for divergence of opinion, except as to the essentials of
Mosaic Law. One such Essenic group believed that Jesus
of Galilee, crucified by Pontius Pilate, had risen from the

---

* צִיר (*tzer*) which could be translated either by ἀπόστολος (*apostolos*)
or ἄγγελος (*angelos*). The latter word could mean either an ordinary messenger or an angel. (Note: the "g" in *angelos* is pronounced hard as in
"go.")

** See p. 20 ff.

dead and would shortly appear as the Messiah. In ways
that elude us, this belief had swiftly spread to the Hellenistic synagogues of Jerusalem. Between the Hellenist believers and the community of James (only a part of which
may as yet have accepted Jesus as the Messiah) there were
tensions. Among other things, the Hellenists had attacked
the Mosaic Law and disparaged the sacrifices of the Temple. This (and perhaps other offenses that are not clear to
us) were more than could be tolerated and had provoked
official condemnation, followed by a persecution.

Foremost among the persecutors was Paul. Then, suddenly, in a way and at a time unknown to us came the shattering moment of conversion. Paul heard Jesus speaking to
him; he believed that he saw him. Paul was commissioned
as the apostle to the Gentiles. How it may have happened
we have conjectured in an earlier chapter.* But as the
reader now knows, nothing is certain except that somewhere, sometime in the mid-thirties of the first century,
Paul first persecuted what he calls "God's community,"
then became converted to it and believed himself appointed to be the chief apostle of the Risen Jesus to the
Gentiles. We have assumed, as most scholars do but many
do not, that the persecution was in Jerusalem. We have
said that the conversion may also have occurred there but
that recent scholarship tends to place it in Damascus.[50]

From Paul's own testimony, we know that he was in
Damascus soon after his conversion even if it did not take
place there, and that he went from Damascus to Arabia
(Gal. i, 17). Many writers have imagined that this sojourn
in Arabia was a wilderness ordeal in which Paul sought
complete solitude while adjusting himself to his new convictions. There is no real reason for this supposition; the
term "Arabia" covers a wide territory which contained any
number of cities and settlements to which Paul could have
repaired and in which, for that matter, he could have

* See p. 32 ff.

preached as he later did in Damascus. Our own view, which we think has plausibility but cannot be supported by much evidence, is that there were encampments of Essenic sects no great distance from Damascus and that Paul, for a time, took refuge in one of them. The *Damascus Document*, earlier mentioned,* can be interpreted as supporting this hypothesis though many scholars would dispute it.[51]

It is conceivable that Essenic encampments in this area were more hospitable to Hellenistic thought than those at Qumran or Jerusalem. Josephus tells us that there were more orders than one of Essenes and both he and the Qumran documents give indications of Hellenistic influence (*Wars*, Book II, viii, 2-14). Paul may therefore have found encouragement in such a community. It is true that he says that after his conversion he "conferred not with flesh and blood" (Gal. i, 16), but this need only mean that he did not submit his claim to apostleship to be approved by the leadership of the movement, not that he did not talk to anybody about his conversion or discuss questions of religion. In Arabia, or in Damascus, or in both, Paul brought upon himself the wrath of the authorities, resulting, he tells us, in King Aretas sending a patrol to try to capture him as he left the city gates. But he escaped by being let down over the walls (II Cor. xi, 32).

After three years in Arabia and Damascus Paul came to Jerusalem privately, to consult with Peter and James. What they talked about we do not know, or how much agreement there was between them. Paul, who confessed that he could be "all things to all men" if it furthered his mission, need not have confided to the Jerusalem leaders all that was on his mind. But he must have gone searchingly into the testimony of Peter and would surely have put his own evaluation on what he was told.

* See p. 185.

From Jerusalem he went home to Tarsus. What he did there we do not know. But whether he was actively conducting missions or merely pondering the purpose to which he was committed, there must have been, at least as he saw it, a continuity in his apostleship which his stay in Tarsus did not interrupt. The best reason for thinking that he was actively preaching is that Barnabas came to Tarsus to ask him to join them in the work at Antioch. Barnabas must have had cause for his confidence in Paul's ability and, unless it was Paul's work in Damascus that had given him a favorable reputation (which in view of the outcome seems uncertain), it must have been work in Tarsus.

Why was Paul needed in Antioch? In a curious and unexpected way it was because of an action of Gaius Caligula, the Roman emperor. Gaius had insisted that his statue be set up in the Temple at Jerusalem. Petronius, the legate of Syria, who had received the order to perpetrate this outrage was much alarmed, knowing that it might bring upon him a Jewish revolt. As long as he could he temporized, and finally, preferring the emperor's wrath to a senseless slaughter of protesting Jews, he wrote Gaius, begging that the order be rescinded. Gaius replied that for his insubordination Petronius must commit suicide. But before this letter arrived, the half-mad emperor had been assassinated (41 A.D.) and Petronius was free to grant himself a pardon. All of which appeared marvelous in Syria and a testimony to the God of the Jews.

Furthermore, before his death Gaius had suspended the order to erect the statue (but not his instruction to Petronius to commit suicide) at the pleading of his friend, Herod Agrippa, to whom he had awarded the Jewish crown. Most astonishing of all, on the day Petronius agreed to entreat Caesar to change his mind about the statue, a severe drought ended in heavy showers of rain.

Petronius himself was deeply impressed. A few months

earlier, it had seemed certain that a great persecution was about to begin against the Jews. There had been a horrible pogrom in Alexandria. There were likely to be others throughout the empire. Now, suddenly, the Jews had triumphed; Caligula was dead, his statue was not in the Temple, Petronius was allowed to live, there was a Jewish king again, and—surely a miracle—the drought was over: Jehovah had sent rain!

The Gentiles flocked to the Antioch synagogues. Barnabas and the Antioch believers saw their opportunity. They knew who best could cultivate it, whose voice would be most persuasive, who knew how to preach to Gentiles with passionate conviction the gospel of the Risen Lord. They sent Barnabas to Tarsus in search of Paul.

2. *The Campaigns in Cyprus and Asia Minor*

When Syria was ruled from the East, Damascus was the capital; under Western powers, the seat of government was Antioch. By the time Paul came to work there at the behest of Barnabas, Antioch had had four centuries in which to become magnificent. Five miles of its streets were lined with statuary, much of its paving was white marble, it was famous throughout the empire for its splendid temple of Apollo of Daphne. Here on the banks of the Orontes, the redemptive death of Adonis, followed by his resurrection "on the third day," was annually enacted in a drama that went back to the slaying of the King.[52] Here the emasculated priests of the Great Mother performed their frenzied dances, gashing their arms with knives and bespattering onlookers with their blood. Here were temples of the deities of fertility with their sacred prostitutes the reward of whose hire maintained the temple treasury.

Here too was a large and vigorous Jewish colony which from time to time brought added turbulence to a population that was already noted for its restlessness. Somewhere in this colony a community of Essenic New Covenanters had for some time been awaiting the promised Messiah. To this community had come refugees from the persecution of Stephen's Hellenists, bringing with them the gospel of the Risen Jesus. It was a community with a close relationship to the Jerusalem New Covenanters superintended by James. But there was also rivalry. Antioch was a greater city than Jerusalem and had long been deeply imbued with Hellenism, of which indeed it was the cultural focus in the eastern empire, so that we may be sure that the New Covenanters of Antioch were not as rigorously Judaic as those of Jerusalem. Soon there would be tensions between the two centers but at the time of the ingathering of the Gentiles after the death of Caligula it was natural for the Antiochians to send to Jerusalem for aid, and in response came Barnabas.

This apostle, of whom unhappily we know very little, was undoubtedly a man of great ability to whom the new movement owed much more than is conveyed by our Scriptures. Many scholars regard him as nobler-minded than Paul, to whom the book of Acts unjustly subordinates him.[53] Whether he was sent to Antioch by James, as Acts reports, has frequently been questioned since James seems only to have tolerated (rather than welcomed) Gentile incursions and would scarcely have encouraged what was going on at Antioch. Some scholars, including Goguel, even think that Barnabas was not sent for at all but was in Antioch already when the Gentile believers began to be added, and that he was the leader of the Antiochian community.[54] Perhaps so; but it is evident from Galatians as well as Acts that Barnabas held James in high regard (Gal. ii, 1). If, as seems likely, this regard was mutual, James could have sent Barnabas to the Syrian capital to see to it that the mass influx of Gentiles was orderly and that due respect was paid to the minimum Judaic regulations.

In any case, under Barnabas, the Antioch society became large and prosperous. This could not have been favorably regarded by the Jews of the Pharisaic synagogues, who were themselves eager to receive proselytes, but for the time being at least there was apparently no conflict. Probably the sect of John the Baptist was also actively making converts, and there must have been other such movements. We must not think of the movement of which Paul and Barnabas were apostles as though it had only the synagogue to contend with. Nor must we think of the Jewish groups as the only evangelizers; there were Hermetics and Gnostics, and always and everywhere the mystery religions.

But in spite of its rivals the Antioch community was soon strong enough to finance missionary campaigns in the adjacent territory. After a year or so, it was possible to send Barnabas and Paul to Cyprus, the former's homeland, where, according to Acts, Sergius Paulus, the proconsul, was converted. In Cyprus there seem to have been no communities of New Covenanters as there were in Antioch and Damascus, and it is in the synagogues that Paul and Barnabas do their initial preaching.

In Cyprus something of importance happened in which Paul was controversially involved but which the composer of Acts decided not to reveal to us. Paul down to now has been subordinate to Barnabas but henceforth he takes the lead in extending the mission to cities in the south of Asia Minor. Although Barnabas goes with him, it is no longer as senior partner in the team of "Barnabas and Saul" but as a member of the mission called "Paul and his company" (xiii, 13). One of the original group—John Mark—refuses to remain with Paul, and in evident disapproval of what Paul was doing—or contemplating—returned *not to Antioch* but to Jerusalem! There was something that John Mark wanted to report—and urgently. Whatever it was, Paul never forgave him for it; never again would he take John Mark with him on a missionary campaign (xv, 37,38).

If we wish to form some opinion of what it was that had happened on the island of Cyprus we must first take note that the story of the conversion of the proconsul is not inherently improbable. He, like many other Romans, may have been much impressed by the successful resistance of the Jews to the edict of Gaius Caligula. Surely their Jewish God had been with them. If Paul, in explaining his gospel to Sergius, had placed the emphasis on Jewish monotheism, dispensing with Mosaic regulations, the proconsul may well have been unusually responsive. On the basis of his having made so important a convert (or if he did not actually convert him, on the basis of having gained his favor), Paul may have taken the leadership from Barnabas. It may also have been at this time and at the hands of Sergius Paulus that Paul received his Roman citizenship and took the name Paulus from his benefactor (it is precisely at this point in the narrative that the change of name is made—xiii, 9).* And the grateful proconsul may have given Paul money with which to conduct a new mission.

Irrespective, however, of whether the above conjectures are correct, Paul must have made a new departure, thoroughly objectionable to John Mark but not so much so to Barnabas, and this undoubtedly was in the extent to which he had departed from Judaic obligations. Probably he had told Sergius Paulus that he could enter the Covenant with Jehovah God simply by faith in Jesus the Messiah. This would have been sufficiently offensive to Mark, though he may equally have objected to Paul's offering a place among "the elect" to a Roman proconsul on any terms whatever. Was not Rome the enemy the Messiah would overthrow? Paul was revealing through his attitude to the proconsul that he was attached to ideas of his own rather than to those of the original apostles. This we may be sure was

---

* See p. 12 f. for other theories about the names Saul-Paul.

true from the beginning. In Antioch, Paul had held back some of his thinking and had preached as the situation required; now, where he found greater freedom, he was preaching more of his own gospel.

This was the gospel he took with him to Iconium, Lystra and Derbe, first to the synagogues where he was repulsed and expected to be repulsed; then to the Gentiles among whom he found believers. At Lystra, he was stoned by the infuriated Jews and left for dead, but upon being revived escaped to Derbe. Barnabas, it seems, was left unharmed and does not appear to have aroused the enmity that was directed against Paul, doubtless because he was not going as far as Paul in his view of the Law and Mosaic regulations. It is not necessary to suppose that both preached precisely the same doctrine, provided they remained together in believing that the Risen Jesus was the Messiah they were anticipating.[55]

What other campaigns Paul engaged in during this earlier period we cannot even guess; but there must have been such. The beatings and shipwrecks that he enumerates in Second Corinthians (xi) cannot all have taken place in the later period. But however many the campaigns or where they took him, this earlier activity was centered in Antioch. The later campaigns were also Antioch-centered until the quarrel with Peter. As a general basis, recognizing that no assured chronology of Paul's life and work is possible, we might place the activity in Antioch itself in 41 A.D., the campaigns in Cyprus and Asia Minor (and others of which we have no information) from 42 to 45 A.D., the campaign around the Aegean Sea from 45 to 53 A.D., interrupted in 51 by a visit to Jerusalem.

3. The Early Message: "Maran Atha"

For the New Covenanters as a whole, whether they believed in the Risen Jesus or not, the basic and unifying belief is summed up in the short prayer, *"Maran atha!"* "Our Lord, Come!" or "Our Lord cometh!"* The followers of John the Baptist may also have prayed this prayer. As it stands, it does not necessarily refer to the canonical Jesus, though it does, of course, on the lips of the early believers and Paul. Messianists of many different shades of belief were held together by the one uniting, fervent expectation that the Messianic reign was near.

It is difficult for the modern mind to view this expectation in its actual context. In the first century it seemed to be an inevitable consummation to which events were swiftly and inexorably tending. Revolts and riots, droughts and famines, the attempt of a mad Caesar to erect his image in the Temple, were all portents that "the Day" was near. To the Catholic scholar, Grollenberg, it was an outlook comparable to that of contemporary Christians who believe that now in the atomic age they are living "in the closing phase of world history."[57] Probably, however, for the Messianists of the first century, the expectation was more intense.

How much the New Covenanters differed from other Jewish Messianists in this expectation cannot be clearly determined but it seems evident that they surpassed the Jews of the synagogues in piety, differed from them in espousing poverty as a virtue, exceeded them in the vigor of their call to repentance ("Repent, for the Kingdom of Heaven is at hand," was the basic theme of both John the Baptist and Jesus), in benevolence, ("Love one another" was the typical admonition of all the New Covenanters as it was of James and Peter and equally of Paul), and in con-

---

* The Aramaic or Syriac מָרַן אֲתָא (Maran atha) transliterated into the Greek of I Cor. xvi, 22 as Μαρὰν ἀθά (*Maran atha*) (Westcott and Hort) cannot be construed with complete certainty but it is not to be doubted that it is an ejaculatory prayer, widely used by the New Covenanters, conveying the wish or the affirmation that the Messiah will soon come.[56]

sidering themselves a chosen instrument of God, a spiritual elite of the Jews.

The early message of the canonical apostles was thus, *as preached to Jews,* a call to repentance because the "Day" of the Messiah was near, and *as preached to Gentiles,* essentially the same message coupled with an appeal to forsake idols and worship the one true God. Both Jews and Gentiles were exhorted to live worthily of the great hour that was now imminent, restraining "the evils of the flesh" and, through loving-kindness, subduing all malice, envy or hostility one toward another. The one vexed question as we have repeatedly seen, in calling Gentiles to repentance was the extent to which faith in the Messiah was sufficient for salvation without imposing the regulations of the Mosaic Law.

In the view of the New Covenanters, or at least of some of them, Gentiles had been given a place in the Messianic Community to make up for the apostasy of a large number of unworthy Jews. When the Messiah came, it would be found that each of the twelve tribes had assembled 12,000 of the faithful, totaling 144,000, and that of Gentiles there was "a great multitude which no man could number" (Rev. vii, 9), which, as Schonfield has pointed out, means "ten thousand times ten thousand" or 100,000,000 since "the highest figure capable of being represented in the Greek alphabetic notation was 99,999,999, so that the addition of one yielded a number which no man could number."*[58]

All of these, however, both Jewish and Gentile, were "sealed" (Rev. vii, 3,4) or elected in advance to the Messianic community and it was assumed by most of the New Covenanters (apparently without regard to the improbability of mustering as many as 100,000,000 of them) that the Gentile believers would be found among the "God-

* This rather formalistic computation could not have been kept consistently in mind by the New Covenanters, although it is a perfectly sound exegesis of the passage in the book of Revelation.

fearers" of the synagogues, a restriction which Paul refused
to share, this being one of the reasons for the antagonism
he aroused, beginning with the disaffection of John Mark.

Whoever he may have been to others, to the canonical
believers and their apostles, the Messiah was Jesus the
Nazorean, he who had overcome death on the cross and
was now their "Risen Lord." To prove that he was indeed
the Messiah they relied very largely upon a demonstration
from the Scriptures (our Old Testament which to them was
the entire Bible) that Jesus had fulfilled the prophecies of
the One who was to come. To modern minds, these demon-
strations would appear exotic and the fulfillments of
prophecy wildly improbable, but at the time it was considered that God had given to his elect a special insight or
gnosis, so that they could say, as does the writer of the
Epistle of Barnabas, "Blessed be our Lord, brethren, who
put in us wisdom and understanding of his secrets" (Barn.
vi, 10).[59]

From the beginning, even when he was preaching under
restraint and was not free as yet to proclaim his whole
gospel, Paul's emphasis was salvation by faith in the Messiah Jesus. He made much use of the story of Abraham,
who "believed" God long before there was a Mosaic Law,
and in fact before he was circumcised. His circumcision
was but an evidence of his faith. His righteousness was
neither by Law nor by circumcision but by faith. He accepted the promise of God that his posterity should inherit
the earth and—according to Paul—his posterity was not the
nation physically descended from him, many of whose
members had forsaken the Covenant, but all believers,
Jewish or Gentile, who had faith in God's Messiah. This, so
far as we can recover it, was Paul's early message, his supplement to the announcement that the *parousia* of the
Messiah was at hand; and for most of the Judaic believers
it went too far. God still had a special province for the
Jews, they said, another for the Gentiles. Paul, by effacing

the distinction, was destroying the special mission of Judaism.

But in his own thinking Paul went even farther. That he was holding back the gospel he would later preach is beyond question. He had milk for babes, meat for those who were grown up (I Cor. iii, 1, 2), he tells us. To the Jews he became a Jew that he might "gain Jews"; to "them that are without law, as without law" that he might gain these also. He was in fact "all things to all men" that he might "by all means save some" (I Cor. ix, 20-22).

Paul has been much criticized for this and even accused of dishonesty. The charge is uncomprehending and inapposite. To Paul, it was salvation that counted, whether of Jew or Gentile, and it was achieved by faith in the Messiah-Redeemer. Whether the approach to this faith was through Old Testament prophecy, Gnostic theology suitably adapted, or the myths and rituals of the mystery religions scarcely mattered, provided the faith itself was real. The Jew had one background, one way of thinking, the Gentile another. The Lord Jesus could make his way to the heart of a believer through any of these avenues. He was more than all of them. The gospel must be fitted to the cultural antecedents and intellectual and spiritual capacity of those who received it.

Such was the audacity of Paul's thinking, and such his misunderstood genius. Even in the early period we may be sure that he had gone far in this process, for from the beginning he was *the* apostle to the Gentiles. That was the commission that Jesus had given him in his special vision. It was for this that Paul had known himself fitted even before the vision. Once he had received his commission his thought was set free, and in the fiery furnace of his ardent mentality, white-hot with devotion to the Lord Jesus who had loved and saved him, the "rigors" of Judaic Law, supported by exclusive claims, melted and flowed into molds that he had prepared for the reshaping of them, resulting in his "new Judaism."

For the present, he was being "all things to all men" by keeping himself under restraint. There were "degrees" of understanding in the gospel corresponding to the "degrees" through which the initiate must ascend in the pagan cults and Gnosticism. That Paul's gospel was "graduated" and multifaceted seems strange and inconsistent to us: but to him it was all one gospel. And the burthen of it in the early period was the same with him as with the others: "*Maran atha!*"—"Our Lord, come!"

The distinctive rite through which believers were received into the movement was baptism. The use of the Greek word *baptitzo* for this rite is very strange since it was never used by Greek writers for a religious ceremony or for purification but for such things as the *sinking* of ships, or being *immersed* in debt, or *drenched* in wine. But evidently it was given a special meaning by the believers, and Josephus also knew of it since he speaks of John the *Baptistēs*. As Enslin remarks, we have here an instance of the many "gaps in our knowledge—linguistic as well as historical—of the early centuries."[60] In some of the mystery cults the same rite was used, as it was for proselytes to the synagogues, but for the believers baptism was "into the name of the Lord Jesus."

The sacred meal at this time was much simpler than it became in Paul's later formulation, and for most of the communities it remained simpler even through the first half of the second century, as we discover from reading the gospels and Acts. Indeed, as we noted earlier,* some scholars have felt that since Paul's formulation is so highly developed it cannot really be his but must be assigned to the period following the writing of the gospels; but it belongs so integrally to the Pauline corpus that we should have to

* See pp. 133 f.

say the same thing of everything else ascribed distinctively to Paul, which is impossible since his letters place him squarely within the first half of the first century. Here again then, we see how far ahead Paul was, as compared with his contemporaries, in achieving a synthesis; but this was only barely apparent in his earlier missions.

4. The Aegean Campaigns and the Visit to Jerusalem

As we have several times noted, Paul's missionary activity is not completely reported in Acts; nor is it fully covered in those of his letters that have come down to us. Since these two sources are all we can draw upon for information—and in the case of Acts often with uncertainty —it is futile to pretend that we can fill in the blanks; there is nothing upon which to build up even a probable conjecture.

Let us then acknowledge that we do not know where Paul "five times received" the Jewish "forty stripes save one," or where he was three times shipwrecked, or spent "a night and a day in the deep." Nor do we know of his "hunger and thirst," his "cold and nakedness" (II Cor. xi). To these events we can assign neither time nor place but can only hope that in the intervals between them the afflicted apostle was sometimes in safety and that his weary body, if not his mind, occasionally found rest.

If we leave this insoluble problem and follow the general pattern of Acts, we see that Paul, perhaps in about 45 A.D. or a little later, visited Phrygia and Galatia. He seems to have gone into the Galatian highlands because of a sickness contracted in the lowlands, possibly malaria (Gal. iv, 12 ff.). He is grateful that the Galatians did not despise his infirmity on this first (or former—the Greek can mean either) visit, indicating by the adjective that he had made at least two visits before he wrote this letter. At that time, he says, in contrast to their present attitude they would have "plucked out their eyes and given them to" him.

This suggests that as well as the malaria, Paul had something wrong with his sight. The blindness in the legend of the Damascus journey may hint at this. It is also reported in Acts that he did not recognize the high priest even though he stood before him (xxiii, 4, 5). And he never writes his own letters but dictates them to an amanuensis. To certify to their authenticity, however, he autographs a salutation at the end, but it is in "large letters" such as a person with poor sight might make (Gal. vi, 11). It may therefore have been an ophthalmic condition that was his famous "thorn in the flesh," rather than the epilepsy so confidently asserted by commentators. Whatever it was, it seems to have come upon him with unusual severity following his visions and he calls it "a messenger of Satan" (II Cor. xii, 1-10). To know how much it handicapped his work we need only reflect that a prophet was supposed to cure diseases, especially those that caused seizures, not fall victim to them. Paul's "thorn in the flesh" must therefore have been a sore embarrassment.

From Galatia Paul went to the Asian seaport of Troas, accompanied by Silas, who may have been with him all the way from Antioch, and Timothy, a young convert whom he treated almost as a son and who was of immense service to him. They were "forbidden of the Holy Ghost" to preach in the province of Asia, which most likely means that in Ephesus, its capital, the "God-fearers" to whom in the first place they would have gone had been successfully evangelized by the preachers of John the Baptist. From the guarded reference in Acts (xix, 1-7) we may infer that between Apollos, the envoy of the Baptist, and Paul and his party there was sharp rivalry, and this, as we saw in a previous chapter,* is confirmed in the letters (I Cor. i, 10-17).

At Troas Paul had a vision of "a man of Macedonia"

* See p. 193.

beseeching him to "come over and help us" (Acts xvi, 9) and he and his companions sailed to Samothrace and Neapolis and thence overland to Philippi, thus inaugurating what we have called the Aegean campaigns since they embraced both the European and Asian cities that line the Aegean Sea. Here we shall not follow the Acts pattern further, not because it may not be correct as far as it goes but because there must have been both additional land travel and an unknown number of unrecorded voyages. Paul could not have been shipwrecked three times without doing considerably more sailing than he does in Acts. Let us suppose then that after his first Aegean campaign in which he established communities of believers in Philippi, Thessalonica, Beroea (in Athens he fails), and Corinth (and perhaps in other places), he sails for Ephesus and, Apollos now being in Achaia, makes sufficient headway to be able to establish the Ephesus "church" as his Aegean headquarters from which for a while he and his fellow workers campaign both by letter and by personal mission in the province of Asia and across the Aegean Sea. (See map, p. 41.)

As we see from Acts, and as Paul himself testifies, they were constantly in trouble with the Jews of the synagogues and with the civil authorities. There was more reason for this than our Scriptures convey. Paul and his campaigners were in the Aegean area at a time when numerous Jewish emissaries, many of them the *apostoloi* of the Temple treasury, were going about plotting sedition. The Emperor Claudius, as a security measure, had expelled a great number of Jews from Rome. In Judea itself, one incident after another was inflaming the populace and crucifixions had become increasingly frequent. Messianists in particular, most of whom looked for a quite earthly and warlike Messiah to lead them in revolt against the Romans, were suspected of conspiracy. And Paul and his colleagues were, of course, Messianists.

This made them very objectionable to the soberer elements in the Jewish colonies who were afraid that they would attract the hostile attention of the authorities not only to themselves but to the entire Jewish community. Mere denial that they were secretly plotting a revolt against Rome was unconvincing; if they were Messianists they were almost certainly subversives. This was the view of the civil rulers too, who had learned to their sorrow how painful the consequences could be if they relaxed their vigilance in Jewish matters.

Paul and his fellow workers were therefore not often given the benefit of the doubt. Scholars increasingly believe, with Schonfield, that they "were ignorantly or deliberately identified with the Jewish nationalist agitators" who were fostering rebellion against the empire.[61] Certainly, to Jews whose real objection to Paul was his attitude to the Mosaic Law and his reception of Gentiles into "the true Israel," nothing could have been easier or a more obvious device for getting rid of him than denouncing him to the authorities as an insurrectionary agitator.

That there was much trouble with the priests and wardens of the pagan cults, or even with silversmiths such as Demetrius (Acts xix, 24) who made their living by selling idols, we well may doubt. The new movement as yet was far from strong enough to challenge the worship of the six-breasted Diana (Artemis) of the Ephesians. These stories, as one scholar gently puts it, "raise historical qualms."[62] The purpose of the Demetrius story with its riot fomented by the silversmiths and the subsequent pacification of the mob by a magistrate is to show how the civil authorities ideally should deal with riots against Christians at a much later time—the time that Acts was written (xix, 23-41).

To what kind of people did Paul take his gospel? Sometimes to rather substantial citizens like Lydia, the "seller of purple" in the Roman colony, Philippi (Acts xvi, 14, 15). Sometimes to fairly prosperous artisans like Aquila and his wife, Priscilla, who, when they had been expelled by Claudius from Rome, migrated to Corinth, where Paul, to earn his living, joined them in the craft of tentmaking (xviii, 2, 3). But undoubtedly it was more often the poor who received his gospel, those whom the Jews called *'amme ha-'aretz* (people of the land) and the Greeks *hoi polloi* (the many or the majority). The former, though Jews, were lax in their keeping of the Mosaic Law[63] and were thus particularly accessible to Paul's message, while the latter sometimes had no regard for law of any kind and were much in need of a gospel of salvation.

With many of these people Paul had his difficulties even in establishing ordinary standards of decent behavior. In Corinth in particular, where sexual vice of every kind flourished without hindrance, he has to rebuke the believers—who had become calloused by their environment—for their easygoing toleration of a particularly bad case of "fornication" (I Cor. v). He wants the believers to cease keeping company with "fornicators," which means not only severing their relationships with people of lax morals but also giving up friends who belong to cults where sex rites are practiced. From these same cults, of course, must have come some of his converts, and doubtless from those of them to which *hoi polloi* could afford to belong, in which a low social status encouraged a low order of morality.

It is evident that Paul had more success in his Aegean campaigns than in the earlier ones, although he could never be really confident that the newly founded communities would be loyal to his own leadership or that they would not stray from his gospel. To describe the conditions he had to meet, city by city, and the situations he was required to deal with in his letters would take up many pages and is beyond our purpose. What we need to see is the general nature of his campaigns, radiating out from Ephesus, which produced the first Gentile communities of believers which would later become Christian churches.

These communities were as different from that of Jerusalem as Paul's gospel was different from Peter's or James's. To this we shall come in the next section, but first we must note that it was this difference that was causing Paul ever-increasing trouble, so that when he returned to Antioch, perhaps in about 51 A.D., he was compelled to seek a determination of the issue through negotiations with James at Jerusalem.

As we saw when we inquired into this Jerusalem conference, there was no real settlement.* The evidence Paul produced for the acceptance of his converts by the Risen Jesus into the Messianic community was that they "had the Holy Spirit." The same ecstasy which had testified to the presence of the Spirit of Jesus with the Judaic believers had been conferred upon his Gentile communities. The latter were also "showing forth Jesus" by their way of life. This was not to be disputed. On the other hand, there was the Law and how could Gentiles really belong to the following of the Jewish Messiah and repudiate the Judaic regulations which were the sign of the Covenant? As we have seen, James and Paul came to no agreement. It is even doubtful whether the *full* measure of the divergence between Paul and the Jerusalem leaders was ever openly debated between them. Barnabas remained on Paul's side during the discussion, but later, when put to the test at Antioch, forsook him. How well had he understood Paul's real position? The fact was—though no one quite wanted to face it—that neither Barnabas nor any of the apostles had gone anything like as far as Paul in opening up the movement to the Gentiles.

The end of the conference was merely personal amiability—"the right hand of fellowship"—and an agreement by Paul to take up a collection for the Jerusalem community (Gal. ii, 9, 10). This we sufficiently discussed in our

* See p. 47.

initial study.* Paul was eager to do it and James apparently was more than willing to receive the money.

When Paul returned with Barnabas to Antioch, Peter soon followed (to escape arrest in Jerusalem) and upon the basis of the Jerusalem discussions, even though there had been no agreement, he joined with the Gentile believers in the common meals (or possibly the sacrament of bread and wine). Then came the messengers from James who, no matter what he would countenance in the communities founded by Paul around the Aegean, insisted that the Jewish and Gentile believers be segregated at Antioch.** For Paul this was a crucial test. If the Gentiles at Antioch were not eligible to join the Jewish believers in one united fellowship, their status was inferior. They did not belong to the true Israel. In this case his own converts were also outside the true Israel, which he could not concede without disowning the very heart of the gospel he had preached to them—salvation by faith and baptism into the Messianic community of the new Judaism in which there was "neither Jew nor Greek" but only a new creation in Christ Jesus. It was to this gospel that Paul had been commissioned by the Risen Lord himself and to deny it was to deny his apostleship.

Thus came the quarrel with Peter and never again did Paul set foot in Antioch. Undoubtedly, as an Antioch missionary he was dismissed. He was on his own now, isolated from the other apostles, doomed to increasing loneliness.

Paul returned to Ephesus. He had not been there long when he learned that Judaizers had undermined him in his congregations in Galatia. That this was instigated from Jerusalem we cannot be absolutely sure, but it seems all too likely that not only in Galatia but at Ephesus and in all

---

* See p. 51 f.

** Did James feel a special concern for Antioch because the believers there were a part of the Essenic society which had long been in communion with the Jerusalem Essenes that he superintended? Was this the basis of his authority outside of Judea? Jerusalem being the headquarters?

the Aegean congregations Jerusalem agents were opposing Paul. According to some scholars—a minority but not un-impressive in their argument—a systematic campaign was "devised and organized by James and directed by Peter."[64] But is this possible while at the same time Paul was raising a collection for the Jerusalem community?

In any case, Paul's situation was one of utmost anguish. These were the congregations that *he* had gathered, with untiring labor and at the risk of his life. For their sake he had been flogged and beaten with rods. By letter and by visit he went from one community to another exerting him-self beyond measure to restore them to the gospel he had preached. In doing this, we must remind ourselves, he was also beset by the synagogue Jews and the followers of the Baptist, though with the latter, judging from his letters, he may eventually have formed a more friendly relationship (I Cor. i, 11ff.). That he largely succeeded we may infer from his intention of going on to Rome. But this had to wait until he had carried his collection—perhaps in 53 or 54 A.D.—to the patriarchate at Jerusalem.

5. *The Later Message: "Christ the Redeemer"*

It was at Antioch that the believers were first called Christians (*Christianoi*), a name given them in derision (Acts xi, 26). As we know, *Christos* is merely a Greek trans-lation of the Hebrew *Mashiach,* which we pronounce *Messiah.* This would be well understood by Greek-speaking Jews. To them *Christos,* like *Messiah,* meant "anointed with oil," the allusion being to such ceremonial anointings as those of the Jewish kings and priests. The distinction of the "Awaited One" was that he surpassed all earlier "anointeds" in rank and significance and thus was *the* "Anointed." But to the Greek-speaking Gentiles who knew nothing of this, the word made no sense. They "anointed" with oil only for medication or "rubbing down" athletes.

So the word *Christianoi* as they applied it to the believers was intended as ridicule and meant something like "those who are rubbed with salve."* But like other names given by scoffers (such as "Quaker" and "Methodist"), the word *Christianoi* became in the end the accepted name of the movement and even a term of esteem.

To those who were first called by this name it meant only that they believed in a Messiah, and to some of them that the expected Messiah was the Risen Jesus. But to Paul from the beginning it meant far more. It is true that he can think of there being other Christs (*Christoi*) or even another Jesus (*Iēsous*), as we saw earlier, yet for him the two words *Iēsous Christos* are the distinctive name of *his* Messiah-Redeemer, just as they are for modern Christians in the form "Jesus Christ." Not that Paul's connotation was the same as that of modern Christians, of course, but to him as to them the emphasis was on the *person,* Jesus Christ, rather than upon the *office.* However easily he may think of other *Christoi* as concepts or as Messiahs that others may believe in, for him there is only one *Christos* who actually exists, his Lord and Savior, Jesus Christ.

This is perhaps the best way of indicating briefly what his later message was. We have already inquired into its sources and have seen something of how Paul achieved a synthesis of Jewish Messiah and pagan redeemer.** This we shall not repeat. But we shall note once more that to Paul, no matter how much pagan theology, sacramentalism, or ritual he absorbed into his thinking it was still a Judaic Messiah-Redeemer that he preached and that *to him,* however it may seem to us, what he was proclaiming was the new and universal Judaism that was the crown and culmination of the whole of Jewish history.[65]

How much the more tragic was it therefore that in his

---

* χριστός (*christos*) is from χρίω (*chriō*) which means *to be rubbed on,* as φάρμακα χριστά (*pharmaka christa*) or *salves.*

** Part Two, Chaps. I and II.

last campaigns even more than in his first, he was never-ceasingly contending with the Judaizers. To the latter, of course, he was a dangerous, pernicious heretic, betraying Jewish nationalism and subverting the true faith. Looking at it from the normative Jewish viewpoint, this was a just accusation. But to Paul it was sheer blindness and per-versity.

Much of his time had to be given to this conflict, both in personal campaigns and in his letters. His gospel itself is largely formulated in terms of it, particularly in Gala-tians. It was by faith, not by Law, that they were saved. They, the Gentile believers, are the true Israel, the chil-dren of Abraham. Circumcision means nothing; they are to be "in Christ, a new creation." But this is not his sole theme, even in Galatians. Christ must be "formed" in them, the Christ whom "the world has crucified unto him" and he "unto the world" (vi, 14).

He has by no means given up the Messianic expectation, but when he finds that some of the Thessalonians have stopped working and are living in idleness, waiting for the *parousia*, he tells them not to take leave of their senses, for those who will not work, neither shall they eat. Nor are they to listen to a "spirit-possessed" member who tells them that the coming of the Christ is at hand. Before the Christ can come, he continues (introducing ideas that he had not previously transmitted and perhaps had not him-self fully worked out until then), the Lawless Man, the Doomed One, Anti-Christ must be "revealed" (II Thess. *passim*).

With the Corinthians he takes up a wide variety of ques-tions, the resurrection of the dead being perhaps the out-standing one. There is a terrestrial "body" and also a celes-tial. It is the celestial one that is immortal "for flesh and blood cannot inherit the Kingdom of God." Here he thinks in Gnostic and mystery cult terms but adapted to Judaic theology. It is the "First Adam" that is the prototypal man and the Savior is the "Last Adam." Here we might note in passing that Christians who believe in the resurrection of the same body in which they pass their earthly lives would have shocked Paul profoundly. It was of the essence of his doctrine that the flesh (*sarx*) must perish as the flesh of Jesus did on the cross, carrying evil with it. The new body, although material, was not made of flesh (I Cor. xv).

It is in a letter to the Corinthians that he gives his formula of the Sacrament of the Lord's Supper which he "received of the Lord"—i.e., by special communication or vision (I Cor. xi, 23-26)—which is not at all the simple ceremony of Jewish usage, whether normative or Essenic, but a fully developed mystery religion ritual.

It is in Romans that his theology is most fully worked out, a remarkable letter in that it was sent to a community of believers that Paul had not founded and which, when he arrived in Rome as a prisoner, seems not to have existed —or at least it left Paul severely alone. In the letter, however, Paul is hoping that the Roman congregation will not only receive him warmly but will help him on his way to Spain (finance him?) (Rom. xv, 24, 28). This is one of the mysteries of the Pauline chronicle that must remain such: there is no satisfactory explanation of it. There are also a number of other ways in which the letter to the Romans poses difficult problems and it seems certain that as it comes to us it is a composite document only a part of which was originally addressed to a congregation in Rome.[66]

But it was in fetters that Paul was to go to Rome. His last campaigns were in the cities of the Aegean (and perhaps in some of the inland Asian cities—Hierapolis, Philadelphia, Sardis, Thyatira, Pergamum, and possibly others). We cannot follow his itineraries or know how many times each congregation was visited. Nor can we—and it is time to remind ourselves of this—completely understand Paul's gospel. Even though we could give a thousand pages to it instead of this brief outline, at the end we would have to confess that no modern mind has fully understood Paul. In many ways he remains an enigma, and more so to those who have studied him intensively than to those who have never discovered how darkly obscure are many of the problems to be solved.

But for our own study it is sufficient that we see that in his later missions he preaches his own full gospel, not merely of the coming of the Messiah but of salvation through his crucified and resurrected Savior, Jesus Christ, whose *gnosis* has been imparted to him by a special revelation, and with whom the believers are united in one *body* through faith and the sacraments, and by whom they are led through his *holy spirit*.

CHAPTER III

THE NARRATIVE COMPLETED

1. *The Call of Jerusalem*

Paul was well aware of the risk he took in visiting Jerusalem. In about 53 or 54 A.D. when he made this last visit, Jewish nationalism was running higher than ever and his offense against it had become insufferable. The *apostoloi* of the Temple treasury and the provocateurs who had been ranging through the empire now knew him well and had reported his "pro-Gentile" activities to their superiors at Jerusalem. The Zealots must also have known of him and, since they more than all others were impatient to begin the revolt against Rome, must have been deeply incensed against him.

As for the more moderate elements in high circles in Jerusalem—and among these we must count the leaders of the Pharisaic party whose realism and semipacifism disinclined them to insurrection against Roman rule—Paul as they saw him was a traitor to the Jewish faith. As the time draws near, he is not even confident that the collection he has taken up in the Aegean and Asian congregations will be well received by James and his community. He asks the Roman congregation to pray for him that he may be delivered from his enemies in Judea and that his "ministration" (the collection) "may be acceptable to the saints" at Jerusalem (Rom. xv, 31).

Nonetheless, to Jerusalem he is determined to go. He hopes somehow to plead his cause successfully and yet not compromise the independence of his apostleship. His need of recognition, although he will not acknowledge it, is great. Moreover, he could not admit himself to be an exile, no longer free to visit the Holy City. We must keep always in mind that *to himself* he was the most loyal of Jews and was giving to Judaism a new and vastly expanded significance.

If he could in any way make the Jerusalem visit harmonious, it would be serviceable to his cause. In his further campaigns he could mention that he had just returned from a conference with James and the patriarchate and there had been no trouble. On the contrary, they had received at his hands a large fund contributed by his congregations. If he could say this, it would tend to undermine the Judaizers.

For some reason, undisclosed by the composer of Acts, in his voyage to Judea Paul goes out of his way to omit a call at Ephesus. Evidently Ephesus had become too dangerous for him. He tells us—or seems to tell us: the passage is ambiguous—that he had once fought with wild beasts at Ephesus (I Cor. xv, 32). There is a strong tradition of his imprisonment there and he may narrowly have escaped execution. So that in the end, Ephesus, his second headquarters, was as unavailable to him as Antioch, his first. According to Acts, it was because he was in haste to get to Jerusalem that he did not stop at Ephesus (xx, 16) but since, also according to Acts, he sent for the Ephesian elders to come and confer with him at Miletus, two days' journey south of Ephesus, no time was saved. As Goguel concludes, "the compiler of Acts wanted to throw a veil over" the real reason for avoiding Ephesus.[67]

Paul's sorrowful speech of farewell to the elders in which he says that after his "departing, grievous wolves shall enter in among" them (xx, 29) and that some of themselves would forsake him is a prophecy after the event.[68] Here once more we have a speech by the composer of Acts, who knew what had happened at Ephesus and in the Asian churches after Paul's death. Nonetheless, we can well believe that Paul was uneasy. If the elders came down to Miletus to meet with him he was still *persona grata* with the Ephesian congregation but evidently not with the civil authorities. Or it may be that it was the Jews who had made Ephesus too perilous for him. Or both together.

Upon disembarkment at Caesarea, Paul is warned of the danger of going on to Jerusalem, and his traveling companions who had come with him to safeguard the money and to be witnesses of its transmittal to James try to dissuade him from completing the journey. But he is determined to go on and in a few days is received by James and the "elders" (there is no longer any mention of Peter or the original apostles) and, although Acts does not say so since it is the intention of the composer to suppress all mention of it, he hands over to James the collection. It must have been a moment of great satisfaction for Paul, in spite of his anxieties: he had promised this fund to James, he had raised it in his own congregations, he had now delivered it.

The circumstances of his arrest, as described in Acts, have been interminably debated. The composer is determined to show that Paul was innocent of any offense against either Judaism or the empire; he was the victim of Jewish fanaticism, one whom the Roman procurators, first Felix, then Festus, could convict of no crime and whom the unprejudiced Agrippa II could say might have been set at liberty if he had not appealed to Rome (xxvi, 31). We must keep always in mind the readership for which "Luke" was writing, half a century after the events he was describing, and that his purpose was to prove that Gentile Christianity was the true Judaism directly descended from a legally innocent *believing* Jewish movement at Jerusalem. It was always the *unbelieving* Jews who were the villains of the story.

Written for this polemical purpose, it is a story very difficult to reconstruct.[69] It has been suggested that Paul was arrested in the Temple because, as one who had abandoned his Judaic faith, he had no title to be there and was in fact committing an act of desecration of which Gentiles were warned by inscriptions on the Temple walls and for which the death penalty was prescribed. In Acts, the accusation is that Trophimus, an Ephesian, was taken into the sacred precincts by Paul, a mistaken charge based upon the circumstance that the two men had been seen together in the city streets (xxi, 29). But those scholars are surely right who regard this as an explanatory interpolation, an original marginal gloss, the equivalent of a modern footnote added by an editor.[70] All that we can be sure of is that something happened that caused Paul's arrest in the Temple.*

What the narrative tells us is that Paul, on the advice of James, paid the expense of four members of the community who had taken a Nazarite vow, he himself joining with them in the "purification," after which, on the seventh day their heads were to be shaved and the "offering offered" (unless the head-shaving came at the beginning of the seven days). The purpose of observing this ascetic rite was to prove Paul's fidelity to Jewish ritual in an extreme and dramatic way, and we must admit that Paul in his role of being "all things to all men" may possibly have fallen in with the suggestion.**

But it did not work. Before the seventh day was reached Paul was recognized in the Temple and a mob attacked him. He would doubtless have been killed then and there

---

* The inscription on the Temple walls is known from a stone found by Clermont-Ganneau near the end of the last century; it may be translated as follows: "No alien is to enter within the balustrade and enclosure around the holy place. Whoever is caught will be answerable for his own death, which will ensue."

** The vow was normally for thirty (not seven) days, so Paul may have taken it on his own initiative at the beginning of the voyage to Jerusalem.

had not the Roman tribune in the Tower of Antonia come to his rescue. The latter suspects him of being the Egyptian insurrectionary who had recently led a revolt which the Romans had suppressed though the Egyptian himself had escaped. Paul identifies himself as a Tarsian Jew and begs leave to speak to the people. The composer of Acts here introduces a speech of his own contriving and in his own style so that Paul can prove his faithful Judaism and the mob can cry out against him as soon as he says that he was commissioned to preach to the Gentiles. As Loisy points out, this speech is quite plainly an interpolation and at xxii, 23-24 we are back where we were before the speech at xxi, 34-35.[71]

We can be sure, however, that the Acts story is substantially correct in its report that the Sanhedrin demanded that Paul be handed over to its jurisdiction. Since Paul was a Jew, the Sanhedrin, the supreme Jewish Council, was well within its rights in making this demand, but Paul foresaw with perfect clearness what the verdict would be if the Council judged him: he would be sentenced to be stoned to death. So he took a desperate step: he declared himself a Roman citizen. At once his chains were taken off and he was ordered to be sent to Felix, the procurator, at Caesarea.

2. The Roman Citizen

That Paul was a Roman citizen is not to be doubted. But when and how did he become one? Perhaps we should believe Acts which has him declare that he acquired this citizenship by birth (xxii, 28). There were probably Tarsian Jews who were Roman citizens ever since the time of Pompey, who received Tarsian assistance which he may well have rewarded by conferring Roman citizenship. But how does this accord with Paul's having been a strict Jew in his early life, a "Pharisee of the Pharisees"? Did strict Jews accept citizenship in the empire they hated? What did they do about joining a Roman *tribe*—which was the only method of acquiring citizenship—since the *tribal* ritual involved a worship which to them was idolatry? Or was there a Jewish *tribe* which was allowed to use a ritual of Jehovah?

We cannot answer these questions. Perhaps we should reaffirm our earlier suggestion: that citizenship was conferred on Paul by the Cyprus proconsul, Sergius Paulus. But in this case—and the same argument applies if he was born a Roman—why did Paul permit himself to be three times "beaten with rods" (II Cor. xi, 25) when he might have escaped it by announcing that he was a Roman? (We are assuming that these beatings were later than the Cyprus visit and that Paul had not been in trouble with the civil authorities before the first campaigns reported in Acts.) How did one prove his Roman citizenship? We know from Seutonius that there were severe penalties for false claims to citizenship: "Those who usurped the privileges of Roman citizenship he [the Emperor Claudius] executed in the Esquiline field" (Claudius, XXV, 9). But how, without sending to the Tarsian municipal authorities for a transcript of the record, did Paul's captors confirm that he was a Roman? Were there passports?

We can answer none of these questions. We cannot even be sure that Paul did not purchase his citizenship before leaving Corinth as insurance against trouble with the Jews when he reached Jerusalem. There is a reasonable doubt, of course, that he could have afforded the large sum needed, although Felix, the procurator, according to Acts, believed that Paul had considerable funds and might give him a bribe (xxiv, 26).*

However all this may be, it is plausible that Paul had

---

* That Paul was not penniless, even when he arrived in Rome, seems to be corroborated by his having the means to pay the rent (for two years) of "his own hired house" (Acts xxviii, 30).

concealed his Roman citizenship until he needed to declare it to save his life. Perhaps he had been in this extremity more than once.* In any case, the assertion of his right to be tried under Roman law by the procurator had now completely cut him off from his people. It had also cut him off from the Jerusalem believers, apparently, for there is no sign that they did anything to help him. (The composer of Acts would eagerly have included any story of help from James if there had been any.)

Felix heard the Sanhedrin's case against Paul, then merely adjourned it, keeping Paul in custody. He was not closely confined, however, and his few remaining friends were free to come and see him. To Felix this was doubtless a quite satisfactory arrangement: it kept Paul from making trouble and it kept a Roman citizen out of the hands of the Sanhedrin. What was the charge against Paul? At first it must have been sacrilege and heresy and it would have been this again if Paul had been handed over to the Sanhedrin. But before the procurator he was accused of being "a mover of insurrections among all the Jews throughout the world" (xxiv, 5) and thus the charge was treason.

Felix evidently doubted that Paul was a *provocateur*— or he may have asked himself what Jew (in some degree) was not? During this very period when Paul was in custody in Caesarea, the Jews of the city were trying to curtail the civil rights of the Gentiles (Caesarea had been rebuilt by Herod the Great as a Hellenist city) and riots had broken out. Although married to a Jewish princess (whom he had

* The story in Acts xvi, however, where he and Silas allow themselves to be severely flogged and imprisoned and then, when they are told that they are at liberty to leave, refuse to do so until the magistrates themselves come to release them because the magistrates have inflicted an illegal punishment upon them—*both* Silas (!) and Paul being Roman citizens—is quite incredible. The time for declaring Roman citizenship was before the flogging, not afterward for the trivial purpose of embarrassing the magistrates; and indeed, this story raises the question of Paul's Roman citizenship afresh. If he was flogged at Philippi, why had he not prevented it by insisting upon his legal rights? In Philippi particularly, such rights would have been respected, for Philippi was a Roman colony.

persuaded to divorce her former husband), Felix was not popular in Judea. His suppression of the fanatical Zealots, who were eager for war against Rome, had resulted in the rise of the *Sicarii*, "dagger-men" who had so cultivated the art of stealthy assassination that no Roman or Roman-sympathizer ever felt safe. Even the high priest, Jonathan, was not immune but fell to *Sicarii* knives because of his supposedly pro-Roman policy. (There is also a bewildering tradition that Felix hired the *Sicarii* for this murder!)

Under such conditions, Paul's status was truly precarious. The Jews hated him as a traitor to his nation, the Romans were not sure that he was not a traitor to the empire. He was a Messianist, and although his Messiah was supposedly in heaven, no Roman ruler could overlook the possibility that what was described to him as a heavenly Messiah might suddenly turn out to be a rebel "Deliverer" on earth.

To what extent did Paul, in the various hearings, plead that he was still a loyal Jew? That he described himself as still a Pharisee, as Acts says he did, is beyond belief (xxiii, 6). As Windisch correctly sums up this matter, "If Paul could have behaved as Acts represents him here, and then [later] write the sharp invective (Phil. iii) against Pharisaism, he would have been a hypocrite." And he goes on to say that reconciling the Paul of the letters with these Acts passages, besides being impossible, is insulting to Paul since it means that he was "denying his convictions in order to save his life."[72] Yet, without going as far as Acts says he did, Paul may well have made out the best case he could for his Judaism.

When Felix completed his term as procurator and was succeeded by Festus (57 or 58 A.D.) the Sanhedrin made another application to have Paul placed under its jurisdiction. Festus, whose natural wish must have been to begin his administration on the best terms possible with the Jewish Council, called Paul before him and after a short interrogation was ready to yield to the Sanhedrin's demand. That he asked Paul whether he would go up with him to Jerusalem "and there be judged of these things before me" (xxv, 9) is impossible; Paul had no choice in such a matter if it was Festus who was going to judge him, and he could just as easily give his verdict at Caesarea as at Jerusalem. What we have in this passage is the disguised fact that Festus was surrendering Paul to the Sanhedrin.

Only one recourse was left. "I appeal," said Paul, "unto Caesar!"

3. *"Unto Caesar Shalt Thou Go"*

Paul's appeal was a difficult one to refuse. The main question was one of jurisdiction. Should a Jew who was a Roman citizen be tried by a Jewish council against his will? But there were other questions. Of what force was a Jewish charge of heresy when made against one who was entitled to be judged under Roman law? Was there any truth in the accusation of treasonable activities against Rome? The matter was not simple. It was well to submit it to the supreme tribunal.

How much hope Paul had of being declared innocent at a trial in Rome we can only surmise. There was no want of Jewish influence in the imperial capital. Nor was Roman sensitivity to Jewish questions any less there than in Judea. Increasingly there was the fear of Jewish revolt not only in Palestine but throughout the empire. If any color could be given to the charge that Paul was an insurrectionary the death sentence would be automatic. On the other hand, if in Roman eyes Paul seemed to be accused by the more responsible elements in his own nation of some gross offense against Judaism, or if he was believed to be fomenting disorder among the Jews, the inclination to grant jurisdiction to the Sanhedrin would be very strong.

Paul must have known all this. But if the prospect was

dim in Rome it was completely hopeless in Jerusalem. The appeal to Caesar was all that was left. Festus too must have realized that Paul's chances in Rome were not likely to be much better than they had been in Caesarea. But his appeal was lawful. He was a Roman citizen charged with offenses for which, if guilty, he must forfeit his life. He was entitled to exhaust his legal resources. Festus consulted briefly with his advisors. In a few moments he turned back to Paul. "Thou hast appealed," said Festus, "unto Caesar: unto Caesar shalt thou go."

4. *Last Journey*

Once Paul had decided to carry his case to the imperial tribunal, the matter was ended so far as Festus was concerned. The story of the further interrogation in the presence of Agrippa II, Bernice, his queen, "with great pomp . . . with the chief captains and the principal men of the city" (xxv, 23) is, in the forthright words of the Abbé Loisy, "mere editorial padding intended to provide a setting for a new speech by Paul in his own defense and a new testimony to his innocence in which the Herodian prince backs up the Roman procurator."[73]

The statement placed in the mouth of Agrippa to the effect that Paul could have been set free if he had not appealed to Caesar (xxvi, 31) is quite impossible. If Agrippa had wanted Paul to have his liberty he could easily have arranged it. What we have in this invented incident is the effort of the composer of Acts to dignify the status of Paul as a highly important prisoner in whom even royalty had taken an interest. The tone of the remark attributed to Agrippa does, however, let us know that Paul was not eventually set free, just as does the speech composed for him in his conference with the Ephesian elders at Miletus.

In the story of the voyage to Italy, Acts returns to the "we" source, as we noted in our study of the traditional narrative,* and we are given a stirring, largely eyewitness account of the long and hazardous trip to Italy.

Upon arrival at the port of Puteoli, we are told that Paul "found brethren" (xxviii, 14), with whom he and his friends who were with him "tarried seven days," a rather remarkable proceeding for a prisoner under guard and implying that the patrol that had Paul in custody was exceedingly indulgent to him. We are also told that "the brethren" came from Rome as far as "the Market of Appius and the Three Taverns" to meet the captive apostle, which brought him much encouragement (xxviii, 15). Who these brethren were we are not told, and perhaps could not have been told, since they were doubtless created by the composer of Acts so that there would be something of a procession when Paul entered Rome. The composer, however, cannot entirely conceal from us the true nature of things. There is no welcome for Paul from any community of believers; only a gathering of Jews to whom Paul is supposed to have said that he has nothing of which to accuse his nation and that "because of the hope of Israel" he is "bound with this chain" (xxviii, 19, 20). That this is the Paul of the letters speaking is entirely beyond belief. He had been wont to accuse his nation both freely and frequently and he was the apostle to the Gentiles, not the representative of "the hope of Israel."

The truth is that Paul came to Rome, a forlorn and tragic figure, and so far as the believers were concerned was received, to quote one scholar, "with marked indifference."[74] The realities of his last days are most reliably indicated by the tradition repeated in the Second Letter to Timothy. Few scholars believe that this letter was written by Paul.[75] But its writer may very well have been drawing upon accurate information in letting us know that at his trial Paul was completely forsaken (iv, 16), and that in order to find him in the prison to which he was committed after he was

* See pp. 54; 82 f.

no longer allowed (or could not afford) his private lodging with its armed guard, his friend Onesiphorus has to make a diligent search, for which Paul is grateful, as he also is that Onesiphorus was not ashamed of his chain (i, 16, 17). Evidently the community of believers to which Onesiphorus would naturally have made his way when he reached Rome, and from which he would have expected information about Paul, had completely abandoned him and did not even know where he was. This must have been near the end, for in Philippians he describes his situation (doubtless a year or so earlier) as much less desolate, having found "brethren" even in the Pretorian Guard ("Caesar's household"—iv, 21).

Much has been written about Paul and Peter perishing together in the Neronian persecution (64 A.D.), Paul by decapitation as befitted a Roman citizen, Peter by crucifixion. But nothing is known. The Catholic critic, Duchesne, expresses the opinion that the tradition usually maintained by scholars of his communion that the church in Rome was founded by Peter "lacks sufficient foundation to win the assent of history."[76] Many Protestant scholars would fully agree with him. Yet the tradition remains—as a tradition. For ourselves, we have no basis upon which to pronounce upon it.

What was the drift of Paul's mind as he saw the end coming? What was his hope for his congregations? The fact is that from the standpoint of our modern thought-world, Paul had no reason whatever for believing that his work would endure. "All they that are in Asia are turned away from me," says the Timothy tradition (i, 15). But his thinking was not ours; his thought was cast in an altogether different mold. "I have fought the good fight, I have finished the course, I have kept the faith: henceforth there is laid up for me the crown of righteousness which the Lord, the righteous Judge, shall give to me at that day: and not only to me but to all that have loved his appearing" (iv, 7,8).

Paul believed his own gospel. There was no room in it for despair. In chains, he is still the apostle to the Gentiles. In his dungeon, dictating to an amanuensis, he is still preaching: "Rejoice in the Lord always: again I say, Rejoice. In nothing be anxious; but in everything by prayer and supplication and with thanksgiving, let your requests be made known unto God. And the peace of God, which passeth understanding, shall guard your hearts and your thoughts in Christ Jesus" (Phil. iv, 4-7).

PAUL AND CHRISTIAN ORIGINS

1. *The Beginnings of a New Religion*

However much Paul thought of the gospel he was preaching as the culmination of Judaism, it was in fact a new departure in religion. Judaic in inspiration and to a great extent in composition, it was nevertheless Mediterranean rather than Palestinian and its concept of the Christ as the Son of God was Greek. So also was its modus of salvation. In the mind of Paul, the rabbinic thinking with which he had begun and the Nazorean elements he had acquired were cast in a Hellenistic mold and the result was not a new Judaism but a universal faith: not the Messianic hope of his nation but Gentile Christianity.

While Paul did not foresee that he was founding a church in our sense of that word but looked for the fulfilment of his gospel in the reign of Jesus, the Savior-Messiah who would soon appear, he nevertheless did found a church and provided the distinctive basis of its sacramental cultus and theology.

Much was still to come before Christianity had clearly defined itself as a new religion but in Paul we see already the beginnings of the Great Synthesis. In the words of Johannes Weiss, "all the spiritual currents of the time have met in him: Old Testament prophetic piety and rabbinical Judaism; Hellenistic-Jewish enlightenment and Stoic ethics; syncretistic Hellenistic mysticism and dualistic, ascetical Gnosticism."[1] To this must be added whatever he had derived from the early believers at Jerusalem and the movement led by Stephen; whatever he had absorbed from the Jewish apocalyptic and didactic literature and the Scriptures of the Essenes; also the Nazorean eschatology— the proclamation of the end of the age and the reign of the Messiah as preached by John the Baptist and Jesus; and finally, the conviction that in Jesus, crucified and risen, the new age had already begun and that for all who had faith, even now (not after the Messiah had come) there was salvation.

To Klausner, who sees Paul from the standpoint of Jewish scholarship, this synthesis in the apostle's thought was not based upon a comparable harmony in his inner life. "His soul was torn between Palestinian Pharisaism . . . and Jewish Hellenism—and in a certain measure also pagan Hellenism," he writes, but in any case it was Paul who was "the cause of the complete overthrow of historic Judaism" in the Gentile world of the first century.[2] This judgment, quite valid from the Jewish standpoint, is put a little differently by Christian scholars, as for example, Knox, who says that it was "Paul more than any other man who was responsible for the fact that Christianity was not a Jewish sect but an independent body with an independent life."[3]

As a completed achievement this did not occur within Paul's lifetime. On the contrary, after his death the congregations he had founded seem to have half-forgotten him. It was the rediscovery of his letters, stimulated by the publication of Luke-Acts, that brought him his greatest triumphs.[4] From this time forward all Christian writings would be strongly marked by his influence and Christian theology would be based upon his thinking. However much Peter might be exalted in the eventual *mythos,* it was not in his mind or in that of any Palestinian that the new religion had taken shape: in the development of Christianity the decisive personality was Paul.

Not even the identification of the Pauline *corpus* with the dangerous campaign of the heretic, Marcion, could shake Paul's dominance. Marcion, in the middle of the second century, had prepared an edited collection of Paul's letters which he called the *Apostolicon* and a revised version of Luke's gospel which he called "the" *Gospel,* upon the basis of which he attempted to discredit the Old Testament and detach Christianity from its Jewish origin and from the Jewish God, Jehovah. From his Gnostic standpoint, Marcion saw Jehovah as the Creator God who had brought the world under sin and under the Law that condemned sin, and it was not he but the Supreme God who had sent his Son to be crucified for man's salvation. This, Marcion argued, was Paul's theology as revealed in his letters, a contention for which he argued so persuasively that his adherents became numerous.

This identification of Paul with Marcion heresy would surely have reduced his influence upon more orthodox thinking if it had been possible to reduce it; but the fact was that there was no alternative to Paul unless the Church were to change its character drastically and give up its tradition and its history. So the church fathers had no option but to repudiate Marcion and at the same time defend Paul from Marcionite interpretations, which meant in the end a still further advance in Pauline influence.

It was in its struggle against heresies that the church defined itself, so that at last it was neither a new Judaism nor a Gnostic sect nor a mystery religion, though all these elements had entered into its composition. But the beginning of the development was itself a heresy, and the great heretic who was responsible for it was the man who was rejected not only by rabbinical Judaism but in the end by the New Covenanters themselves: the Apostle Paul.

2. *The Church and the Empire*

The inner causes of the triumph of Christianity over the Roman Empire have long been debated. What was it that the new religion supplied that nothing else did and which the empire in all its might could not successfully resist?

We know of the spiritual emptiness and formalism of the imperial rites. As long ago as the beginning of the second century B.C., the senate had so little real respect for the religious ritual it maintained that in annoyance at having its proceedings interrupted while the consuls officiated at the propitiatory observances which followed an earthquake, it ordained that only one earthquake was allowed to be reported on any given day![5] By the first Christian century, official Roman religion was no more than a shadow, and as we saw earlier in our study, Caesar worship was instituted in the hope of supplying something more substantial. But it failed.

It is not farfetched to suppose that Judaism could have captured the Roman Empire if it had not been for the nationalism that was inseparable from it. Indeed, this in a measure is what happened in the triumph of Christianity, although we must emphasize the qualifying clause "in a measure" since Christianity was not merely Judaism without its nationalism but a fusion of its Judaic core with all the other elements that had entered into its composition.

Mithraism might have become the dominant religion if it had been less military and had made more room for women; in this case, no small number of its characteristics would have been identical with those of Christianity, though of course it would have had neither Paul nor Jesus.

The intense struggle of the Church with the Gnostic sects proves that here, too, were viable alternatives; one or other of the mystery religions might have become ascendant—or the Hermetic faith, or a synthesis of these movements considerably different from the synthesis achieved by Christianity. But none of these things happened. The alternatives were all either overcome by the Church or absorbed into it.

Or at least this is true in major matters. It is easy to forget that pagan beliefs and practices tenaciously hung on for many centuries, surviving side by side with the Christian ones. Isaac of Antioch (fifth century) complains that both clergy and laity alike, instead of invoking "the blessings of the saints, lo, they carry about the incantations of the magicians; and instead of the holy cross, lo, they carry the books of devils . . . one carries it on his head, another round his neck, and a child carries about devil's names and comes [to church]."[6] In such matters also as calling the "Lord's Day" the "Day of the Sun" (Mithraic), and in Easter observance and in numerous points of ritual and symbol, pagan and Christian dualism continued for a long while before the Christian image was finally stamped upon them.

Nonetheless, in the main, in spite of all the persecutions and the attempts to stamp it out, Christianity had triumphed by the time of Constantine (325 A.D.). One reason for it was undoubtedly its universalism, a conception which had already won at least theoretical acceptance. Seneca could write to his brother, Gallio, in 52 A.D., "I know my country is the world"[7] and Epictetus (c. 90) was soon to write, "If what philosophers say of the kinship of God and men be true, what remains for me to do but as Socrates did; never, when asked one's country to answer, 'I am an Athenian or a Corinthian,' but 'I am a citizen of the world.' "[8]

Besides its universalism, which it owed chiefly to Paul, Christianity had the immense advantage of having inherited Jewish monotheism, a high conception of one God in a world that was wearying of its idolatries. But would this monotheism have won such wide acceptance if it had not carried with it the Redeemership of Jesus, which was not a Jewish conception except to the extent that it was a Jew who first developed it—again the Apostle Paul? Here we have perhaps the precise combination of Judaic and Gentile theology that the peoples of the Mediterranean area were ready to receive as meeting their needs. With the worship of one God came also salvation from sin and death through the one God's Son, the crucified and risen Savior.

But besides appealing to the mind and exalting the spirit, the new religion appealed powerfully to the heart. It was a religion of love. This was so whether it was Pauline or the Jerusalem community. It must be traced to the Essenic sects which, besides the high ethical standards which they inculcated and which Christianity took over, relied upon love as the solvent of conflicts between man and his neighbor and as the supreme ethical motivation. It was this love that Jesus preached and invoked in his followers. It was not *erōs* (desire), or even *philos* (affection), but *agapē* (spiritual love), a kind of love for which no word existed in classical Greek but which was expressed by *agapē* in New Testament times and carried the sense of unselfish benevolence and sympathetic insight as well as personal fondness or affection. *

It cannot be said, unfortunately, that this or any kind of love was always evident in the controversies of the theologians. Nor was there any lack of power-hungry bishops in the developing Church, or of domineering personalities. Nevertheless, this love of which Paul so frequently speaks in his letters and to which (in spite of intervals of very human hostility and even fiery anger) he gave so much room in his own life, was an important element in early Christianity.

So was the dignity of the individual person, for he was the child of God, the beloved of the Savior, Christ Jesus.

* These Greek words do not have precise English equivalents and their shades of meaning vary with the context. Ἔρως (*erōs*) is not by any means used only for sex-love but, e.g., for the love of beauty; there is φῐλανθρωπία (*philanthropia*) for a general friendliness to all mankind; and ἀγάπη (*agapē*) can have other meanings than those given above, but what it meant in Christian usage is well conveyed by Paul's famous poem in I Cor. xiii.

As such he was a brother of all other Christians, a member of a communion of souls all of whom had the same value in the sight of God. Inconsistent with Christian love was the belief in retribution for the wicked, either in a future life or on earth after the *parousia* of the Savior-Messiah. But this kind of inconsistency, whatever it may be in logic has long persisted in life, and the thought that the injustices of the earthly dispensation would be redressed in the heavenly cannot have been unattractive, particularly to the impoverished and oppressed.

With all this to offer, Christianity made rapid progress, and because of the extreme fidelity of its believers to their faith, many of whom became martyrs rather than compromise their salvation "in Christ," the empire soon recognized that although the Church had no military weapons it had a "might" of a new and extremely menacing quality against which Rome might pit her strength in vain. As Gilbert Murray phrases it, "Such a movement brought union among the oppressed and at the same time roused terror in society generally" because it did two things, both expressive of its noblest qualities: "It represented the cry of the poor in a suffering and harshly administered world, and it proclaimed a great, if temporary, liberation of the human mind by its wholesale denial of false gods and idolatrous pietisms."[9]

And thus Paul, who thought he was proclaiming the new and universal Judaism established by Christ Jesus, his Messiah-Savior, had in fact founded a universal church against which the empire would strive in vain. In the words of Loisy, "As the third century unfolded, Roman paganism more and more came to resemble a vast hoarding behind which the Christian religion was gradually being built up."[10] Soon the hoarding would collapse by its own weight and reveal the triumph of Christianity.

In his prison cell awaiting execution Paul had no way of knowing how marvelous was his victory; but not only had he vanquished the Sanhedrin and the Judaizers who had charged him with treason to his nation: he had defeated the Roman Empire!

Those who look to miracles as the foundation of their religion, thus basing their faith upon what in the end their intelligence must always question, might well consider how little they would lose if they gave up miracles and contemplated in its full, astonishing extent, the wondrous way of history.

3. *Farewell to the First Christian*

We can learn a good deal about Paul and, in a measure, we can understand his work. But we cannot really know his mind or recapture his thinking, even though we have his words. Only the superficial student will believe otherwise. The more thoroughly we go into the Pauline concepts, the more we know that his mind lived in *his* world and that the modern mind can only partly penetrate it.

Paul was not consistent. No original thinker ever is. How he could believe in all the things he did at one and the same time is a mystery to us. There is much that we can never know. Yet of what happened we can have clear glimpses; and we can be sure that Paul was the most important factor in making events shape themselves as they did.

Whether he betrayed Judaism is a question that can be debated but never settled. It depends entirely upon the point of view. That he betrayed Jesus, though often charged, is a senseless accusation. There were no circumstances in which he could have served Jesus the Galilean other than he did. To say that he "let down" the teaching of Jesus is to forget the 13th of First Corinthians. And it must be remembered that Jesus, in his own view of his mission, was the Jewish Messiah. As the world viewed it, the mission of Jesus failed. He was crucified. But in the fervent faith of Paul the crucifixion was itself the moment of mankind's salvation and Jesus the triumphant Savior.

The utter dedication of Paul to his work and the immense suffering he was willing to endure in its performance are beyond question. He asks the Corinthians—a little self-consciously—whether, since others are boasting, he too may boast a little. We have quoted his words before; we quote them again in concluding. "Are they Hebrews?" he asks. "So am I. Are they Israelites? So am I. Are they the seed of Abraham? So am I. Are they ministers of Christ? I more. In labors more abundantly, in stripes above measure. In deaths oft. Of the Jews five times received I forty stripes save one. Thrice was I beaten with rods, once was I stoned, thrice I suffered shipwreck, a night and a day have I been in the deep; in journeyings often, in perils of rivers, in perils of robbers, in perils from my countrymen, in perils from Gentiles, in perils of the city, in perils in the wilderness, in perils in the sea, in perils among false brethren, in labor and travail, in watchings often, in hunger and thirst, in fastings often, in cold and nakedness. And besides all those things which are without, there is that which presseth in upon me daily: anxiety for all the churches" (II Cor. xi, 22-28).

Who can read this chronicle and not be moved? Who can say that this man—no matter how by modern standards we evaluate his work—ever let anybody down? In considering his poem on love (I Cor. xiii), commentators have often called it an interpolation. But no one who tries to live for a while in Paul's world, following his travels, pondering his thought, trying to enter into his life as a Jew, as a Greek, as an apostle of the Christ he loved with his whole soul, can accept any such thesis. The poem on love is not an interpolation. It is the self-portraiture of supreme insight as Paul extended himself in his labors and grew in his comprehension. It came out of his life as he lived it. It is the distilled essence of what he had learned in toil and tears and the bloody sweat of tortured flesh and anguish of the spirit.

Though he has the tongues of men and of angels, the gift of prophecy, the command of all knowledge, the faith that moves mountains; though he bestows his goods to feed the poor, gives his body to be burned—it is nothing! All of it! Nothing! For what avails in the end is love, and it is love alone that "prevaileth."

Here indeed he is "neither Jew nor Greek," but just *man* breathing deeply of the breath of God, and it might be well if all men, no matter what their faith—or for that matter, if they have none—would come even to the outer rim of this tremendous comprehension!

And so we watch him, man of controversy, center of storm after storm, toiling up the river beds of the Taurus mountains, waiting through the night to be rescued from the perilous sea, baring his back to the whip and the rod, falling before the stones that are flung upon him—and then, in the dark hours while he rests somewhere, wondering about his congregations, feeling the burden press down upon him, his "anxiety for all the churches."

We can see how he learned about love. And though in the mists of that ancient time so much has vanished and we shall never know its shape or test its substance, we can see what it was that lifted one man above others. Something there is that "beareth all things, believeth all things, hopeth all things, endureth all things"—and it is this alone that "never faileth." For faith is mighty to prevail, and hope is a light that no darkness can ever put out, but the final victory is not in either of them. Greater than both is love.

BIBLIOGRAPHY

General:

The Beginnings of Christianity, F. J. Foakes Jackson and Kirsopp Lake, London & New York: Macmillan, 1920-1933, 5 vols.

The Birth of Christianity, Maurice Goguel, trans. from the French by H. C. Snape, New York: Macmillan, 1954.

The History of Primitive Christianity, Johannes Weiss, trans. from the German by F. C. Grant & others, New York: Wilson-Erickson, 1937, 2 vols.

The Birth of the Christian Religion, Alfred Loisy, trans. from the French by L. P. Jacks, London: George Allen & Unwin, Ltd. New York: Macmillan, 1948.

Christian Beginnings (Parts I and II), Morton S. Enslin, New York: Harper, 1938 (Torchlight Edition, 1956).

The Beginnings of the Christian Church, Hans Lietzmann, trans. from the German by B. L. Woolf, New York: Scribners, 1937.

Christian Beginnings, F. C. Burkitt, London-Univ. Press, 1924.

Primitive Christianity In Its Contemporary Setting, Rudolf Bultmann, trans. from the German by R. H. Fuller, New York: Meridian, 1956.

Studies In Early Christianity, S. J. Case, New York & London: The Century Co., 1928.

Paul and His Interpreters, Albert Schweitzer, trans. from the German by W. Montgomery, New York: Macmillan, 1912 & 1948.

The Mysticism of Paul the Apostle, Albert Schweitzer, trans. from the German by W. Montgomery, New York: Henry Holt & Co., 1931.

The Life of St. Paul, F. J. Foakes Jackson, New York: Liveright, 1926.

St. Paul and the Church of the Gentiles, W. L. Knox, Cambridge: Univ. Press, 1939.

From Jesus to Paul, Joseph Klausner, trans. from the German by W. F. Stinespring, New York: Macmillan, 1943.

Contemporary Thinking About Paul. Edited by Thomas S. Kepler, New York: Abingdon-Cokesbury, 1950.

253

The Jew of Tarsus, Hugh J. Schonfield, New York: Macmillan, 1947.

Myth, Magic and Morals, F. C. Conybeare, London (1910) & Boston: Beacon Press, 1925.

The Mission and Expansion of Christianity in the First Three Centuries, Adolph Harnack, trans. from the 2nd German edition by James Moffatt, New York: Putnam, 1908. (4th German edition, Leipzig: Hinrichs, 1923.)

The Primitive Church, B. H. Streeter, New York: Macmillan, 1930.

New Testament:

The Beginnings of Christianity, Jackson & Lake: *supra*.

The Origins of the New Testament, Alfred Loisy, trans. from the French by L. P. Jacks, New York: Macmillan, 1950.

An Introduction to the New Testament, Edgar J. Goodspeed, Chicago: Univ. of Chicago Press, 1937.

The Literature of the Christian Movement, Morton S. Enslin, New York: Harper, 1938 (Part III of *Christian Beginnings*).

The Authentic New Testament, H. J. Schonfield, London: Dobson, 1956.

The Vocabulary of the Greek Testament, J. H. Moulton and G. Milligan, Grand Rapids, Mich.: W. B. Erdmans, 1950.

A Jewish Understanding of the New Testament, Samuel Sandmel, Cincinnati: Hebrew Union College Press, 1956.

A Fresh Approach to the New Testament and Early Christian Literature, Martin Dibelius, New York: Scribner, 1936.

The Making of Luke-Acts, H. J. Cadbury, New York: Macmillan, 1927.

Varieties of New Testament Religion, Ernest F. Scott, New York: Scribner, 1943.

The Judaic Background:

Introduction to the Old Testament, Robert H. Pfeiffer, New York: Harper, 1941 & 1948.

Judaism in the First Centuries of the Christian Era, George F. Moore, Cambridge: Harvard Univ. Press, 1927-30, 3 vols.

The Messianic Idea in Israel, Joseph Klausner, trans. from the Hebrew by W. F. Stinespring, New York: Macmillan, 1955.

Paul and Rabbinic Judaism, W. D. Davies, London: S.P.C.K., 1948.

Religious Development Between the Old and New Testaments, R. H. Charles, New York: Henry Holt & Co., 1913.

History of New Testament Times, with an Introduction to the Apocrypha, Robert H. Pfeiffer, New York: Harper, 1949.

The Jewish World in the Time of Jesus, Charles Guignebert, New York: E. P. Dutton & Co., 1939.

The Jews and Judaism During the Greek Period, W. O. E. Oesterley, London: S.P.C.K., 1941.

Studies in Pharisaism and the Gospels, Israel Abrahams, Cambridge: Camb. Univ. Press, 1924, 2 vols.

Judaism and Christianity, W. O. E. Oesterley, H. Loewe & E. J. Rosenthal, New York: Macmillan, 1937.

The Jewish Antecedents of the Christian Sacraments, Frank S. B. Gavin, New York: Macmillan, 1928.

Also Jackson & Lake, vol. I; Enslin, Bultmann, &c., *supra.*

The Hellenistic Background:

Paideia: The Ideals of Greek Culture, Werner Jaeger, trans. from the German by G. Highet, Oxford: University Press, 1945, 3 vols.

Alexander the Great, W. W. Tarn, Cambridge: University Press, 1948, 2 vols.

Cambridge Ancient History Series, vols. 6 & 7, Cambridge: Univ. Press, 1927.

Hermetica, W. Scott, Oxford: Univ. Press, 1924, 4 vols.

Forerunners and Rivals of Christianity, Francis Legge, Cambridge: Univ. Press, 1915, 2 vols.

The Mystery Religions and Christianity, S. Angus, London: John Murray, and New York: Scribner's, 1925.

Pagan Regeneration, H. R. Willoughby, Chicago: Univ. Press, 1929.

Relation of Paul to the Mystery Religions, H. A. A. Kennedy, London: Hodder & Stoughton, 1913.

Paganism to Christianity in the Roman Empire, W. W. Hyde, Phila.: Univ. of Penn. Press, 1946.

The Golden Bough, James G. Frazer, abridged edition, London & New York: Macmillan, 1925.

Five Stages of Greek Religion, Gilbert Murray. Oxford: Univ. Press, 1925 (New York: Columbia Univ. Press, 1930).

Prolegomena to the Study of Greek Religion, Jane Harrison, New York: Meridian, 1955.

The Greek Way to Western Civilization, Edith Hamilton, New York: Norton, 1930; & New American Library (Mentor), 1948.

Hellenistic Civilization, W. W. Tarn, London: Arnold, 1927; revised 1952.

Hellenistic Religions: The Age of Syncretism, F. C. Grant, New York: Liberal Arts Press, 1953.

Gnosticism, Robert M. Grant, New York: Liberal Arts Press, 1957.

Some Hellenistic Elements in Primitive Christianity, W. L. Knox, London: Milford, 1944.

Fragments of a Faith Forgotten, G. R. S. Mead, London: Theosophical Pub. Soc., 1907.

The Influence of Greek Ideas on Christianity, Edwin Hatch, New York: Harper, 1957.

Miscellaneous:

The Apocrypha and Pseudepigrapha of the Old Testament in English, R. H. Charles, Oxford: Clarendon Press, 1913.

The Apocrypha (King James Version), Edited by M. Komroff, New York: Tudor Press, 1946.

The Apostolic Fathers, trans. E. J. Goodspeed, New York: Harper, 1950.

The Apostolic Fathers, trans. Kirsopp Lake, London: Heinemann, 1914.

The Apocryphal New Testament, trans. M. R. James, Oxford: Univ. Press, 1924.

The Decline and Fall of the Roman Empire, Edward Gibbon, Milman Edition, New York: Harper, 1850.

The Dead Sea Scrolls, Millar Burrows, New York: Viking, 1955.

The Jewish Sect of Qumran and the Essenes, A. Dupont-Sommer, trans. from the French by R. D. Barnett, New York: Macmillan, 1955.

The Dead Sea Scriptures, Theodor H. Gaster, New York: Doubleday, 1956.

The Meaning of the Dead Sea Scrolls, A. Powell Davies, New York: New American Library (Signet-Key), 1956.

The Birth of the Gospel, W. B. Smith. Edited by Addison Gulick, New York: Philosophical Library, 1957 ("The Primitive Allegory of the Jesus").

The Cities of St. Paul, St. Paul the Traveller & Roman Citizen, The Church in the Roman Empire, &c., by Sir W. M. Ramsay are older standard works of limited value to the modern student but are occasionally useful. London: various dates.

The New Testament Background: Selected Documents, C. K. Barrett, New York: Macmillan, 1957. For Greek and Latin literature not included in Barrett, consult the *Loeb Classical Library,* or if this superb collection is not available, try the *Oxford Library of Translations*.

The writings of Justin Martyr, Tertullian, Lactantius, &c., are translated in Clark's Ante-Nicene Library, Edinburgh, Clark, 1867.

Note: Works listed in this bibliography frequently refer to untranslated works in *French* and *German*, of which the following is a selection:

Fourth Edition of *Geschichte des jüdischen Volkes im Zeitalter Jesu Christi*, Emil Schürer, Leipzig: Hinrichs, 1901-9, 3 vols. The English translation of the 2nd edition (1892) is inadequate since the publication of the 4th.

Der Agada der Tannaiten, Wilhelm Bacher, Strassburg: Trübner, 1890. 2 vols.

Hauptprobleme der Gnosis, Wilhelm Bousset. Göttingen: Vanderhoeck & Ruprecht, 1907.

Les Mystères païens et le mystère chrétien, Alfred Loisy, Paris: Nourry, 1913 & 1930.

Les Mages hellenisés, Joseph Bidez and Franz Cumont, Paris: Les Belles Lettres, 1938.

Fourth Edition of *Les Religions orientale dans le paganisme romain*, Franz Cumont, Paris: Geuthner, 1929. (The 2nd edition, trans. G. Showerman, Chicago Univ. Press, 1911, is inadequate since the 4th was published.)

Die Religion der Griechen, Otto Kern, Berlin: Weidmannsche Buchhandlung, 1938, 3 vols.

Atlases:

Westminster Historical Atlas to the Bible, George E. Wright and Floyd V. Filson, Phila.: Westminster Press, 1945 & 1956.

Atlas of the Bible, L. H. Grollenberg, O.P., trans. J. M. H. Reid & H. H. Rowley, London & New York: Nelson, 1956.

Rand McNally Bible Atlas, Emil Q. Kraeling, New York: Rand McNally, 1957.

Suggestions for Further Reading

The available literature bearing directly and indirectly on St. Paul and Christian origins is enormous. Even that part of it which may justly be called scholarly is exceedingly large. Of the latter, however, only a portion would be of interest to the general reader, and the following suggestions, except where otherwise noted, are drawn from this portion.

First, there should be some background reading. *Hebrew Origins* by T. J. Meek (New York, Harper & Brothers, 1936) would be a good beginning. R. H. Pfeiffer's *Introduction to the Old Testament* (New York, Harper and Brothers, 1948) is a little technical but excellent. The present writer's *The Ten Commandments* (New American Library paperback, 1956) gives a brief survey of Old Testament criticism. Joseph Klausner's *The Messianic Idea in Israel* (New York, Macmillan, 1955) provides most of the Judaic background that the reader will need at this point (it covers the Apocrypha and Pseudepigrapha and some of the rabbinical writings as well as the Old Testament). This might be followed by W. O. E. Oesterley's *The Jews and Judaism during the Greek Period* (New York, Macmillan, 1941).

For the Hellenistic background, the reader should by all means begin with Gilbert Murray's *Five Stages of Greek Religion* (Boston, Beacon Press reprint, 1952), then read Edith Hamilton's *The Greek Way to Western Civilization* (New York, New American Library reprint, 1948). W. W. Hyde's *Paganism to Christianity in the Roman Empire* (Philadelphia, University of Pennsylvania Press, 1946) might come next, followed by chapters XXVIII to XLVI in the one-volume edition of J. G. Frazer's *Golden Bough* (London and New York, Macmillan, 1925). If the mystery religions are a special interest, a beginning might be made with S. Angus' *The Mystery Religions and Christianity* (New York, Scribner, 1925). This treatise (like others of the books recommended) has an excellent bibliogra-

phy, by the aid of which, together with references in the foot-
notes, the reader can discover further resources suited to his
needs.

At this point, the encyclopedias should be mentioned. Any
good public library will have *Hastings' Dictionary of the Bible*
and *should* have the *Encyclopedia Biblica* (which is better).
The former is in five volumes, the latter four. Then there is the
indispensable *Encyclopedia of Religion and Ethics* (twelve volumes and index), commonly found in the reference section of
public libraries. The *Catholic* and *Jewish Encyclopedias* are
also valuable, and there are sometimes articles which the reader
may find sufficiently informative in the *Encyclopedia Britan-
nica,* which he may himself possess. For the advanced student,
of course, access to all of these encyclopedias is essential.

For the New Testament and Christian origins, the basic
work in English is Jackson and Lake's *The Beginnings of Christianity* (five volumes, London and New York, Macmillan, 1920-
33). Although some sections of this important study are technical and difficult to follow without a reading knowledge of
New Testament Greek, for the most part (as, for example, all
of volume one) it can be well understood by the general reader.
(Note: This work will only be found in larger public libraries
and in the libraries of theological schools.)

Of New Testament introductions, Goodspeed's *An Introduction to the New Testament* (Chicago University Press, 1937) is
brief and among the most easily read; for background history,
Pfeiffer's *History of New Testament Times* (New York, Harper
and Brothers, 1949) covers the subject from the political, literary and religious standpoint in about as short a treatment as is
practical. Pfeiffer also provides a good bibliography.

Coming now to standard works (other than Jackson and
Lake *supra*) on Christian origins (in which Paul is studied in a
larger or lesser degree according to the emphasis of the writer),
Enslin's *Christian Beginnings* (with which his *Literature of the
Christian Movement* is continuous in a second volume) may be
recommended (Harper, Torchlight Edition, New York, 1956).
The Abbé Loisy's *Birth of the Christian Religion* and *Origins of
the New Testament* (English translations, London and New

York, Macmillan, 1950) should not be overlooked. If Loisy sounds dogmatic, it is only because in a brief treatment, he cannot always stop to give his reasons; he is a sound scholar with a Gallic style which L. P. Jacks has adequately rendered. Of full-size treatments, if the choice must be limited to a single work it might well be Maurice Goguel's *The Birth of Christianity,* published in English translation in 1954 (New York, Macmillan). A standard work which many would prefer to Goguel's is Johannes Weiss's *The History of Primitive Christianity* (English translation, New York, Wilson-Erickson, 1937). It is better to read both these works than to make a choice between them. A brief treatment of almost the entire field, including Pauline theology, will be found in Rudolf Bultmann's *Primitive Christianity in its Contemporary Setting* (English translation, New York, Living Age Books, 1956). For a very different interpretation of Christian origins—and in the estimation of most scholars one that is too radical—the reader might consult W. B. Smith's *The Birth of the Gospel* (edited by Addison Gulick, New York, Philosophical Library, 1957).

If he follows these suggestions (or enough of them), the reader will at this point be finding his own way in the literature of Paul and Christian origins and further guidance will not be needed.

REFERENCES

ABBREVIATIONS

EBi—*Encyclopedia Biblica,* edited by T. K. Cheyne and J. S. Black, 4 vols., London, 1899-1903.

HDB—*Dictionary of the Bible,* edited by James Hastings, 5 vols., Edinburgh and New York, 1898-1904.

DCG—*Dictionary of Christ and the Gospels,* edited by James Hastings, 2 vols., Edinburgh and New York, 1907.

Jos. *Ant.*— ⎰ *Antiquities of the Jews* and *Wars of the Jews,* by F. Jo-
Jos. *Wars*— ⎱ sephus (circa 37-100 A.D.), in one vol. trans., W. Whiston, London, 1873.

J & L—*The Beginnings of Christianity,* edited by F. J. Foakes Jackson and Kirsopp Lake (also J. H. Ropes and H. J. Cadbury), 5 vols., London and New York, 1920-1933.

ERE—*Encyclopedia of Religion and Ethics,* 12 vols. & Index, edited by James Hastings, Edinburgh and New York, 1908-1926.

INTRODUCTION

1. Goguel, M., *The Birth of Christianity,* trans. Snape, H. C., New York, 1954, p. 37.
2. Weiss, J., *The History of Primitive Christianity,* trans. Grant, F. C. and others, New York, 1937, vol. 1, pp. 5-6.
3. Bultmann, R., *Primitive Christianity in its Contemporary Setting,* trans. Fuller, R. H., New York, 1956, pp. 11 and 175 (hereafter referred to as Bultman; similarly other authors).
4. Enslin, M., *Christian Beginnings* (with which *The Literature of the Christian Movement* is continuous, with pages numbered accordingly), New York, 1938 and 1956 (Torchlight Edition), p. 147.

PART ONE—PROLOGUE

1. For an extensive description of Tarsus, see Ramsay, W. M., *The Cities of St. Paul,* London, 1907. Briefer and more recent: Glover, T. R., *Paul of Tarsus,* London, 1925, pp. 5-23. Also EBi and HDB, "Tarsus."
2. Lipsius, R. A. and Bonnet, M., *Acta Apostolorum Apocrypha,* vol. 1, 1891. Slightly different translations in HDB, vol. 3, p. 700; James, M. R., *The Apocryphal New Testament,* Oxford, 1924.
3. Jos. *Ant.* Book XX, chap. xi (p. 549b).
4. Weiss, p. 675.

261

CHAPTER I

5. Schonfield, H. J., *The Authentic New Testament*, London, 1955, p. 204, footnote (hereafter referred to as *Auth. N.T.*).
6. Enslin, p. 179. See also Goguel, pp. 167-176.
7. J & L, vol. 5, p. 59 ff.
8. Schonfield, *Auth. N.T.*, p. 204.
9. Loisy, A., *The Birth of the Christian Religion*, trans. Jacks, L. P., London, 1948, p. 114 ff. (hereafter referred to as *Birth of*). *The Origins of the New Testament*, trans. Jacks, L. P., London, 1950, p. 174 ff. (hereafter referred to as *Origins*).
10. Headlam, A. C., in HDB, vol. 1, p. 33b.
11. Schweitzer, A., *The Mysticism of Paul the Apostle*, New York, 1931, p. 41 (hereafter referred to as *Mysticism*).
12. Enslin, p. 420. See also "The Speeches in Acts," Cadbury, H. J., J & L, vol. 5, p. 402 ff.
13. Loisy, *Origins*, p. 175.
14. Enslin, p. 169.
15. Many scholars, particularly German; but cf. J & L, vol. 5, p. 188 ff.
16. Loisy, *Birth of*, p. 129.

CHAPTER II

17. Grollenberg, L. H., *Atlas of the Bible*, London and New York, 1956, p. 139.
18. Many scholars adapt the information given in Acts to a broad pattern of two chief periods of missionary activity. See, e.g., Weiss, pp. 203 ff., 277 ff.
19. Inge, W. R., *Outspoken Essays*, London, 1921, p. 208.
20. Barnes, E. W., *The Rise of Christianity*, London, 1947, p. 196.
21. Headlam, A. C., in HDB, vol. 1, p. 25 ff.
22. Goguel, p. 89.
23. Weiss, p. 143.
24. Borguet, J., *De rebus delphicis imperatoriae aetatis capita duo*, Montepassulano, 1905.
25. E.g., Loisy, *Les Actes des Apôtres*, Paris, 1920, pp. 474-476, 498 ff., 571.
26. Weiss, p. 5. The question is exhaustively examined by Kirsopp Lake in J & L, vol. 5, p. 195 ff.
27. Discussed by Goguel, p. 297; and in many studies of the New Testament text. See J & L, vol. 5, p. 196 ff.
28. See Goguel, p. 303 ff.; Weiss, p. 273 ff.; and most modern scholars.
29. Nock, A. D., *St Paul*, New York, 1938, pp. 118-119.

CHAPTER III

30. Schweitzer, *Mysticism*, p. 45.
31. James, M. R., *The Apocryphal New Testament*, Oxford, 1924.
32. Nock, p. 236.
33. For this entire section, inclusive reference is made to: J & L, vol. 2; Dibelius, M., *A Fresh Approach to the New Testament and Early*

Christian Literature, London, 1936; Bultmann, R. and Kundsin, K., *Form Criticism,* trans. Grant, F. C., Chicago, 1935; Taylor, V., *The Formation of the Gospel Tradition,* London, 1933.

34. Eusebius (Pamphili), *Historica Ecclesiastica,* iii, 39, 15.
35. James, p. 519.
36. Enslin, p. 392.
37. See e.g., Bacon, B. W., *Studies in Matthew,* New York, 1930.
38. Goodspeed, E. J., *Introduction to the New Testament,* Chicago, 1937, p. 180 (hereafter referred to as *Intro.*).
39. Robinson, J. A., *The Study of the Gospels,* London, 1902, p. 42.
40. James, pp. 92-93.
41. Knox, J., *Chapters in a Life of Paul,* New York, 1950, p. 120.
42. Loisy, *Origins,* p. 145. For a full discussion of the textual problems of which the foregoing is an example, see J & L, vol. 3.
43. For discussions of the Galatians problem, see (older view) Ramsay, W. M., *The Church in the Roman Empire,* London, 1905; EBi and HDB "Galatia" and "Galatians"; J & L, vol. 5; (newer view) Enslin, pp. 217-232; Knox, chaps. 3-5; Goguel, *passim.*
44. Schonfield, *Auth. N.T.,* p. 190. See also Torrey, C. C., *The Composition and Date of Acts,* New Haven, 1916.
45. Goguel, p. 212.
46. Knox, p. 36.
47. See #24 *supra;* also p. 40 in text.
48. See, e.g., J & L, vol. 2, p. 174 ff.; Goguel, p. 152 ff.
49. HDB, vol. 2, p. 679b. For a fuller account see Mead, G. R. S., *The Gnostic Baptizer,* London, 1924; also ERE, vol. 8, p. 390b ff.
50. Goguel, p. 492.

PART TWO—CHAPTER I

1. Frazer, J. G., *The Golden Bough,* abridged edition, London, 1925, p. 352.
2. *Ibid.,* pp. 336 and 346.
3. See, e.g., Sellin, E., *Introduction to the Old Testament,* New York, 1923; Pfeiffer, R. H., *Introduction to the Old Testament,* New York, 1948.
4. Discussed by Pfeiffer, R. H., *History of New Testament Times,* New York, 1949, p. 9 ff. (hereafter referred to as *Hist. N.T.*).
5. See Dupont-Sommer, A., *The Jewish Sect of Qumran and the Essenes,* trans. Barnett, R. D., New York, 1955; innumerable articles. Discussed in Davies, A. P., *The Meaning of the Dead Sea Scrolls,* New York, 1956, pp. 70-79.
6. For ancient Hebrew history see (e.g.) Meek, T. J., *Hebrew Origins,* New York, 1936; or Oesterley, W. O. E. and Robinson, T. H., *A History of Israel* (2 vols.), Oxford, 1932. For the later period see Pfeiffer, *Hist. N.T.,* pp. 1-45; J & L, vol. 1, part 1. Both periods, articles, EBi, HDB.
7. Quoted in conversation with H. G. Wells in his *Outline of History,* New York, 1920, p. 353.
8. Quoted in Hamilton, E., *The Greek Way to Western Civilization,* Mentor Edition, New York, 1948, p. 30.

9. Dodd, C. H., *The Bible and the Greeks*, London, 1935.
10. In Philo, *The Embassy to Gaius*, XXXVI, 282.
11. In Jos. *Ant.*, XIV, 7, 2.
12. Klausner, J., *From Jesus to Paul*, trans. Stinespring, W. F., New York, 1943, p. 321 (hereafter referred to as *Paul*).
13. *Ibid.*, p. 24.
14. Juster, J., *Les Juifs dans l'empire romain*, Paris, 1914, vol. 1, p. 203. Mentioned by Klausner and others.
15. Klausner, J., *Philosophim ve-Hoge-De'ot*, Jerusalem, 1930, I, p. 65 ff.
16. Papyrus, London, 1912 (H.E. 212), given in Barrett, C. K., *The New Testament Background: Selected Documents*, New York, 1957, p. 45.

CHAPTER II

17. See, e.g., ERE, vol. 6, p. 231 ff.; Bultmann, *Primitive*, p. 162; Loisy, *Birth of*, pp. 219-334; Legge, F., *Forerunners and Rivals of Christianity*, Cambridge, 1915. For a sympathetic treatment of Gnosticism, see Mead, G. R., *Fragments of a Faith Forgotten*, London, 1900.
18. Murray, G., *Five Stages of Greek Religion*, New York, 1930, p. 196.
19. See Loisy, *Birth of*, p. 265 ff.
20. Robinson, J. A. T., *The Body*, London and Chicago, 1952, p. 38.
21. Davies, W. D., *Paul and Rabbinic Judaism*, London, 1948, revised 1955, p. 20.
22. Tertullian, *De Baptismo*, 5. Cited in numerous discussions of Christianity and the mystery religions. See, e.g., Enslin, p. 194; Pfeiffer, p. 164; Loisy, *Birth of*, p. 205 ff.
23. Justin Martyr, *Apologia*, I, 66, 4. See Halliday, W. R., *The Background of Christianity*, Liverpool, 1925, pp. 312-323.
24. See Harrison, J., *Prolegomena to the Study of Greek Religion*, Cambridge, 1903, *passim*.
25. For a full account, see Angus, S., *The Mystery Religions and Christianity*, New York, 1925 (hereafter referred to as *Myst. Rel.*); ERE, vol. 9, p. 70 ff.
26. Frazer, *Golden Bough* (abridged edition), chaps. 25 and 26.
27. Ramsay, W. M., *Cities and Bishoprics of Phrygia*, Oxford, 1896-1897, I, p. 92 ff.
28. Enslin, p. 189.
29. Apuleius, *The Golden Ass*, trans. Graves, R., New York, 1951, p. 238 ff. Also citation in Barrett, p. 97 ff.
30. Frazer, pp. 347-356.
31. *Ibid.*, pp. 362-385. A brief account in Pfeiffer, *Hist. N.T.*, p. 156 ff.
32. Harrison, p. 496.
33. See Cumont, F., *The Oriental Religions in Roman Paganism*, trans. (2nd Edition) Showerman, G., Chicago, 1911, p. 100.
34. Frazer, p. 346.
35. *Ibid.*, p. 479 ff.
36. *Ibid.*, p. 376 ff.
37. Robinson, J. A. T., *passim*.
38. Enslin, p. 197.

39. Bultmann, p. 201.
40. Loisy, *Birth of*, chaps. 7 and 8.
41. Schweitzer, A., *Paul and His Interpreters*, 1912, trans. Montgomery, W., New York, 1951, p. 226 (hereafter referred to as *Interpreters*).
42. Maurenbrecher, M. and Gunkel, H., discussed by Schweitzer, *Interpreters*, p. 232 ff.
43. Loisy, *Birth of*, p. 243 ff.
44. Cumont, F., *The Mysteries of Mithra*, trans. McCormack, T. J., Chicago, 1910, *passim*. See Hyde, W. W., *Paganism to Christianity in the Roman Empire*, Philadelphia, 1946, p. 46 ff.; Angus, *Myst. Rel.*, *passim*; ERE, vol. 8, p. 752 ff.
45. Dieterich, A., *Eine Mithrasliturgie*, Leipzig, 1923.
46. Inge, p. 354.
47. Annotated translation in Barrett, p. 80 ff.
48. ERE, vol. 12, p. 315b.
49. Angus, *Myst. Rel.*, p. 20.
50. Frazer, p. 351.
51. Loisy, *Birth of*, ref. 26, p. 402.
52. Angus, S., *Environment of Early Christianity*, New York, 1920, p. 103.
53. Murray, *Five Stages* (1930 edition), p. 155.
54. Harrison, p. 480.

CHAPTER III

55. A tabulation of Paul's use of the Old Testament is given in Prat, F., *The Theology of St. Paul*, Westminster, Md., 1946, vol. 1, pp. 411-414. The tables are also reproduced in Kepler, T. S., *Contemporary Thinking about Paul*, New York, 1950, p. 197 ff.
56. See, e.g., Davies, W. D., *passim*.
57. Klausner, J., *The Messianic Idea in Israel*, trans. Stinespring, W. F., New York, 1955, p. 446 ff. (hereafter referred to as *Messianic*).
58. Schweitzer, *Interpreters*, p. 227.
59. For an exhaustive treatment, see Klausner, *Messianic*.
60. *Ibid.*, p. 229 ff.
61. *Ibid.*, p. 520.
62. E.g., Brownlee, W. H., "The Servant of the Lord in the Qumran Scrolls," *Bulletins of the American Schools of Oriental Research*, Nos. 132 and 135, New Haven, 1953 and 1954.
63. Murray, G., Preface to Loisy, *Birth of*, p. 7.
64. Harrison, p. 479.
65. Bultmann, p. 177.
66. Davies, W. D., p. 114 ff.
67. Pliny's Letters, ix, 21, Bosanquet trans., London, 1914.
68. Charles, R. H., *The Apocrypha and Pseudepigrapha of the Old Testament in English*, Oxford, 1913, II, pp. 282 and 291 ff.
69. These Talmud quotations (b.31a, etc.) are frequently quoted. See Davies, W. D., p. 64; Branscomb, B. H., *Jesus and the Law of Moses*, New York, 1930, p. 256.
70. Enslin, p. 191.

PART THREE—CHAPTER I

1. Enslin, p. 170.
2. Weiss, p. 8.
3. There is now a large literature on the Dead Sea Scrolls. For a semi-technical exposition, see Burrows, M., *The Dead Sea Scrolls*, New York, 1955. See also footnote, p. 170.
4. See Howlett, D., *The Essenes and Christianity*, New York, 1957, *passim*.
5. Cross, F. M., "The Scrolls from the Judean Desert," in *Archeology*, vol. 9, No. 1, pp. 41-53.
6. See articles in EBi, HDB, "Nazareth," "Nazarene."
7. Loisy, *Origins*, p. 34.
8. See Bacon, p. 163 ff. Also ERE, vol. 9, p. 260.
9. Bultmann, p. 175.
10. See Davies, W. D., p. 285 ff.
11. Jos. *Wars*, II, viii, 11.
12. See Brownlee, W. H., article, "The Servant of the Lord" (#62 *supra*).
13. Cullman, O., quoted in Bultmann, p. 214.
14. Weiss, p. 52. See also his analysis in 716 ff.
15. *Ibid.*, p. 661.
16. Kundsin, K., in Grant, *Form Criticism*, p. 112.
17. In *The Institutions: Historia Ecclesiastica*, II, 1 (Reliquiae Sacrae, Oxford, 1814-1818).
18. Massebiean, L. and Spitta, F. are cited by Enslin as pioneering this view in 1895 (*Revue de l'Histoire des Religions*, xxxii, Paris, 1895, pp. 249-283).
19. Gaster, T. H., *The Dead Sea Scriptures in English Translation*, New York, 1956, p. 16 ff.
20. *Ibid.*, p. 17.
21. Pfeiffer, pp. 40 and 42.
22. See art. "Jesus" in DCG, p. 859 ff.
23. Davies, A. P., p. 75.
24. James, p. 511.
25. *Ibid.*
26. For the argument for the Teacher as a single individual, see Dupont-Sommer, chap. 3 and *passim*; Allegro, J., *The Dead Sea Scrolls*, London, 1956, chap. 6 and *passim*; Howlett, chap. 5. For the opposed argument see Gaster, p. 24 ff.
27. Howlett, chap. 5.
28. Millar Burrows' translation, p. 401.
29. Mead, G. R. S., *Did Jesus Live 100 B.C.?*, London, 1903 (hereafter referred to as *100 B.C.*).
30. Goldstein, M., *Jesus in the Jewish Tradition*, New York, 1950, p. 74.
31. British Museum, Orient. Dept. M.S. Add. 26964. Quoted and text printed by Krauss, S., in *Das Leben Jesu nāch judischen Quellen*, Berlin, 1902.
32. In Neubauer's *Medieval Jewish Chronicles*, Oxford, 1887, p. 53.

33. Epiphanius, *Patrologia Graeca*, XLI, Migne Edition, Paris, 1863, cols. 392 and 393.
34. Claudius xxv. Barrett, p. 14.
35. Tertullian, *Apol.*, iii; Lactantius, *Instit.*, iv, 7.
36. Mead, *100 B.C.*, p. 51, note.
37. Weiss, p. 177.
38. Goguel, p. 310, note.
39. Weiss, p. 32 ff. See also J & L, vol. 1, part 3.
40. See Schonfield's reconstruction, *Auth. N.T.*, p. 286 ff.
41. Ramsay, W. M., *The Teaching of Paul in Terms of the Present Day*, London, 1913, p. 21 ff.
42. Weiss, J., *Paul and Jesus* (quoted in Ramsay, *Teaching of Paul supra*), p. 22.
43. Klausner, *Paul*, p. 315.
44. Graves, R., and Podro, J., *The Nazarene Gospel Restored*, New York, 1954, p. 970 ff.
45. As estimated by most modern scholars. See, e.g., Enslin, p. 158.
46. Conybeare, F. C., *Myth, Magic and Morals*, Boston, 1925, p. 8 ff.
47. Schweitzer, *Interpreters*, p. 245 ff.

CHAPTER II

48. Schonfield, H. J., *The Jew of Tarsus*, New York, 1947, p. 46 (hereafter referred to as *Tarsus*).
49. *Ibid.*, p. 47.
50. E.g., Loisy, *Birth of*, p. 129. For a different view see Weiss, p. 190 ff.
51. See Burrows, p. 199 ff.; Howlett, p. 112 ff.
52. Glotz, in *Revue des Etudes Grecques*, xxxiii, 12, quoted by Loisy, *Origins*, p. 109.
53. See, e.g., J & L, vol. 2, p. 371; Loisy, *Birth of*, p. 127 ff.
54. Goguel, p. 191.
55. For a discussion of the differences of belief among the New Covenanters, see Schonfield, *Tarsus*, p. 177.
56. See Weiss, p. 37; Enslin, p. 192.
57. Grollenberg, p. 139.
58. Schonfield, *Tarsus*, p. 155.
59. Goodspeed, E. J., *The Apostolic Fathers, An American Translation*, New York, 1950, p. 29.
60. Enslin, p. 193.
61. Schonfield, *Auth. N.T.*, p. 233.
62. Enslin, p. 275.
63. Barrett, p. 163.
64. Leitzmann, H., *Die Reisen des Petrus*, S.B.A., 1930, pp. 153-156; discussed by Goguel, p. 316.
65. For a more recent (Jewish) discussion of Paul's Judaism than Klausner's, see Sandmel, S., *A Jewish Understanding of the New Testament*, Cincinnati, 1956, Part II.
66. For a discussion of the Romans problem, see Enslin, pp. 262-272; or Goodspeed, *Intro.*, pp. 69-87.
67. Goguel, p. 219.
68. See Enslin, p. 421.

69. See J & L, vol. 2, p. 187 ff.
70. See Schonfield, *Auth. N.T.*, p. 244.
71. Loisy, *Birth of,* note 59, p. 391.
72. Windisch, H., in J & L, vol. 2, p. 333.
73. Loisy, *Birth of*, p. 172.
74. Goguel, p. 319.
75. Goodspeed, *Intro.*, p. 327 ff.
76. Duchesne, H. A., p. 55.

CONCLUSION

1. Weiss, p. 650.
2. Klausner, *Paul*, p. 312.
3. Nock, *St. Paul*, p. 247.
4. Goodspeed, *Intro.*, chap. 13; and most modern New Testament introductions.
5. Hyde, p. 27.
6. Burkitt, F. C., in Proceedings Soc. Bib. Arch., 1901, p. 77, quoted, Angus, p. 51. See also ERE, vol. 4, 578 ff.
7. In *De vita beata ad Gallionem*, 20, quoted in Hyde, p. 29.
8. In Discourses I: 9, 1, Schenkel Edition, Leipzig, 1898.
9. Murray, G., in the Preface to Loisy, *Birth of*, p. 9.
10. Loisy, *Birth of*, p. 217.

INDEX

Abraham, 215
Abraham ben Daud, 190
Acts, book of
    catechesis in, 69-77, 83-89
    composer and sources of, 45,
        75-77, 80-84, 177, 194
    date of, 82f.
    and *Galatians,* 31f., 39, 45
    relation to Luke's gospel, 69
    speeches in, 23, 30, 39, 231,
        234
    "we" passages, 82
Acts of Paul and Thecla, 14
Adonis, 94, 129, 208
Aelia Capitolina, 105
Agrippa II, 30, 232, 239
Ahriman, 136
Ahura-Mazda, 136
Akiba, Rabbi, 113, 152, 162
Alexander the Great, 97f., 105
Alexander Janneus, 101, 115,
    186ff.
Alexandra, 101, 188-191
Alexandria, 62, 107-108, 117,
    139, 208
Alexandrinus, Codex, 76
Allegro, John, 170n.
Ananas, 62
Ananias (of Damascus), 26, 29
Angus, S., 140
Antioch, 17, 42, 86, 94, 121,
    208f.
    "community" of, 16f., 42, 45,
        48-50, 174f., 207f., 209f.,
        224
Antioch source (of *Acts*), 45, 82
Antiochus Epiphanes, 98-100
Antipater (of Idumea), 102

Apocrypha, New Testament, 59,
    184
Apollos, 87, 219f.
Apostles, the, 15n., 21, 31, 70,
    174, 177
Apostolos, 16, 204, 230
Apuleius, 127
Aramaic, use of, 13, 18
Aretas, 27f., 206
Aristobulus, 100f.
Athens, 220
Attis, 33, 94, 127f., 140
Augustus (Octavian), 103, 117

Bacon, B. W., 172
Baptism
    Essenic, 170
    of Jesus, 67, 70
    Jewish use of, 112, 217
    by John, *See* John the Baptist
    New Covenanters, 170, 217
    pagan, 126, 137, 140, 217
Baptist, John, *See* John the Bap-
    tist
Bar Kochba (Kozibah), 105, 152
Barnabas, 30, 35, 38ff., 42f.,
    44-48, 177, 207, 209-212
    and *passim*
Barnabas, letter of, 59f., 215
Barnes, Bishop, 39
Ben Assai, 162
Bethlehem, and Adonis cult, 129
Bezae, Codex, 76
Biblical criticism, 58ff.
Bultmann, Rudolf, 2, 133, 156,
    172, 174
Burrows, Millar, 170n.

269